# Reflections
# of a Pilot

For Margaret

# Reflections of a Pilot

## LEN MORGAN

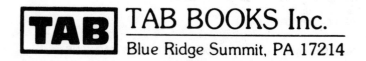

TAB BOOKS Inc.

Blue Ridge Summit, PA 17214

All of the chapters in this book were originally published in *FLYING*.

Books by Len Morgan
**The P-51 Mustang**
**The AT-6 Harvard**
**Crack Up!**
**The Boeing 727 Scrapbook**
  with T.L. Morgan
**View From the Cockpit**

FIRST EDITION
FIRST PRINTING

Copyright © 1987 by A.G. Leonard Morgan

Printed in the United States of America

Library of Congress Cataloging in Publication Data

Morgan, Len.
    Reflections of a pilot.

    1. Aeronautics.   I. Title.
TL559.M67   1987      629.13      86-23164
ISBN 0-8306-2098-2
ISBN 0-8306-2398-1 (pbk.)

Cover photograph by Gordon Bowen and FLYING MAGAZINE.

# Contents

# Introduction

Back in the 1930s when I caught flying fever, *airplane* and *dangerous* were words of the same meaning—at least, in the popular view. This notion was not entirely baseless though insiders joked that starvation was the greatest peril. Like many boys in those Depression times, I read everything I could find about planes and pilots. Dime pulp magazines and the occasional silent Hollywood epic were the only sources of information.

I was 14 before I saw a plane close up. It was a Waco 10 with an OX-5 engine flown by a threadbare barnstormer. We boys were strictly forbidden to accept the free rides he offered in exchange for distributing his leaflets, so we sat in the cockpit inhaling the heady aroma of gasoline, dope, and leather.

According to aviation writers, piloting was work for extraordinary men. Air movies confirmed this notion. Unless you were good in technical subjects, a born athlete and saw Robert Taylor in the mirror, your chances were slim. Squarely facing up to my situation left me with little hope of being a pilot. Except for the war, few of us would ever have learned the truth—that most of what we had read and watched on the screen was pure bunk.

Technical mindedness is not a prerequisite. I know veteran pilots with spotless records who couldn't wire a doorbell. Athletic ability counts for little. You'll likely find more good pilot material on the chess team than on the football squad. Appearance means nothing. I can think of few pilots who fit the popular physical image. You'd take most of them for anything but what they are—professionals whose careers are flying.

To be sure, professional pilots share certain attributes—good health, the ability to quickly master and adapt to new concepts, the knack of total concentration, sound judgement and imagination. Most important is an abiding interest in the work and the challenges it presents. A keen sense of humor is essential for on occasion the flying life is utterly frustrating.

The term *pilot* is no more descriptive than *doctor* or *engineer*. Modern aviation includes a thousand special skills in a thousand quite different areas. Bear in mind that I can only try to tell it like it was in the small corner of the big picture I was fortunate enough to occupy.

# Bowman Memories

My earliest memories of flying date back to 1937 when we moved from rural Georgia to Louisville. Our new home was a half hour by bike from Bowman Field, the state's largest airport—a square mile of bluegrass surrounded by tall trees. On the south side was a neat brick terminal flanked by two hangars, one for private aircraft, the other for the Army Reserve. The terminal contained the small offices of American and Eastern, a waiting room with twelve seats, and a cafe that served up a stupendous hamburger for the outrageous price of 30 cents.

By the measures of that day, Bowman was a bustling facility, yet it was not unusual to lean on the steel fence for an hour and see nothing flying but birds. Patience was often rewarded by an unmistakable sound in the distance, a dot in the haze growing and sinking low over the trees. It would be a Stinson Reliant or Stearman coming in for gas, or government men from Cincinnati in a Bureau of Air Commerce Fairchild 24, or a pair of P-12s, or something really unusual. One day a creaking old Keystone bomber paused enroute to its demolishment at Wright Field in Dayton and was joined minutes later by a sharp B-10 with retractable main wheels. I stood close enough to hear their leather-helmeted pilots talk.

Louisville Flying Service was strictly off limits. We fascinated boys were rarely permitted in that hangar and never could we touch an airplane, much less climb inside. The Army was more understanding and sometimes left the gate open. More than once I stood next to the fire bottle when an O-43 fired up. I can still hear that awesome Curtiss V-12 come to life, see the curl of smoke and flash of flame from its short stacks; if that didn't give you flying fever nothing could.

One memorable Saturday the sky was suddenly filled with the angry snarling of many big engines. Eighteen spanking new Seversky P-35s sped across the field at tremendous speed, peeled off and three-pointed on the grass—a training exercise out of Selfridge Field up near Detroit. I walked between the shiny pursuits, feeling their cold curves and listening to the boisterous talk of the young stalwarts who flew them. Then they were gone, bouncing across the turf in pairs, forming up and vanishing to the north, leaving but an echo of their magic in the silent hangar and an emptiness in the heart.

I remember the occasional ungainly Bellanca C-27, the handsome Northrop A-17, the dashing little P-12 and Curtiss P-6E, a creation of breath-taking beauty, but the Army ramp was usually deserted except when one of the local BT-2B's was pushed out for a hop. Oh yes, toward the end of those spectator days one of the first monstrous Flying Forts came in, flown by colonels. The unbelievable monster was quickly towed inside, the doors rolled closed and gate locked.

Louisville Flying Service hangared most of the big names of that so-called "Golden Age" of civil flying, some almost forgotten now—Stinson, Waco, Cessna, Rearwin, Aeronca, Beech, Dart, Culver, Monocoupe, Fairchild, Spartan. It was obviously a dandy club for the handful wealthy enough to pay the dues. They played and we watched from behind the fence. An aging Curtiss Fledgling, an antique even then, was tied down outside; it lifted almost within its length and soared aloft at incredibly slow speed. One day a Stearman-Hammond dropped in, drawing much attention. With pusher Menasco engine, twin rudders and tricycle landing gear, it seemed all wrong, a flying freak. So much for my feel for the future.

The arrival of airline DC-2s and -3s was attended by more fanfare than greets today's Concorde from Heathrow. On a summer evening large crowds would await Eastern's Number 7 southbound from Chicago to Miami, Louisville being the second of 10 enroute stops. Someone would point and all would look for the tiny nav lights. Three minutes later the glistening marvel would stop beneath the floodlights and we would read, "The Great Silver Fleet," above the windows and study the passengers walking off. How could they be so nonchalant after such high adventure?

Such American Airlines hotshots as "The Southerner," "The American Mercury" and "The Sun Country Special" bypassed us, racing from coast to coast along the main line through Nashville and Memphis. By 1939 we had five AAL trips per day flown with the same glamorous "Flagships" with little admiral's pennants above cockpit windows. Once in a while a DST sleeper would roll up and we'd look at the extra row of windows and imagine riding in an upper berth. Wow!

From this distance it is clear that C. R. Smith and Eddie Rickenbacker shared a boyish enthusiasm for flight. All that razzmatazz was right off the cob, but it worked. It sold a lot of folks besides me.

There were special events like the week trans-Atlantic hero Clarence Chamberlin hopped passengers in his big Condor and the day "Wrong Way" Corrigan landed in his Robin. He delayed the parade in his honor until satisfying all requests for autographs. I still have mine pasted inside his book.

Kentucky Derby week was the high point of the Bowman year with all kinds of aircraft flying in. I still have snapshots of a Stinson Model A trimotor, an Orion, Boeing 247D, 10A Electra and a civilianized Boeing biplane fighter said to have been piloted by one Howard Hughes. American and Eastern ran extra sections, affording my first chance to go aboard. Mike Murphy came in with his fleet from Kokomo, Indiana, to tow banners and print "Pepsi Cola" against the sky, always dotting the i. It's funny the things you remember. At night he flew his Boeing 80A trimotor, to the broad lower wing of which was attached a neon sign board.

It's still all there at Bowman, the brick terminal, the two hangars which seem to have shrunk and of course a lot of newer buildings. The airlines and military moved out long ago. It's all different now; it's all tricycles for one thing. On my last visit only one airplane seemed right in those old surroundings, a polished Cessna 195, someone's prized antique. New look or not, I'm still fond of the old place and aware of what I learned there. Bowman was real fun in those lean post-Depression years, offering a free grand performance to the patient and observant.

It convinced me that pilots have the edge on everyone else. Nothing has changed my mind in the half century since.

# Airmanship

$W$ay back, in that first ground school, we were lectured by a Royal Air Force retread. Thoroughly miffed at not being posted to a Spitfire unit, the old vet (he must have been all of 35) was nonetheless doing his bit for new chaps in distant Ontario. The course was "Airmanship," the intent being to instill a proper airman's viewpoint in each of us. By slyly challenging the hard data we got in other classes, he made us think. He raised questions rather than giving answers. He should have done a book.

Never since has the pilot's life been so sensibly approached in any school I've been to. Had such sessions been part of all ground-schooling and retraining from then until now, we might not need remedial safety clinics today.

To perform safely and efficiently on an all-season basis, a pilot must be knowledgeable in a number of subjects. He has to understand the theory and practice of flight; he must appreciate his airplane as a machine, including its complex internal machinery; he has to know about weight-and-balance; he must learn weather and communications; he must concern himself with economics, in most phases of civil flying, at least, and be mindful of public relations; he requires an awareness of the law. And he will find most useful general information on many other topics.

In traditional training each phase is taught by a specialist, an instructor who is understandably prone to regard his field as the most important in the curriculum. Unless you keep the machine running smoothly and expertly cope with in-flight malfunctions, nothing else matters, says the fellow who teaches engines and systems. Of what value is mechanical savvy if you can't steer it unerringly from A to B, asks the navigator. Mechanics and nav are important, says the meterologist, but they'll count for naught if you don't pay close attention to me. All very true, says the performance expert, but if you don't load it correctly and fly by my charts, those other things won't matter because you'll lose control, run short of fuel or bankrupt the operation. On and on it goes until the student wonders about the overall picture.

Each expert is—in his own way—right, and so obviously right that the beginner is confused. Where should emphasis be placed? What are the real priorities? It would be appropriate to send in an old hand to wrap it up, an experienced pilot to pull it all together—to teach airmanship, that is.

Among other things he would remind students that classroom instructors are rarely pilots and therefore see things from completely different points of view. The knowledge they impart is vitally important (though often overloaded with detail; you don't need to know how an oil pump functions so long as you know what to do when it malfunctions—and be certain that sooner or later it will.) The relative importance of the several aspects of flight varies rapidly, even wildly, the trick being to immediately evaluate a given situation and concentrate on the problem while not losing sight of the total picture.

Pilots fiddling with sick engines have flown back into the ground; pilots engrossed with weather radar have run their tanks dry; pilots busily attending to cockpit chores have collided; pilots fretting over fuel have become lost. All failed to keep the big picture in mind.

He would further suggest that all classroom information, including that in published manuals, be regarded with some reservation. To be sure, the verbal and printed material passed out is the best available at the time, but the mere fact that it is repeatedly revised should be thought-provoking. A pilot works in a fluid environment and must quickly adapt to new ways as experience makes them advisable. Indeed, he should anticipate such change.

During the war we were taught how to fly through line squalls by well-meaning experts who seemed to know exactly how thunderstorms were constructed, though none had actually been inside one to verify his theories. They told us that towering CB's sometimes rose to 25,000 feet but even the big ones could be penetrated. A lot of sheet metal fell out of dark clouds, proving they sometimes contained forces that could stop even the Army Air Corps.

We were also taught that the only procedure for multi-engine departure was to bend it over, clean it up and build speed, which worked well enough in such primitive types as the C-47 and B-17. The basic fallacy of it was revealed with the advent of high-performance equipment. If a B-26 engine died during the stay low, clean-it-up routine, it usually crashed. It was "one a day in Tampa Bay" down at McDill Field where B-26s crews were trained. Airline pilots bent postwar Convairs learning the same lesson.

The point—that a pilot can get into trouble while doing precisely what he was taught to do—should be made clear in school, yet I've never heard it mentioned. The facts and procedures for a new airplane are handed down as were the Ten Commandments. Memorize the numbers, go by the charts, fly it by the book and you'll be okay was the thrust. In airline circles a new man often seeks out a senior with time in the ship. "I've got the rating; now tell me what I really need to know." He wants no surprises. The following hour is invariably blunt, meaty and time well spent.

The information dispensed in typical training is indeed a most useful guide to good practice but you never heard that stressed in class. In fact, the tone is usually this-is-the-way-it-is which leads the inexperienced to accept everything as the gospel truth. Airplanes, routes, numbers, airports, procedures, everything is in a state of flux.

Since a student eventually will recognize the facts of life, he might as well learn them from the start. The new world he enters consists of two kinds of people, ground and air. The ground crowd design, construct, dispatch, maintain and otherwise control and regulate all flying, civil and military. The air people are the airmen who actually operate the machines which deliver the services.

Ground people wield clout not only because of their number but because they control the money and write the rules. They call the shots in overall strategy. A few try to dictate tactics, but that's our department. While the relationship between us is, for the most part, cordial, some contention is unavoidable. In general, they regard us with respect, tinged with question and envy. We regard them with respect, question and a certain suspicion. Each view is entirely normal and understandable.

It is important for us to understand why they are the way they are. Each of them, in his own corner, labors under considerable pressure. In my (the airline) area, executives wanted smooth, on-time, economical completion of schedules—those loomed in their thinking as prime considerations; the maintenance people wanted deferral of trivial (to them) repairs until the next hangar check; city fathers demanded noise abatement departures; controllers expected strict compliance with complex terminal routes, insisting that we avoid VFR traffic all the while.

The service itself is delivered in a machine to which the builder has appended a thick manual of instructions, restrictions, limitations, warnings and procedures which are to be followed to the letter. Its fueling and dispatch are based upon weather data which is, at best, an educated guess and, on occasion, wildly inaccurate.

There is no pleasing everyone every time; in fact, it is virtually impossible to complete a flight without violating one or more of the ambiguous federal rules which govern all operations, not to mention company policies. The pilot who tries will only end up frustrated and dangerous.

The ground type, being immersed in his own specialty, is unlikely to grasp the total picture. He is apt to regard flying as an overrated calling because he thinks of it in the narrow terms of his own expertise. Were fuel burn the sole pilot concern, much more could be conserved; were traffic avoidance the only worry, there would be fewer collisions, were it not for other distractions, we'd not forever be asking, "Was that for us?" We must keep all of the aspects in mind all of the time.

The ground fellow reckons in absolutes; two plus two equals four. In flight, however, two and two can come up three or five. When it happens there is no help in the manuals for the people who assembled them say such a thing can't happen. The positive statement is the trademark of the ground man. Considering history, he should be more honest with himself—and us. There is a considerable list of airliners on which the original round arithmetic was faulty. General and military aviation history confirms numerous similar design embarrassments.

Airmanship, as the old RAF fellow saw it, involves far more than flying skill. It suggests a mature personality, a well-rounded, thinking individual capable of enjoying his trade in a difficult, unrealistic and sometimes hostile atmosphere. It is knowing what is useful and what is irrelevant, what to believe and what to ignore, when to listen, when to think on something else. It is recognizing that the aviation community is machine-orientated to the point of machine worship. So intense is the desire for the system to work that, when there is trouble, it is instinctive to point to men—usually crewmen—as the cause. Even we who fly are often guilty of baseless snap judgement.

It is recognizing the interests which motivate ground people and remembering that we often understand their world better than they understand ours. It is clearly seeing that poor communication remains the root cause of most problems and placing the blame where it belongs—on us. Our public relations record is deplorable. We know—or we think we know—what is wrong with the system but we waste too much time comparing complaints, agreeing on the need for change, grousing to each other.

The fine features which make flying a fascinating and rewarding way of life are largely the result of constructive pilot suggestion or insistence. Whenever we settle for less, we have only ourselves to blame. It's too bad we have to spend a lifetime flying to learn what should have been taught from the beginning—in Airmanship.

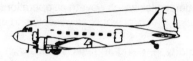

# Aerial Shutterbug

In aviation there is no older business than show business. The first aeronauts discovered, along with the wondrous properties of hot air and hydrogen, that people would pay to watch or, better still, to go along for the ride. Bob Hoover and the Blue Angels ply a trade established more than 200 years ago.

The second oldest flying specialty is aerial photography. Frenchman Felix Tourachon, spruce in top hat and frock coat, ascended to shoot Paris in 1863, four years before Wilbur Wright was born. This use of aircraft continues to the present.

It is interesting work. Desperate to continue flying in that bleak post-World War II time when pilots were ten cents a hundred, I grabbed an offer from a small outfit doing "aerial surveys." There was more to it than simple picture taking, much more: we shot broad areas straight down from high level, producing overlapping exposures of extremely high quality. The results were used to update maps and otherwise keep track of changes of the face of the Earth. Our clients were federal agencies and large cities. There's a word for the whole painstaking process: photogrammetry.

The boss had used Cessna Airmasters before the war and was starting up again with surplus AT-6s. How high had I flown one, he asked. I guessed 16,000 feet. Would it make 20,000 with two aboard and a camera? I thought it might. The average airplane can surprise its pilot when flown to its limits. Forty-five minutes after takeoff we struggled through 20,000 and eventually pegged out at 21,500, slopping along nose high with manifold pressure reading 17 inches. I fiddled with RPM and mixture controls seeking maximum thrust. Reversing course was a challenge. On the second try we only lost 200 feet. "Good enough," said the boss.

Aerial mapping is the world's safest flying employment. Acceptable pictures required near-perfect conditions and could be shot no sooner than three hours after sunrise and no later than three hours before sunset. Smoke, haze or the smallest puff of cumulus cloud spoiled the day; the slightest turbulence made it impossible for the photographer to keep the camera level. You couldn't get away with fudging; with magnifying lenses a photogrammetrist measured shadows and computed exposure time to within ten minutes and altitude to within 200 feet. In Kansas you could count on four "good" days a month on the average, in some coastal regions half a day.

My ship was stripped of antennas, paint and most rear seat equipment. A large hole was cut in the belly and a plexiglass window installed. Oxygen bottles, camera mount, film racks and a low seat were installed in the rear cockpit and off we went to Denver to map for the U. S. Forest Service. On nine cloudless mornings the cameraman and I broke ground early only to see tiny cu forming in mountain valleys just as we leveled off. I grew to hate clouds. Understand that we were paid a small base salary plus a mileage bonus for acceptable work, such bonus being reduced for reruns—of which there were many. In theory at least, you could earn a living.

We flew "lines" red-penciled on large scale (and often inaccurate) county maps, north and south so as to crab the bulbous nose into prevailing westerly winds and out of the way. The trick was to visualize a line as actually running across the ground and to stay directly above it. The maximum allowable deviation from a line on that job was—get this—1,200 feet. Exposures were timed to provide a 50% overlap and lines spaced to give a 30% sidelap. There were 360 negatives per roll, 9″ by 9″ each. Overlap was the photographer's problem, sidelap the pilot's.

There were frequent headaches. Once a minor oil leak fogged the belly window; then the camera's shutter jammed; next, while foolishly hurrying a turn, the ship flicked upside down and I lost 3,000 feet recovering from a spin. The cameraman remained silent; the previous day he had discovered, just as we leveled off, that his racks contained empty film cans. It was not a pursuit for the short-tempered.

Those were the first days of pressurized air travel. More than once we spied a new DC-6 or Constellation lumbering along beneath us. If we built speed to the red line and timed it just right, we could fly loose formation for long enough to give their drivers something to talk about, but who would believe them?

We spent time with Forest Service experts examining the product. From it they measured the water in remote mountain lakes, counted deer, identified tree diseases, figured the runoff of melting snow and discovered unauthorized use of public lands (cabins, stills, traps) and redrew road and trail maps. Few secrets eluded the airborne eye.

When all went well we could wrap up a city like Cincinnati in a day, several counties in a week. With a surplus Cessna C-78 we ran tests on a captured German camera that leveled itself. We got that old "Bamboo Bomber" up to 17,000, as I recall. In an effort to trim fuel and maintenance bills, the boss bought a Beech 35, one of the original Bonanzas, for just over $9,000. It was indeed economical, but tended to hunt in the slightest chop at a rate too rapid for pilot or cameraman correction. The resulting trail of shots zigzagged beyond acceptable limits.

A line shot along the Ohio valley contained an odd sequence. A DC-3 was spotted on the ramp at Louisville's Bowman Field. In the following shot it was taxying, in the next it was on the runway and so on throughout its scheduled run to Cincinnati. It appeared in every exposure, the last showing it parked at Lunken Airport.

We did occasional aerial views of factories, schools, distilleries and the like, shooting these small jobs down low from a J-3 with side panels removed. In winter that was as cold work as in the AT-6 at high level anytime. More than a few enterprising private pilots still earn operating expenses and more taking "oblique" shots of farms and factories.

A local fellow told me recently that he has been in aerial surveying for three years with his father who has been at it for 33, after taking over the business from his father. They fly Cessna 185s powered by turbocharged, fuel-injected Continental engines and operate routinely at 25,000 feet. I got our tired old AT-6 to 24,500 once on a very cold day and was inching toward 25,000 when my frozen photographer demanded that we go home immediately. It was the only time he lost his temper.

World War II veterans I've told about that strange job give me a funny look. Everyone knows an AT-6 won't climb that high.

# On Shooting Pilots

One piece of advice I'd give a student pilot just starting out is, "Take pictures. Get a camera and don't leave home without it." My regret is that so many planes, places and people in my flying career can now be recalled only from logbook entries. What a shame.

Initially, it is aircraft that will intrigue you most; the urge is to aim at nothing but machines. Take pictures of the people—your instructors, pilots you fly with, the airport crowd. And places—the fields, hangars and scenes you now take for granted—for in time you will value these mementos much more, believe me. There is virtually no aircraft I have flown or seen or heard about that cannot be found in a picture book, but many of the old fields have vanished and many a familiar face that is forever gone.

Keep your photographic record in some sort of order, identifying shots as to date, locale and names. The few minutes this takes will answer a lot of questions thirty years from now. When you do shoot planes, make sure you get the registration in the frame. The importance of this will become apparent years later.

My wings were pinned on by a genial and very senior RCAF officer who afterwards posed with any cadet who asked. I didn't bother. Today I'd prize a picture taken with him because of the occasion and because he was Gerry Nash, one of five remarkable Canadians who, flying Sopwith Triplanes as the legendary "Black Flight" in 1917, shot down 87 enemy aircraft in as many days. I shook his hand but what I'd give for a shot of that moment.

Had I taken my camera along I could show you a snapshot of my airplane being blown out of the sky. Did you ever hear of a PQ-8? Neither had I but the orders said go to Topeka and fly one to a North Carolina coastal base. It was in fact a prewar Culver Cadet with spindly fixed tricycle gear, its right seat stacked with black boxes. The fire engine red PQ-8 was a radio-controlled target. At the destination, an artillery school, I watched with mixed emotions as an incredibly lucky student gunner converted my little plane into a rain of kindling. I have no pictures of that strange episode—or of him.

Your snapshots will probably assume historical significance with the passage of time. The notion that manufacturers, corporations and government agencies keep vast photo files is mistaken. Space considerations lead to the destruction or dead storage (same thing) of most old film. The average airline can produce few shots of retired equipment; builders often dump "obsolete" files, priceless photos included. While the services do keep up huge picture collections, mistakes happen. A memorandum concerning inflammable celluloid caused one base to burn thousands of irreplaceable negatives of early Army types, the news of which left historians in tears. Researchers often find the best pictures in private hands; note the photo credits in most aviation references.

The fluid nature of this game is not apparent to those closely involved. Pictures taken today will seem odd in three years and completely outdated in ten. Go back to snapshots made fifteen years ago and you can hardly believe your eyes. Last night I ran off a box of 1965 slides and saw American Airlines Convair 990s, Trans-Texas DC-3s and Braniff Electras. Of six junior copilots in one shot, five became jumbo captains on international runs and all are now retired. The few snapshots I have of flying school days are almost unbelievable. Where have all the years gone? Why didn't I splurge on a few more rolls of film?

A camera can prove useful in unexpected ways. When a 727's wingtip brushed a baggage cart, its engineer lost no time on obtaining photographic proof that the nosewheel tires straddled the yellow line and that the cart was indeed inside the "circle of safety." They couldn't hang the verdict, "pilot error," on that one.

There is no telling where the camera habit will lead. It is a safe bet that most of the spectacular illustrations seen in books and magazines are the work of people who began as youngsters, shooting at airports for their own amusement. More than one enterprising shutter bug has learned that taking pictures of airplanes is more profitable and less work than washing them and has capitalized on the fact that, while few pilots bother with cameras, most want pictures. The possibilities in aerial photography are limited only by imagination. Any money-making venture may qualify camera/film and flying expenses as tax deductible, by the way.

The camera situation has vastly improved since my first attempts with a box Brownie and, later, a folding bellows affair. Today's inexpensive pocket job with built-in flash serves nicely. It's easy to load, use and takes up little space in flight kit or glove box. Prints or slides—

your choice.

A couple of tips learned from pros: the-closer-the-better is a good general rule, regardless of subject. Use of the flash in daylight close-ups will soften harsh shadows and record more detail. When an airplane is shot, get at least one view that shows the N-number. Be alert for the unusual; one of the best airshow pictures ever published is of expressions in the crowd.

Pictures made inside aircraft can be interesting. Pictures made from inside, through plexiglass, are more difficult, though planning and patience can produce worthwhile results. Don't expect your first work to match the cover of a magazine. Professionals manage such effect, not simply because of skill and expensive cameras, but because they work long hours. A magazine cover is usually the cream of hundred of exposures made during a lengthy session of picture-taking. The amateur might as well compare his home movie with a Hollywood product.

Oh yes, never, but never use up all your film. Leave a few shots on the roll, just in case. In case Air Force One comes in, for example. Gear up, maybe. You'd feel foolish standing there with an empty camera.

# The ABCs

That first hour of dual is vivid in recollection. It was a quiet, clear July morning, I well remember, and the barracks, parade ground and wood hangar are as distinct in memory as if I left yesterday. We walked down the line of yellow trainers and found ours—4568 (that detail from my log, however.)

Mr. Bennett led a preflighting of the Fleet biplane in which, if all went well, I would learn to fly. He removed gas and oil caps to verify levels, even though the fueler had just left. "He's not going to fly this aircraft, we are," he said, "and if a cap is loose, let's find out now and not when we're 100 feet above those trees." Made sense. "You will make this inspection every time you fly, exactly as I did." His use of "you" instead of "we" was faintly encouraging.

We buckled on our chutes. "When I say, 'you have control,' rock the wings; when I say, 'I have control,' hold your hands up where I can see them. One more thing, and this is important: if you ever hear me say, 'abandon the aircraft'—those three words—climb immediately onto the left wing, dive off under the tail and pull your rip-cord when well clear. I will follow. Is that understood?" I repeated the drill, climbed into the front seat and so began 45 years of the finest occupation yet contrived, at least, for one of my disposition.

Also vividly remembered is an electrifying instant three days later just when I was starting to get the hang of it, meaning I could keep us straight and level and manage shallow turns. "Watch where you're going, man!" came a shout through the voice tube; the stick was wrenched from my grip and a lumbering Anson slid by just beneath us, much too close. "We're not up here alone. I can see five other aircraft. Keep your eyes open!" I searched the sky and spotted two. It was the one you didn't see that got you, they said; some fighter pilot I'd make.

In due time and to my surprise, I was "sent solo," as the British say, and flew the circuit without the coaching voice, though I heard the admonishments as though my mentor was still back there. As every pilot remembers, it was a wondrous event. The next day, after more dual, I was sent out alone to flex my wings. "Keep the field in sight, be back in an hour," were the instructions. I took off to the west along with everyone else and frolicked across the Ontario landscape, reveling in the adventure.

During that blissful time the air became turbulent which, had I paid more attention in class, would have suggested a frontal passage and possible wind shift. I was alone on the downwind; everyone else had landed. It took forever to reach base leg, then I whistled across the fence like a Spitfire and slid to a stop with barely enough room to turn. Mr. Bennett was more than a little annoyed. "Damn it, look at the windsock!" he said. It stood out straight in a steady *east* wind. Every student earned a nickname; thereafter I was Downwind Morgan. It didn't happen again.

That blunder induced a tendency to drag it in at low speed which drew a lecture. "It's better to run into the far fence at 20 than the near one at 70. Think about it." Another day I taxied out and swung into the wind 500 feet inside the fence. "Just a minute, hold it right there. Let's use all of the field, shall we? There's nothing more useless than the airport behind you. You're not thinking."

Somewhere in the attic is the map used on the first cross-country, a 100-mile round robin. I spent hours on the flight plan. Admiral Byrd found the North Pole with less preparation. My expedition went off splendidly, however, and with our field in sight I was immersed in self-congratulation when through the voice tube, sharply, "We're supposed to be at 3,000 feet, right? What does your altimeter read? And you're wandering all over the sky; let's get back on course!" Later, my complacency having been illuminated, Mr. Bennett said I'd done a fair job and sent me off solo on a longer voyage.

Flying Officer Thres, an RAF type who had completed an operational tour, was assigned to check student progress. A fair and reasonable man, he strapped into the rear cockpit for the dreaded 20-hour check. I did what he asked, including a spin recovery, all apparently to his satisfaction, there being little comment from him. Then he then said, "I have control. I say, Morgan, has your instructor shown you a slow roll?" I shook my head. Sky and earth swapped places, came right again and we emerged in a power off glide. "You have control," he said. I rocked the wings and took the throttle; it wouldn't budge. He'd neatly tricked me.

Ignoring two fields adequate for the airship Hindenburg, I shoehorned us into a tiny pasture filled with cattle. At 100 feet he advanced the power and we climbed away. Back at the field he said, "Actu-

ally, I think you would have made it but, dear me, those poor cows!"
Old Thres was a good head.

Mr. Bennett then bore down on engine failures, once inflicting
a sudden silence at 200 feet on takeoff. I shoved the nose over, made
a slight turn, glided toward a gap between tall trees and was rewarded
with, "That's the way to do it. Now you're using your head."

We rode in back for instrument training. A spring-loaded hood
shut out the usual view. Pull a catch and it flew back if a quick exit
became desirable. First was taught the lesson still being learned in
the last terrible minutes of life by foolhardy pilots who won't listen to
those who know: the senses are worthless in clouds. Time and again
I tried to stay right side up, only to fall into a graveyard spiral.

The point having been made, the secrets of "blind flying" with
needle, ball and airspeed were explained. With a compass that
bobbed and swung with every bump and an ancient altimeter whose
needle crept an inch per thousand feet, it was clumsy going. Yet the
nimble Fleet could not only be kept upright with concentration but
maneuvered through climbing and descending turns with fair precision. "Relax. Hold the stick with two fingers, roll smoothly into the
turns, scan the panel, don't stare at one gauge." I listened and worked
hard. Recovery from unusual positions and spins under the hood was
particularly great sport.

As the weeks flew by, washouts thinned our ranks. A pal you
sat next to at breakfast was gone by evening and we neither understood his failure nor our own survival. F/O Thres was back for the
"50-hour test" (that's how it's logged) and an instrument check. Here
recorded are the dates of those crucial checks, yet I recall neither hop.

Precious little was learned during those 65 hours or in the 100
to follow in AT-6 Harvards for that matter, yet we emerged as "pilots" and had wings as proof. The mechanical skills needed to fly
larger and faster aircraft could be learned. The seasoning that makes
a pilot worthy of the title would come more slowly.

Serious flying involves a pattern of thinking which is both narrow
and broad, trusting and suspicious. The drudgery of study, training
and preflight preparation is the price of survival. Strict adherence to
proven procedures is essential; complacency is lethal. Certain details demand scrutiny yet must never be allowed to obscure the overall
picture. A pilot is suspicious of his machine and everyone concerned
with its operation, himself included; potentially, he is the chain's
weakest link. The knack of calmly analyzing a problem and reaching
a sensible solution is developed though experience and self discipline.
He must think and think again on what is happening—and what might.

As time passed and the blunt truths sank in, often as the result
of a stupid boner or bad fright, more than once I was less than proud

of myself. I had known better every time. In a sense, every secret of flight had been revealed during those first training hours. But I had not paid attention.

# The Great BAAB Mystery

There are many ways to get lost in an airplane. Here are some that worked for me. Go ahead, have your laugh at my expense, but ponder also on the foolish predicaments that can result from laziness, overconfidence and sheer stupidity.

Upon returning from overseas in 1943, I was assigned to ferrying, the most lackluster of wartime duties. My CO, a stateside warrior who had promoted a command at his home town, took an instant dislike to me because of my ribbons. Not one of them meant anything except that I'd been there, but they clearly made him uncomfortable. So he ordered me to Chicago to pick up a new PT-23, an open cockpit two-seat trainer. In December.

Have you ever flown in an open cockpit plane in Illinois in December? A well digger in the Klondike has it easier. After an hour of exquisite misery I landed for gas and decided there might be less wind blast in the front seat. One problem: there was no compass up front. But nothing could stop the Army Air Corps, not in this toy airplane anyway. Noting only that my destination was clear, I headed south under a 1,000-foot ceiling, sitting on my hands and working the stick with my knees. I was refolding the map one instant and watching it float away in the rain the next, now down at 300 feet to clear the clouds. No map, no sun, no compass and no good plans for the future.

A small town appeared over the nose. I couldn't read the depot name but there was something on the water tank. "Seniors 1942." I hoped all of them were drafted and got permanent assignments to Alaska. I overtook a bus and looked back. "San Francisco." Thanks for nothing, Greyhound. After a considerable search at treetop level, I lucked out, squeezed into a small pasture and slid to a stop just short of a fence. A wizened old man in overalls tottered over and poked the wet fabric. "This one of them guvmint jobs?" he asked.

His wife was a great cook.

The P-51 Mustang's tanks held 269 gallons, enough to make Corpus Christi to Louisville nonstop if you went high. And didn't get lost enroute. The Navy forecaster pointed out a front east of St. Louis but said I could beat it. The wings were full but the fuselage gauge read 25 gallons less than full. No problem. Plenty of places to refuel if necessary. Barksdale Field appeared five minutes early so on to Memphis, then Nashvile, arriving overhead with enough gas left to wrap it up with 15 minutes to spare. I reran the numbers, came up with 20 minutes reserve and talked myself into it. I'd flown this stretch many times and knew it well. I started down in a shallow descent, pressing on.

It was one of those extremely hazy days with no forward visibility, in fact, it was hard to pick out landmarks straight down. Sprawling Ft. Knox did not appear when it should; instead I saw a strange river running due north through hilly country. Guessing that I had picked up a strong west wind (the only thing right I did that day), I reduced power to the minimum, picked up the bisector heading and tuned in the Louisville range. Nothing. A little Mickey Mouse 200-400 kilocycle receiver with a range of 50 miles at 8,000 feet was the sole navigational gear. I was then at 2,000 feet, rapidly burning fuel. I ran the fuselage tank dry, got another five minutes out of the right wing then returned to the left which contained less than 25 gallons if the gauge was right. Suddenly the Louisville range came in loud and clear; I was on the east leg. I landed straight in heavy rain. It took 260 gallons to top the tanks. The fuel truck driver gave me a funny look.

And I might as well tell you the BAAB story, confession supposedly being good for the soul. At a certain southern field a second looie was sent to me for C-47 familiarization. He gazed with wonder at the cockpit and said it was his first ride in an all-metal airplane. He was a primary school instructor inducted into the Army as a staff pilot. Well, he'd come to the right man for answers. Noting only that there was 90 minutes of fuel aboard, I headed for the wild blue to impart my skills.

An hour later I noticed that, one, I was lost, and, two, there were no maps on board. The crew chief pointed to a number of airplanes on the horizon. We ambled over and saw they were circling a large military field. I fished around and found the right tower frequency, joined traffic and landed. On the bumper of the follow-me jeep was stenciled, "BAAB," B_____ Army Air Base, whatever B stood for. "Recognize anything?" I asked my crew. Double negative. It was time to get organized. "Men, we've got a problem," I announced, attempting to distribute the blame. I assigned each man an area of patrol, emphasizing discretion. "Check signs, listen, find a paper, anything. But don't ask whatever you do!''

I went into Operations. No help from the big wall map; everything around the string hole was smudged. No cover on the phone book, needless to say. Try the bulletin board; everything you could dream of asking about BAAB was up there—the base movie schedule, a list of off-limits clubs, an admonition to wear the Class A uniform in the Officers' Club—everything except the blasted name of the place and where it was. There were no clues in the men's latrine, either. Call the chaplain? He would understand. As a last resort but not yet. I met the others outside. No soap. Then it hit me. ''Sergeant, take this nickel, call the operator and ask her where you are.''

''You're kidding, Sir.''

''I'm not kidding. If we don't report in to our home base soon they'll start a search. How can I report in if I don't know where we are? Get on it, Sergeant.''

He was in the booth five minutes, talking fast, but he got the answer.

''Brookley Field!''

''Where's that?''

''Right here; that's where we are.''

''Where's 'right here'?''

''Give me another nickel. I hope I don't get the same operator.''

He hit pay dirt, I reported our arrival to our home base with some manufactured excuse for landing there and, refuelled, we headed home with maps filched from BAAB's files.

Using the authority vested in me as an officer and gentlemen of the Army of the United States, I classified the entire incident as top secret, promising that any divulgence would surely result in an immediate court martial. They wouldn't buy it, shaking their heads in unison, so I bribed the pair with expensive steak dinners. Plus drinks, and they could put it away.

Flying home from Florida one day I looked down at Brookley Field, Mobile, Alabama, long since abandoned as an active air base, and remembered. And, even after all the time gone by since, I winced.

''What are you looking at?'' asked the copilot.

''Just an old field where I landed once, way back, before you were born,'' I said. One copilot knowing about it was enough.

# Drivers, Pilots and Artists

One day the cockpit door was open as we ran through the preflight checklists. A lady looked in. "May my son take a look?" Of course he could. In DC-3 times there was always a skinny wide-eyed kid looking in, asking questions. Such interest dwindled in later years. We desexed flying, turned it into just another job and most boys lost interest. Few youngsters understand that flying remains most things we saw in it when we were boys.

"These are the men who drive the airplane," she told her son. The copilot glanced at me. The boy blushed. He knew. As we taxied out the copilot said, "Who's going to start it off today, Pops? You want me to 'drive' the first leg?" *Drive* is not a term we care for, yet it is a fact that a good number of the people who operate airplanes do indeed drive them.

Major Wilson commanded the Army Reserve observation unit at Bowman Field in the late 1930s. He recognized a few of us high schoolers as true believers and allowed us into the large cool hangar where we admired the trio of ancient BT-2Bs that comprised his small detachment. Once I heard him bless out a lieutenant after they landed. "This is an airplane, not a truck. It's like a violin. You don't *drive* the bow across the strings, you play the instrument. You've got to learn to *fly* this airplane." Having never left the ground I was not sure what he meant, but I thought about it. Looking back, it is clear that Major Wilson was in every sense a pilot. He was a dedicated airman, irritated by rough handling.

My first instructor was from the same mold. His love for the game was infectious. If you didn't come with it, he gave it to you; if he couldn't, you were not cut out to fly anyway. At the end of my clumsy practices he'd say, "I have control, take us home and drop the trainer onto the grass the way a paint brush touches wood." It was beautiful. He had pride in his skills.

Such professionals influenced my thinking. They continuously strove for precision and smoothness. Awkwardness during the first hours was excusable; casualness, corner cutting and lack of interest drew their contempt. You worked every minute or you weren't worth the trouble.

Such a philosophy pervades many fields and is a good thing. It separates jobs from crafts. In flying it drives most airmen to attain a high degree of skill and to work hard at maintaining it. A pilot is good at what he does not simply because it is the proper thing to do but because it keeps him alive. So most of us strived to become pilots. We tried, we worked at it every day, we were reasonably skillful but unspectacular, we got by nicely, we were average. We made up perhaps 90 percent of flying license holders; nearly all of us will die of natural causes.

A handful of our colleagues—perhaps four out of a hundred—rated a special classification. They were the artists whom we all admired and envied, the pilot's pilots, the so-called naturals though there is no such animal. Keen and adaptable, they mastered new techniques and types without apparent effort, breezing through tough schooling and checkrides as though on the third time around. They enjoyed an uncanny rapport with flying machines that made the rest of us feel like all-thumbs bumblers. They could fly anything, anytime, anywhere and they made it look so easy. First-rate piloting is never easy. Had they gone into the arts or sports or business or politics, their names would be household words.

The remaining six percent were drivers, as remarkable in their own way as the artists. Impatience, stubbornness and no apparent feel for machinery were their trademarks. They flog their planes through space with minimum attention to accepted practice, cutting whatever corners they can. They were the despair of their instructors and a joke among their associates. Drivers embarrassed pilots and made artists shake their heads.

Drivers, pilots and artists are to be found in every corner of the picture. You find them on private flying fields and aboard aircraft carriers. They fly executive ships, supersonic fighters, helicopters, airliners, gliders and hot air balloons. All of which raises the question: how do the dirvers hang on, some for a lifetime, in such elite company?

Our measures of each other, while admirably based, are unrealistic. The more you ponder the matter, the better the driver appears. A surprising number of aviation greats were, when the veneer of heroic accomplishment is stripped away, drivers to the bone. Manfred von Richthofen, the vaunted World War I Hun ace with 80 claims, had difficulty learning to fly and was regarded as an indifferent pilot. He was a superb tactician and crack shot who viewed his airplane strictly as a weapon; flying for its own sake did not interest him.

The same holds true for other top aces on both sides of World Wars I and II. It is hard to convince anyone in or out of flying that a pilot who could knock a number of the enemy from the sky was less than a spectacular airman. Yet, many of them perished in accidents caused by stupid mistakes every cadet is taught to avoid. They regarded the plane as a gun platform and had the same regard for it as a soldier for his rifle. The fight was everything, the flight of little consequence.

Which was, and is, as it has to be. Fighter pilots are fighters first, pilots later. They are hunters and killers trained to find and destroy enemy aircraft. The superb exhibitions flown by the Thunderbirds and Blue Angels disguise the real purpose of their colorful mounts. Their shows are staged for taxpayer entertainment. Despite their announcers' claims that the jocks overhead are only showing you what every cadet is taught, they are, in fact, a small band of artists selected after intensive competition. The average military airmen would not try to match them.

Likewise, the record of civil accomplishments from the beginning contains incredible adventures by obvious drivers. The challenge was, the thing, the plane but a tool with which to tackle it. Certain of our idols' planes spent more weeks in repair shops than hours in flight. Had they been more cautious, more aware of the outrageous demands they were making of themselves and their machines, it's unlikely they would have tried at all. But they did, many survived and our hats are rightly off to them.

Needless to add, the hall of fame also includes many artists. With unbounded confidence and rare skill they took on the seemingly impossible, then shrugged off their feats as being all too easy which was the way they made them seem. Pilots are on the list as well, ordinary airmen who for twelve hours or twelve weeks rose above the ordinary to accomplish miracles.

To be fair, there are drivers and drivers. One kind is a bumbling fool. Somehow he got into flying and he remains, arrogant, cocksure, weak in all departments and contemptuous of any talk about more training. To him a plane is another toy dished up by modern society for his selfish use. He operates it (and his car, boat, rifle, etc.) as if he has inherited more skill that the rest of us earn in 20 years. According to him, all the fussing around we do with techniques is nonsense. He feels no responsibility toward anyone his mistakes might harm. This character is as deadly as a cobra. The military wouldn't have him on a bet; he hasn't a prayer with the airlines, he'll never fly an executive aircraft or any other planes whose owners value their property. Those who know him wouldn't rent him a bike but he sneaks by if he buys a plane. If he stays more or less within the law he can keep going indefinitely, or until he rolls his ship into a ball, which is often the outcome. He is a disgrace and an embarrassment. Private aviation usually gets an undeserved bad name because of him.

A pitiful sort is the driver who means well but has no flair for it. He may eventually solo and log a few hours. While his antics make other airmen cover their eyes, he's inept, not stupid. He usually comes to realize the hopelessness of it in time and quits before he kills himself.

Finally, there's the professional driver who makes a career of driving airplanes. He knows his stuff and is as safe as the next fellow statistics-wise. He may log 30,000 hours and never dent a wingtip. He's capable, even expert, insofar as the mechanics of it go. It's just that he doesn't give a damn about the fine points. He's impatient. "This thing is supposed to go from A to B in a straight line—fast," as one saw it.

He's up against the limits, legally and operationally, every mile of flight. He taxies like A. J. Foyt coming out of the pit with great blasts of power and hard braking. Aloft his power remains at maximum and often a hair above. When he changes heading or altitude his riders know all about it. He nails speed on the red line descending and is not overly bothered by chop in the lower levels. After landing he uses the same hard braking and maximum reversing on a 12,000 runway he'd use on a 3,500-foot strip. He has little interest in conserving fuel, lessening airframe strain or making things comfortable for those in back who pay his wages. He regards other traffic as a special challenge, dealing with it in a manner that does credit to a New York cab driver. He plays aerial chicken. While most pilots deplore his attitude, he gets the job done, usually under schedule.

Some of the drivers I've known had the makings of good pilots, even artists in some cases, but it was not in their nature. Flying is an individual exercise, a reflection of personality to a degree. A man who is energetic and aggressive finds the mounting restrictions and limitations of modern flying hard to accept. Much of what must be endured today would tax the patience of a saint, much less a headstrong human.

Many a driver is what he is because he is unwilling or unable to knuckle under. He refuses to conform; he fights the system every time he fires up. He stays within the rules, but barely. Perhaps his is a juvenile approach. Or, it could be that the rest of us take ourselves a little too seriously, put too much emphasis on the details and meekly accept whatever new regulation goes into the book while losing sight of the purpose of it all?

Whatever the truth, we will always have the driver in our ranks, as much a subject of discussion as the artist.

# Lucky, Plucky Pierre

The first pilots were "aeronauts." One of the most fascinating of them was Frenchman Pierre Blanchard. Every "voyage" completed during the earliest days of human flight marked a first of one sort or another. Blanchard's first ascent was no exception. He inflated his hydrogen balloon and was climbing into the gallery with his passenger, a Benedictine monk, when a spectator demanded to be taken along. When refused, he drew his sword, slashed the balloonist on the hand and hacked at the rigging. Gendarames quickly foiled the first of all attempts to hijack a flying machine and the bandaged aeronaut made a successful flight across Paris the same day.

Over the next quarter century the strange little Frenchman was the first many times. While his contemporaries flew for sport or scientific study, Pierre's motive was, purely and simply, profit. He was the world's first professional airman. There were many affluent patrons eager to bankroll an "aerostat," a ride in which cost whatever the market would bear. The novelty of flight was such that all other activity ceased when a balloon went up. The throngs attending these exciting events presented money-making opportunities as Blanchard saw it. Why not rope off the launching site and sell tickets? There were francs to be coined from the new art. And so the original air show promoter, despite the first attempt at skyjacking, made his initial hop in March, 1794, five months after the Montgolfier brothers proved that trapped hot air could lift men from the earth.

Born into a poor Normandy family 31 years earlier, Pierre got little education but showed a flair for mechanics. At 16 he built a crude bicycle then became intrigued with the problem of flight. He constructed a "flying vessel" with a fully-enclosed cabin (another first, perhaps) from which protruded movable wings actuated by levers and treadles. A public demonstration was rained out and, having privately pedaled himself into a lather with no effect, the lad gave up.

The scheme was anything but a failure, however, for his glib claim that his contraption had indeed lifted and born him through space at 75 miles an hour was widely accepted. This false publicity was to pay off later.

The Montgolfier success in September, 1783, and Professor Jacques Charles' ascent under hydrogen 10 days later excited no one more than Pierre. He witnessed the Charles ascent, noticing with interest that the spectators numbered 50,000. Incidentally, these astounding accomplishments took place 21 years before Trevithick built the first steam locomotive and 102 years before the first gasoline automobile.

Pierre enlisted backers and built an aerostat, and a curious affair it was. Beneath the gas bag was an umbrella-like parachute from which hung a gondola equipped with rudder, rotating fan and oars. Should the bag burst, he would float safely to earth, at least, that was the theory. Fortunately, the chute was never put to the test. Though the idea was completely unworkable, credit him with contriving the first emergency gear for an aircraft.

As for the oars, etc., he truly believed he could navigate at will, it being a popular notion among aeronauts that winds aloft flowed in fixed streams, like rivers, and the solution lay in finding one going the right way. Pierre convinced himself that by rowing into favorable currents he could navigate at will. One claim that he had touched down exactly on his launching pad neglected to mention that he had been towed back by a horse. He also boasted that when a flag fell overboard, he valved the gas and dropped quickly enough to retrieve it. It was years before he realized the truth about rowing and abandoned his tiresome calisthenics.

Poor profits were realized from his first hops so he went to England where he was greeted with enthusiasm, his hosts accepting at face value the preposterous reports he brought with him. One admirer was Dr. John Jeffries, a Bostonian with a London practice. The doctor paid Blanchard for a two-hour ride across Kent. Upon landing, the enchanted rider made a startling proposal: let's fly across the channel to which Pierre immediately agreed.

Jeffries paid 800 pounds, which was fair, but paid up front, which was a mistake. The Frenchman locked himself inside Dover Castle and began making hydrogen, having decided to share the glory with no one. Jeffries demanded entrance and a local magistrate finally ordered Pierre to honor his contract. Then it was found that the balloon would not rise and the doctor was on the verge of climbing out when he noticed that Pierre appeared to have put on more weight than the pre-takeoff feast could account for. The cunning Blanchard had attached lead weights to his belt, none of which trickery annoyed the good doctor, a man of incredible good humor, and the two drifted out across the cold sea just after noon on January 7, 1785.

All went well for an hour and a half. Then, with six miles left to go, gas began leaking from the bag. Overboard went all the ballast but the settling continued at a dangerous rate. Next the flags, pennants and "other silk and finery," oars, fan, food, instruments, ropes and anchors. As a last resort, the wine chest was tossed over the side. Judging from the doctor's account that "my noble little captain and I were, God knows how, as merry as grigs to think how we should splatter the water," most of the bottles were empties.

The rapid sinking continued so the pair stripped off greatcoats and "trowsers" and donned cork jackets. At the doctor's suggestion they urinated, though we may guess that worried Pierre needed no prompting. A further suggestion that they throw up the predeparture meal became unnecessary as the balloon finally leveled and slowly drifted over land. Jeffries held onto a tree while Blanchard released the remaining gas and thus ended the first international flight. One letter from the mail carried and the gondola itself may be seen in a Calais museum. (I was sometimes tempted to relate this true story when a passenger complained about our being 20 minutes late during one of my 10-hour international airline schedules.)

Pierre continued flying for another 23 years. He was an unattractive character—vain, jealous, self-serving, a braggart who demanded all the attention—yet there was no doubting his skill and bravery. He was acclaimed a hero and the praise was deserved. He was the first man to fly in Germany, Belgium, Poland, Switzerland, Holland and Czechoslovakia. His record-breaking 300-mile nonstop hop (a fact) was followed by his claim to have climbed to 32,000 feet (a fib). His wife mastered the art and became a celebrity in her own right. It was said she was terrified in traffic, fearing her carrriage would overturn, and sometimes went aloft in a tethered balloon to sleep—another first, if true.

A Blanchard exhibition was preceded by intensive promotion. The couple were born entertainers whose bluster and braggadocio whipped public interest into a frenzy by show time. When the hour arrived, they flew. Indeed, it was dangerous for an aeronaut not to perform as advertised. More than one mob, impatient when a performance was botched or delayed, thrashed the star and destroyed his balloon. Pierre and Marie not only delivered on schedule but made sure that anyone who wanted to watch was accommodated—for a price. Parking was a problem even then, one newspaper advising viewers "to order their Coachmen, after having set them down at the door, to drive on and follow the directions of proper persons."

Following a brush with the police in Austria, Pierre decided to

**Lucky, Plucky Pierre   27**

introduce aeronautics in the new world. He arrived in Philadelphia, the capital city, and signed in as "Blanchard, the celebrated aeronaut." Before light on January 9, 1793, he began inflating his aerostat in the courtyard of Walnut Street Prison (now 6th and Walnut). Sulphuric acid dripped onto iron filings in sealed rum casks, the resulting "inflammable air" being piped into other barrels for washing and drying and into the varnished linen bag. By the appointed hour of 10:00 a.m., all was ready.

Considering the audience, it would have been a bad time for anything to go wrong. President Washington was there with his cabinet, most members of Congress, the chief justices and the four men who would succeed him—John Adams, Thomas Jefferson, James Madison and James Monroe. Henry Knox, Alexander Hamilton and Aaron Burr held front row ($5) tickets, as did Betsy Ross, Martha Washington, Dolley Madison and Maj. L'Enfant, designer of the new capital at Washington. Never before or since have so many American notables gathered to watch an individual perform. The rest of the city's 45,000 citizens waited outside the walls.

Pierre, decked out "in a plain blue suit, cock'd hat and white feathers," received a signed "passport" from the President, clambered aboard and released a few pounds of sand. His balloon rose straight up and drifted away to the south. He looked down on the astonished witnesses, "an immense number of people, which covered the open places, the roofs of houses, the steeples, the streets and roads. What a sight!" he later told reporters. He doffed his hat in salute and waved the flags of France and the new republic. "Then I strengthened my stomach with a morsel of biscuit and a glass of wine."

It was his 45th hop and though it lasted less than an hour and covered but 15 miles, it was the first manned flight made anywhere in the western hemisphere. He landed near Woodbury, N.J., and was driven back to the city where the momentous event was suitably celebrated.

Back in Europe Blanchard continued flying for 15 years. In 1808 he rose from The Hague on his 60th ascent and suffered a heart attack while aloft. He survived the subsequent uncontrolled landing but died a year later. Marie continued ballooning for a decade and made good money at it. Her spectacular and hazardous fireworks displays grew huge crowds. She soared skyward trailing a ball of fire on a cord, then lit sparklers and tossed them out in small parachutes, working with an open flame beneath the bag of hydrogen.

That it didn't happen sooner was a miracle. One evening escaping gas was ignited and the poor woman was suddenly silhouetted against a spurt of flame. With characteristic coolness she lightened the car. It seemed for an instant that the fire was out and she might survive the rapid fall, but the car struck a tall house, spilling her down the roof and onto the sidewalk. It was the final Blanchard first as Marie became the first woman to perish in a flying accident.

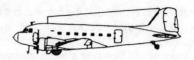

# Experience

Imagine this: it's December and every place from Chicago east has fallen on its face—low ceilings, freezing rain, iced runways, the whole miserable winter bit at its worst. You and I are at Newark Airport with tickets to O'Hare. Outside are three DC-9's, all Chicago bound, and we can take our pick. Their captains have, respectively, 7,500 hours, 15,000 and 22,000. Which airplane shall we take? What safety value can be put on flying hours logged?

Two men walked onto my trip one stormy night, one of whom was obviously nervous. The cockpit door was open. One winked at me and said to his skittish friend, "When you see an old graybeard like him sitting in that seat you have nothing to worry about." I didn't know whether to thank him or slam the door. But it made me think; does longevity in itself guarantee anything?

Much weight is placed on experience as measured by hours logged. A pilot with 7,500 hours obviously has done most things right for a long while: one with 15,000 has done most things right for twice as long and is therefore twice as "experienced," but it need not follow that he's twice as good. In fact, he may be the inferior of the two.

A cursory survey of 21 major airline accidents over a period of years involving several types from the propeller-driven Convair 440 to the jet-powered DC-8 produced these averages: the captain was 43 and had flown 13,200 hours, 3,380 of them in the aircraft concerned. His copilot's figures were 34/6,350/1,130. This impressive experience did not prevent a score of disasters. It is a fact of the flying life that a single stupid mistake can wipe out all the good work of a long and accident-free career.

During my copiloting years it was a pleasure—and, occasionally, onerous duty—to fly with a number of skippers approaching retirement. They reacted in sometimes curious ways. Most seemed unaffected and performed the same predictable solid job until they set brakes for the last time. A few dropped their guard and fretted less over the details that had always concerned them. A handful became increasingly uptight as the final day neared, as if expecting fate to pull a cruel trick just when they had it made. Those good old boys became mean old bears hard to please, and it was impossible to cheer them up.

Experience is like money; the more you have, the better you feel. But while money in the bank buys peace of mind, hours in the log buy nothing until they are spent. The lessons of yesterday must be repeatedly withdrawn and invested in today's work. It is easy to forget and to accept the comfortable illusion that 5,000 or 15,000 hours are in themselves a hedge against trouble.

The nature of his work makes an airline pilot particularly prone to such complacency. He boards his 727 at Los Angeles to fly to Dallas, a run he's made 200 times in the same type in all kinds of weather. He could fly the route without a chart. Today's weather is near perfect and there's the bonus of 70 knots on the tail; the prospects are almost boring. He must prod himself into considering disagreeable possibilities and mentally prepare to deal with them. He is not paid to perform the routine but to expertly handle the unexpected. He is paid to recall the past and apply it to the present, to exercise self discipline and use his experience.

Age is in the experience equation, nearly always as a plus factor, which indeed it should be. Long gone is the notion that flying is a young man's game; the skies are filled with flying grandfathers, many of them driving jumbos. Gregory Boyington and Douglas Bader were more than a match for fighter pilots young enough to be their sons, proving that even combat aviation is not the exclusive province of the very young. Vermont Garrison and George Davis were aces in two wars and there are many other examples.

The point is easily made that age can and should enhance performance along with hours logged. Slowing reflexes are normally offset by increased knowledge and improved judgement. Like all young copilots I was often frustrated by the fussbudget ways of my seniors. Their suspicion, sardonic distrust and endless double-checking would drive a saint to drink. The cautious approach can be overdone, but I came to see that most of their painstaking was based on hard experience. They taught me much.

Do we make too much of age and hours logged? The 7,500 hour captain on the Newark ramp is as qualified, at least, on paper, as the 22,000 hour veteran at the next gate. Deregulation is going to provide answers to such questions. Many captains flying for new entries into the airline picture have less time and seasoning than the average copilot with a long-established competitor. Southwest Airlines, now well into its second decade, has proved that an "upstart" airline can enjoy spectacular success when properly managed and adequately funded. Other newcomers are known to be stretched to the limit. There are stories about overly long crew duty periods, slipshod training, low pay and less than topnotch maintenance that have led corporations to blacklist certain lines for company travel.

The FAA, mindful of the post-World War II debacle when money-strapped new "airlines" flying surplus equipment made the front pages with appalling regularity, keeps a fairly close eye on things. But they cannot inspect every cotter pin and monitor every pilot. A hard-pressed operator can find many ways to cut corners and all insiders know it.

A few years back the airlines of this country flew 26 months without a serious accident, an accomplishment we would all like repeated, and bettered. Perhaps the deregulation upheaval will in time result in a stronger industry and even safer service, though I'm not so sure of these happy results over the long haul. Time will tell.

Meanwhile, they've called our flight. Do what you like, but I'm catching the Nine the graybeard's flying.

# Because He's Got the Job

In multi-engine aircraft operation, a relaxed atmosphere up front goes far in producing consistently good, safe flying. Twenty thousand hours in the left seat, ten in the right and five at the engineer's panel do not necessarily add up to the best possible crew. Certainly, the experience is there, but how well do the three heads work together? The total is not always the sum of its parts.

Those of us who found airline berths after World War II had heard tales of the tyranical captain who made his copilot's life a misery. He was said to be typical. Such rumors caused many World War II veterans to avoid airline work. "I'm not going to sit in the right seat of an old DC-3 and take abuse from some pompous knothead who flew between Nashville and Newark while I was getting shot up over Italy," was heard more than once.

There were eight of us in that early flight engineer class. The CAA (now FAA) had only recently decided to add a third man to DC-6 and Constellation crews. We would be on probation in more ways than one and we knew it. We earned our novel ratings, donned uniforms with two stripes and reported for duty.

Our DC-6 skippers dated back to the early 1930s, the top numbers back to airmail days. Some had been outraged when the Bureau of Air Commerce required copilots in their trimotored Fords and Boeings and had vented their resentment of federal interference upon their unwanted assistants, hence the stories going around.

Like many legends dear to pilots, the despotic skipper stories were not altogether true. Most of the captains we new flight engineers flew with were reasonable and fair-minded men. Each had his pet ways, to be sure, and it was wise to memorize them. Old Charlie wanted the checklist read exactly as printed, Mort wanted you and the copilot to handle it and Porter never wanted to see the thing. "Read me the emergency items if we need 'em," he'd say. "I know the routine stuff.'' Norm went through an elaborate preflight ritual with seat adjustment, gloves, baseball cap, clipboard and a detailed briefing of things to come while Clancy never appeared until the cabin door was closed. ''Turn Three, Morgan.'' he'd say, fastening his belt. No matter what was taught in training, it was understood that the airplane belonged to the captain to run as he pleased. And, if a mistake was made, he would face the music alone. It was his airplane in all respects.

Flying was one-man work according to the premise of that time. No matter what the feds said, the copilot and engineer were seen as standing on the edge of the picture. Our DC-6 skippers (who owned the union as well as the airplanes) saw to it that their pay was kept double the combined wages of their assistants, a clue to their sense of cockpit values. It couldn't last. The complexity of postwar equipment and the rapid increase in traffic made airline flying a team effort. Most of the old heads accepted the third man and gave him a share of the load.

Most, that is. A handful lived on in the past. ''Tell ATC to give me a lower altitude,'' this sort would tell his copilot. He was up there all alone with a dummy on the right who'd get him into trouble if not carefully watched. As for the engineer . . . I flew a month with a captain to whom I was apparently invisible. I raised the gear and dropped the flaps on command but was otherwise completely ignored. During long legs he and the copilot discussed many topics. I listened. When he ordered coffee, he asked for two cups. So be it. The next month I drew a fine old gent who depended on me for engine and fuel management and sought my views when a problem arose. He was, incidentally, one of the sharpest pilots I ever knew.

The engineer had a front row seat at captain-copilot squabbles. More than once I sat between two characters who utterly despised each other. One bitter pair communicated with each other through me. ''Tell him to get me the Tulsa weather,'' that sort of thing. It was ridiculous, of course; it was also an education. Ninety-nine out of a hundred trips were pleasant, often fun. We three ran those schedules as professionals and as our passengers had a right to expect.

Later, as copilot, I flew with younger captains, practically all of whom were cordial working associates. A few aped the handful of hard nosed seniors, forever reminding the world they were God's special gifts to aviation. Every hour was a training hour with such boors, no matter what your background. Happily, they comprised a small percentage of the seniority list, but a month with a fellow who never stops reminding you he's in charge could be a longish 30 days.

After 15 years as a flight engineer and copilot in eight airliner types, I concluded that, next to professional skill, diplomacy is the most desirable attribute of an engineer or copilot. I'm not talking about boot-licking. I'm talking about working with a captain no matter what you think of him because, as the counsel for the Caine mutineers put it in that classic scene, ". . . because he's got the job."

The pilot who goes into most multi-engine flying must serve an apprenticeship, sometimes a lengthy one, under the supervision of pilots who got there earlier. He may find himself teamed with a captain who is younger or less experienced or not quite sure of himself. And, sooner or later, he is certain to find himself teamed with a left-seater who can only be summed up as an equine's posterior. The expert handling of such a misfit is part of the job. The name of the game is not winning friends, but flying safely. No one expects perfect weather every day, nor should he expect jolly companions every trip. Doing the job right despite the weather and regardless of who's in the other cockpit seats is all that matters.

Eventually I made the left seat and only then did I appreciate the many good captains I'd flown with. I came to realize it was their diplomacy, rather than mine, that had made our thousands of hours together safe and enjoyable. They respected me as a pilot and as an individual and I worked my butt off for them. We solved some in-flight problems between us, a few quite hairy, because we worked well as a team when the chips were down. In a word, they were natural leaders who taught by example. They were in charge and had the final say at all times—that was always understood and indeed expected. They knew their jobs and assumed I knew mine; there was rarely a need for talk about who would do what next. Their approach reflected confidence in themselves and in their crews. It produced the best efforts from all of us every time and resulted in the relaxed cockpit atmosphere which is as important as fuel in the tanks.

A few captains never got the big picture. Some today don't have it. Oddly enough, most of the hard heads now giving their copilots and engineers bad times were the loudest beefers during their own right seat days. The left seat tyrant is likely unsure of himself; he needs expert assistance far more than the genial relaxed type, yet he does everything to discourage crew cooperation. He bears watching. Eventually he will encounter a riddle he cannot solve all by himself and that will be no time for his assistants to sit with hands folded and let him sweat. This has happened and it can lead to disaster. During the investigation of a major airline accident in England, it was found that the captain and copilot had had a heated argument prior to the flight.

It is the captain's duty to insist on a relaxed cockpit atmosphere regardless of the different personalities involved. If he is so full of himself or so unsure of himself that he cannot or will not provide proper leadership, it is the copilot's and engineeer's responsibility to see him for the mental dwarf he is and carry on the good work, each on his own. If they cannot work professionally in that unpleasant situation as the crewmen they hope to someday command, they are no more fit for the left seat than the clown who occupies it now.

# Stalls

No pilot can forget his first stall and spin.. My instructor explained the maneuver and told me to follow through on the controls. The top cylinder of the idling Kinner of the Fleet trainer rose toward the sky as the stick came slowly back. Everything got unnaturally quiet, then there was a mild shudder, a violent shake and a lurch to the left as the nose fell through. We were for an instant weightless and then the windshield filled with twisting landscape rapidly rising to meet us. Three turns, then stick forward, full opposite rudder and the Fleet dove back into flight.

What an unkind thing to do to a delightful little airplane that wanted only to fly, I thought. "You want to see another?" asked my instructor through the rubber tube. Not right then I didn't, but I nodded, obviously the expected response. So he did another, I followed through and a few minutes later we landed, thus ending my second hour of dual. The idea at the early stage was not so much to teach as to determine the new boy's reaction and see if, among other things he lost his breakfast. I did not panic, lose anything, or particularly enjoy the experience.

Within two weeks I was routinely doing stalls and spins and reveling in the exercise, though I never quite shook the feeling—and still haven't—that it abuses the airplane. Spin recovery was emphasized in Royal Canadian Air Force training, the word from England being that too many pilots were KIFA (killed in flying accidents), often by spinning out of the overcast too low for recovery. No sooner had we mastered visual recovery than we learned to recover under the hood, using primitive needle, ball and airspeed indications. We were ordered to spin at least twice weekly on solo hops and to certify completion of this requirement by initialing a wall chart in the ready room.

It was more of the same when we advanced to the Harvard (AT-6, SNJ or T-6 to you Army, Navy or Air Force types.) A far cry from the docile Fleet, the Harvard paid off abruptly, wrapped up tight in a spin and came downstairs at an alarming rate while pencils and screwdrivers floated up from the cockpit floor. It captured your complete attention. Following the usual correction, it might respond at once, or continue for another half turn before recovering. One student bailed out, claiming his ship refused to stop spinning. This was put down to inexperience and he was promptly sent back up for more dual stalls and spins.

All of this background raises a question about training which does not include spin recovery. You are not required to demonstrate spin recovery in today's civil pilot training syllabus. Being shown stalls and taught recovery therefrom cannot impress a student half as much as seeing what happens when an airplane is allowed to enter a full blown spin. The sights, sounds and sensations are at first terrifying and capable of fatally confusing anyone who's not experienced them before.

"A properly trained pilot will never get into a spin," a lightplane instructor told me (adding, however, that he showed each student at least one spin and thought it should be a requirement.) Considering certain wake turbulence and wind shear situations, I have less confidence in the it-never-can-happen notion. Supposedly qualified pilots continue to spin in for whatever reasons. I'm hopelessly old school and it's probably just as well that licensing requirements are dictated by more advanced thinkers. If I wrote the book, spin recovery would go back into the requirements and you wouldn't solo, much less get a license to fly solo, until you could recover from a spin as casually as you make shallow turns.

A short, stout little man old enough to be my father introduced me to the C-47, my first multi-engine type. After the usual air work he said, "Okay, I'll show you a stall," and I thought, good Lord, the old fool is going to spin this thing! He wasn't, of course; large transports are not designed for such stress (though many the C-47 was spun, deliberately or otherwise, never with damaging results that I heard of.) He hauled the nose high as we slowed with engines ticking over. With little warning the big instrument panel danced on its shock mounts, we wrenched sideways almost into a vertical turn and the nose fell through. You wouldn't think it to look at those long wings but apparently the tips paid off first. We resumed flight with building speed but considerable altitude was lost in the process. The point was well made: do something right now about deteriorating speed, particularly when close to the ground.

In military training we were shown that a mishandled airplane would stall at virtually any speed. The wings-level, ball-centered payoff was tea party stuff compared to what happened when you horsed back in power-on-maneuvering. A Harvard pulled really tight in a turn might roll further into it—or flick upright and into an opposite direction spin, a truly exciting gyration for the neophyte but a tame one compared to the same blunder in a P-51. Fighter students in World War II were cautioned to commence stall/spin experiments from levels that permitted recovery no later than 10,000 feet above ground level. Power-on and inverted spins were to be avoided. A P-51 might complete six turns and lose 9,000 feet during recovery from a spin entered under power; the P-47 book read, "If you get into an inverted spin, you are in for a hard, violent tussle." The would-be ace read such notes carefully then experimented with his new mount until he could consistently fly it "on the nibble" and, if necessary, use its peculiar stall/spin habits for evasive purposes.

Those of us relegated to transports and bombers forgot actual spinning but we were taught to recover from full stalls. Today's big airplane pilot learns "Approaches to stalls" and recovery with minimum altitude loss. This makes sense; the shake, rattle and roll that results from a full stall is hard on a large airframe and its engine mounts, at least it was when training and proficiency checks were done in the airplane itself. Many's the time I looked from an Electra or 707 cabin window as the student up front wrestled it out of a stall, watching the wing flex and engines twist on their mounts. It made you wince and wonder if the cracks sometimes found in tired old airliners were not induced by such abuse. Now it's all done in the simulator.

The French introduced the Caravelle in 1955, a novel—indeed, radical—departure from convention with engines mounted on the fuselage behind the wing. It caught on and was soon copied by Britain, Russia and us. The new idea offered advantages, but posed one problem: an airplane with all of its powerplant dead weight in the rear tends to remain in a stall, mushing along at slow forward speed as the altimeters unwind and maximum thrust may not be capable of increasing airspeed to the point of elevator effectiveness. One airline twin crashed during stall tests, nose high with little forward velocity. A redesigned wing turned it into a safe airliner.

While modern wing design supposedly insures that current rear-engine types will nose over prior to reaching unrecoverable stalls, all are fitted with stick shakers to warn of impending stall or stick pushers which mechanically shove the nose over when speed becomes dangerously low. These devices are also no-go items on such conventional designs at the DC-8, 707 and 747, but for other reasons. The momentary rapid rate of roll which often follows a stall can sling a pod-mounted engine off the wing. That has happened.

It is assumed that any pilot advancing to high performance turbine equipment is unlikely to corner himself in a low speed situation through carelessness. It is also recognized that the most conscientious can inadvertently approach stalling in certain rare, but possible, conditions involving wind shift, wind shear and turbulence. He must therefore demonstrate immediate recognition of a stall and return his ship to normal flight with minimum altitude loss. It's a part of all multi-engine training.

The stall series used in 747 training and recurrent checks went like this: a Vref (final approach) speed was computed for the landing weight and a movable "bug" positioned next to this number on the airspeed gauges. The first stall was made clean with wings level, the next in a 20-degree bank with 10-degrees of flaps and the third straight ahead with the gear down and landing flaps (30 degrees). In each exercise the engines remained spun up but at low thrust settings. These configurations approximated those seen in near-airport maneuvering.

The real value of such training was lost on me until I flew an airplane with an Inertial Navigation System. Among its readouts are wind direction and speed which proved most useful when approaching a field during unstable weather conditions, as when a front or squall line was near the field. On one approach the INS showed a direct headwind of 25 knots at the outer marker though the tower reported calm surface winds. It was nice to have some warning that you were going to lose that much headwind before you got to the runway. Strangely, this use of the INS was never suggested in our training though it probably is today. In view of such known possibilities, it is not so difficult to understand why modern jet equipment crewed by competent crews has settled into approach lights on short final, or back to earth after takeoff.

Stalling while cruising was a continuous concern of the jet airman trying to milk maximum mileage from his tanks. You had to fly as high as weight and temperature permitted, step-climbing as fuel was burned on long hauls, so you were often right up there in "coffin corner" with stall speed and high speed buffet a few knots apart. No sweat unless you ran into turbulence, in which case there might be no choice but to request a lower level until you were lighter. (When ATC didn't have a lower altitude available, the problem became most interesting.) And it was not smart to try to climb to a higher and hopefully smoother level, not if you were anywhere close to the alt/temp/wt limits already. All maneuvering in the higher levels was accomplished with a watchmaker's touch. You made up your mind about the clouds ahead while 30 miles from them for a shallow turn to avoid them could cross several counties.

Back to the beginning: the tired old relic sat in the weeds, drab and neglected, a fair lady who had known better days, but still a lady and I walked over to visit as I always have and will. I climbed up on the grimy wing and peered into the once-familiar cockpit at the dials and handles I never thought I'd forget. Lo and behold, it was a genuine Harvard by its rusting builder's plate, made in Montreal by Noorduyn. Who knows but that I flew this one in that misting time and rolled it through the summer skies with an exuberance we seemed to share. And spun it, dizzying turn after turn, its windshield filled with rotating farms and roads.

Then I saw the placard pasted on the panel—INTENTIONAL SPINNING PROHIBITED—and I wondered why it was there. The Harvard recovered nicely once you knew the drill.

Oh well.

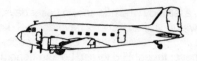

# Wheels, Tires and Brakes

Number 16 in the line for takeoff, we inched along Taxiway Kilo at Kennedy, waiting to launch from Runway 4 Left. It was early evening and moderate rain was falling. We watched with casual interest as the departures roared past on our left, mostly jumbos eastbound, noting the rooster tails thrown high by their mains and the temporary solid cloud left by jet blast.

Then a Laker DC-10 rolled. He was doing 120 knots or so when he went past us and looked good, yet someone behind us saw it happen and called the tower. One or more tires had blown to pieces at the moment of rotation. We heard Laker acknowledge the information and, after a minute or two, advise they would continue to London. "That will give them something to think about for the next seven hours," said the copilot.

We didn't think much about tires or wheels and brakes. Most of our concern centered on airframe integrity and engine health, yet serious accidents have resulted from failures in the complex machinery we raise and lower with a simple cockpit lever. Even on aircraft with fixed ("down and welded") landing gear, these vital components rate more attention than they get.

Strange things happen down there under an aircraft. Old heads among FAA controllers recall the day a single airliner halted all service through the nation's capital for several hours. I was the copilot on board. The wind was from the west, strong and gusty. The captain elected to land north instead of on much shorter Runway 33. He put our big DC-7C smoothly down on the left main, holding us straight with opposite rudder. As we slowed, the right wheels touched and we heard an odd grinding noise. We stopped in the intersection of the two main runways, 35 and 33, and I opened my side window. Both tires and their magnesium wheels were ablaze with a fire too bright to watch. By advancing power on No. 3 engine, we blew the flames horizontally away from the wheel well. The DCA fire equipment appeared within a minute and doused the flames with powder.

No jack of sufficient size could be found, so there the ship sat blocking both main runways, causing scores of flights to divert to other fields. Four hours later a large jack arrived from New York aboard a Martin 404 which squeezed into short Runway 21. When lifted, the two damaged wheels spun freely; why they locked on landing was a mystery. Airplanes sometimes do things that defy explanation.

An airliner's landing gear lives a hard life. It is dragged through slush and water, flogged down rough runways under heavy loads and once in a while is slammed with bone crunching force into unyielding concrete, yet it causes less problems than most other components.

The first Convair 240s had tires with sidewall cups which caught the slipstream and set wheels spinning prior to landing. A step forward, most of us agreed, but this gimmick was abandoned. Engineers say most wear occurs during braking, not at touch down. But, considering the ground-off rubber left in the impact zones of busy runways and the clean surface elsewhere, I'm still not convinced.

Retracting an airplane's landing gear does good things to performance but the apparatus involved occasionally malfunctions. Various alternate means of releasing balky up-locks to allow the gear to fall of its own weight have been devised and they work almost every time. Donald Douglas correctly guessed that his DC-3's wheels sooner or later would resist all attempts at extension so he left enough of them exposed to hold the belly clear, even in a wheels-up landing. A really sharp pilot facing a belly arrival would feather his props on final, nudge each prop to the 8-12-4 o'clock position, and suffer no more than loss of the lower antenna. Yes, the brakes of a DC-3 functioned normally with the gear fully retracted.

Today's heavy airplane pilot, when faced with a gear problem, is usually encouraged to land on those he can extend, rather than land with everything up. Damage will be minimized this way, say manufacturers. And, it was repeatedly shown during World War II that the runway is a better place to land gear up than the grass alongside it, as strange as that may seem.

A thinking pilot babies his tires and brakes as he does his engines. High speed turns place undue side loads on gear parts; hard braking increases tire wear, may warp brakes and cause dangerous heating; pivoting on a main is poor practice. Upon completing a tight turn into a parking slot, it is prudent to roll forward a few feet to relieve twisting stress on gear and tires.

The professional trucker starts his day with a close inspection of tires, brakes and running gear, verifying individual inflation with a hammer. He will tell you that a tire fire is virtually impossible to douse with hand extinguishers. The risk of aircraft tire fires varies with types. The old C-46 was about as much airplane as ever rolled on three wheels, and was a bitch to taxi in a crosswind with its big fuselage and huge rudder broadside to the breeze. One day we taxiied ours a mile along a narrow strip with a strong wind from the right. A lot of left braking was unavoidable. After runup I opened the window and looked back at the left gear. No trace of smoke. As we lifted, someone called, "Don't raise your gear! It's on fire." We hurried around the pattern while the crew chief rounded up three CO 2 bottles. The tire blew upon landing and, fortunately, most of it left the wheel. All three extinguishers were used dousing flames on what was left. Had we retracted that flaming assembly into its well . . .

Heat build up in 747 tires, each of which may support 20 tons prior to takeoff, was something to watch during prolonged taxying, as from Honolulu's terminal to Runway 8R, some three miles from the terminal. Braking is not the cause, but sidewall flexing. One 747 taxied out, had to return for a minor adjustment, taxied out again and blew half its tires at 100 knots during the takeoff run. Flight engineers closely monitor brake temperature gauges. When readings approach the yellow, it is wise to leave the gear extended for a few minutes after takeoff.

General tire condition is extremely critical whenever heavy loads are involved. Once at Kadena Air Base in Okinawa when several airlines were doing Vietnam War charter work for the Air Force, I saw the captain of another line inspecting the tires of his 707-300. Then he asked the tug driver to pull his ship forward three feet. "That guy always wants to see the parts sitting on the ground," said a mechanic, and I guessed there was a tale behind his extra caution. The run from Kadena back to California was the longest we flew. Every takeoff was made at max gross weight—336,000 pounds (plus a bit more perhaps for the wife and kids which we didn't show in the manifest) and that put rotation speed up there at about 160 knots. That's 185 miles an hour on tires tested to 200. That made you tire conscious.

While my own engineers were the fussiest of old maids in their preflighting, I often took a look myself. But I only wondered about the tire surfaces I couldn't see.

# Getting the Habit

It was my good fortune to serve in the same cockpits with many professional pilots, men whose life work was flying airplanes. They came in all shapes and sizes; physically, there was no average. Nor mentally; each approached the problems of flight in his own way, using his own techniques. No two were exactly alike.

From them came a thousand tales which would make, had I only made notes, a book on piloting like none other ever written. My own viewpoint is as influenced by their examples (which were not invariably good) as by personal experience. I learned much about flying from them.

As a newcomer to flying I was somewhat disillusioned to find that pilots were ordinary people. How could seemingly average humans with all their foibles and failings survive long careers in a pursuit so fraught with terrible possibilities? To be sure, there were certain common denominators—knowledge, judgement, skill—but these could be acquired. What was the extra something, the inborn secret—or was there a secret?

Eventually it dawned: good habits separated the men from the boys, and often the quick from the dead. An uncorrected bad habit could spell disaster for the most knowledgeable and skillful; a good one could spell the difference for a pilot of less than average skill and training.

Any serious flying involves the simultaneous accomplishment of several different tasks. Since none of us can consciously think on more than one thing at a time, we must complete the rest subconsciously.

We drive with little conscious attention to car or traffic, continuous practice having made driving second nature. Instrument flying, a far more demanding exercise, also becomes second nature with sufficient practice. We maintain heading, altitude and speed to close tolerances while maneuvering through complex routings with little conscious attention to the mechanics of it, leaving the conscious mind free to appraise the overall situation and plan ahead.

Practice makes perfect, practice keeps perfect and few of us get enough of it. The first really tight approach of winter was often an embarrassment. It was easy to forget weather flying during the summer, to postpone the occasional simulated approach that kept skills honed. The razor sharp instrument fellow had the habit of regular practice.

Unusual and emergency situations quickly reveal a pilot's work habits. Presumably, we all know how to cope with them because of our training or because we thought each one through with aircraft manual in hand. All the proper responses are stored away in the brain cells, right? Yes, but unless periodically dusted off and re-examined, they retreat to the back of the mental shelf and may not be instantly retrievable. When power is lost at lift off, there simply isn't time to rummage through memory for immediate actions. A quick mental review at the head of the runway pulls everything back into focus. A similar review on final approach prevents the cockpit pandemonium which can attend an unplanned go-around. It has been said that an airplane may disappoint a good pilot but it will never surprise him.

No one will argue that it is a good habit to exercise flight controls before every takeoff, full throw, all six ways, and to take a look back up final, no matter what the tower says about taking the runway. It is likewise a good preflight habit to exercise the subconscious, to make sure the filed away data is right there ready to use, to ask blunt questions and get right answers. There is nothing morbid in recognizing and preparing for unpleasant possibilities.

It has also been said that a smart man learns from his mistakes, a wise one from the mistakes of others. Too few of us grow wise. Year after year pilots eliminate themselves and their passengers for the same stupid reasons. We nod knowingly when we learn the causes, but do they always register? We should reflect that the right habits would have avoided nearly all of them.

Aside from collision and structural failure (themselves often induced by less than careful flying), there are precious few problems a self-disciplined pilot cannot solve. Consistent safe flying is the product of creative and imaginative thinking. It is dull, repetitious, tiresome work most of the time; its constructive effect is rarely seen yet it is entirely necessary.

The industry has down played the pilot's role with remarkable success. The public is just about convinced that the modern airplane is a foolproof device that operates itself. Its pilot is portrayed as primarily a monitor who responds to radioed instructions from the ground when he encounters a problem not covered in the book. The airliner is now an "air bus" and the private airplane is a car that flies. As long as your pilot doesn't push the wrong button, he'll get you there intact. "Pilot error" causes most accidents, federal and industry aviation experts keep reminding everybody.

I couldn't care less about the image this nonsense produces. If laymen equate me with the fellow who wants to do all the driving, so be it. If they imagine that flying a Beech involves no more than driving a Buick, let them. It's when a pilot swallows the line that the trouble starts. He becomes complacent.

Today's airplane is almost foolproof. Day after day throughout the seasons it serves with a degree of reliability undreamed of a few years ago. Today's typical airline squawk is that a seat won't recline or a water tap drips. There are margin notes in the logbooks of my recip days that can still make me sweat. It's a different world now, isn't it?

Not really, and it is dangerous to think so. The basic man-machine equation remains unchanged. The aircraft has not been built which will not sooner or later present its pilot with a serious problem which only he can solve. Something unusual, one of those things the ground people will tell you can never happen. When it does happen, all of the automatic gadgets on board won't help; all of the cute verbal warnings and bells and lights become distractions and any attempt to get assistance by radio is a waste of time. When it does happen, only old fashioned stick-and-rudder work will save the day.

It happens. Little public attention is given to successful salvage jobs, those hairy instances when machinery fails a pilot and he alone fills in the blanks, yet they are not uncommon. "Design error" is not often found in the written reports.

We Americans are the most blessed of aviation people. Our system has produced the finest aircraft on earth and provided a freedom of flying activity envied everywhere else. But all is not sweetness and light. Economics remain the bottom line and selling the product is the name of the game. Our delirious infatuation with science has created an aura of machine worship in which man plays a supporting role. The computer outwits its inventor and (it seems to follow that) the airplane has become safer than its pilot.

I wouldn't change any part of it, being a card-carrying free enterpriser myself. I do want to know where I stand in the big picture. Strip away all the baloney and what's left? There's me, the pilot, a fallible human with a full list of faults. There's the machine, the airplane, a magnificent device. The odds against it failing me are perhaps one in 100,000, but I cannot bank on that. Today the odds may be one in one. We are the equation which has not changed since Orville wrestled his contraption across 40 yards of Carolina sand.

I pen these thoughts with no notion of advising, dear reader, but as a personal reminder. It is an old habit of mine to ponder these things.

# The Departure

The take off is said to be the most critical phase of flight. If we accept the definition, "crucial; of decisive importance with respect to the outcome," critical is exactly the right adjective. Another definition which reads, "involving uncertainty, risk and peril," need not apply if we remind ourselves of the potential for uncertainty, risk and peril. An uneventful departure calls for careful planning.

Most of the reasons why the departure is critical are obvious; the aircraft is at its heaviest and most sluggish; the powerplant(s) are running at full power; airframe, landing gear and tires are under maximum stress. And, any abnormality or emergency must be dealt with at low altitude when considerable attention is required simply to keep the beast airborne. It is wise to ponder these things before releasing the brakes.

A pilot's frame of mind is the most important aspect of all. None of us quits being a driver and starts being an airman simply by climbing out of a car and into a plane. The casual attention to auto and road that got us to the field won't necessarily get us safely into flight. The pilot who flies regularly is obviously less prone to making a silly mistake than the one who flies infrequently. But no matter how long it's been since I last flew, I must start thinking like a pilot and imagining myself in flying's exacting environment before I fire up. This is no problem once the right habits are adopted.

We airline pilots had it made. Most of the dull work of preflighting had been completed when we reported for duty. We had only to review these preparations and double-check the numbers. A pack of papers bearing our trip number was already on the Operations counter. It contained a wealth of information—sequence reports, forecasts, radar plots, upper winds and two or more computer flight plans. There was more—PIREPS, NOTAMS, Special Advisories, a list of inoperative equipment and recent repairs, the nature and location of hazardous cargo—the extent of the paperwork depending upon trip distance and complexity. No item of pilot interest was omitted.

Outside stood the airplane, cleaned, provisioned, fueled, thoroughly inspected. That was the white collar way to go flying. Few in the trade appreciated all this good help. I'll admit I never did until we bought a Bonanza. Suddenly I was gas boy, inspector, baggage buster, dispatcher, loader, operations clerk and caterer. Preflighting was a tedious and time-consuming nuisance.

In C-47 freighting days we made sure the heaviest crates were over the wing, that everything was tied down securely, then drove down the runway at full bore until the ship felt ready to fly. There is much more to it now. No pilot can "eyeball" today's weight-weather-runway equation and come up with a trustworthy solution, no matter how many times he has flown his type from the same runway on similar days.

There are many factors to consider—weight, wind, temperature, runway length and elevation. Runway slope and condition are crucial; standing water or slush can add hundreds of feet to a jet's take-off run. Near-airport obstructions may dictate a rapid rate of climb and thus restrict take off weight. The load manual prepared by an airline's engineering staff contains a page for every runway at each regular and alternate field on which are shown all possible situations. It is a simple matter determining if today's proposed operation is, in fact, safe and legal, all things considered. You follow that book every time.

Immediately following push back, the final weights of passengers and cargo and the distribution of the underfloor load are radioed to the cockpit. Adding payload to aircraft and fuel weights, the appropriate V-speeds along with the proper setting for stabilizer trim are determined. Other factors peculiar to a given departure must be reckoned with. The use of engine and/or wing anti-icing during take off robs engine power and thus involves a weight penalty; runway water or slush may involve down-loading; an inoperative anti-skid system or thrust reverser can have similar effects. And it must always be remembered the trip must arrive at its destination at no more than its maximum landing weight which is considerably less than the maximum gross weight at which it may legally depart.

A different wing flap setting can, in certain situations, increase take off weight; turning off engine bleeds which supply air conditioning systems increases thrust. It's the crew's job to examine all the facts, and find the right numbers. These calculations are very carefully reviewed by all crewmen. Take off power settings require equal attention. An airliner may be fitted with more than one model of the same basic engine, in fact, four sets of numbers for take off thrust are sometimes required. Whenever conditions allow, reduced power is used for departure to conserve fuel and prolong engine life.

All departure performance figuring in large turbojet equipment is based upon two rather unpleasant assumptions: that an engine is going to flame out during the ground roll or immediately after lift off. The aim is to load and operate the airplane in such a way that if an engine fails prior to V1, it can be stopped on the remaining runway. And, if it fails after V1, it can continue the take off and climb at a rate sufficient to clear obstacles. How much can we weigh today in this airplane on this runway? That is the question. The answer is in the load manual.

Pilot confidence in the take off numbers thus determined varies with individual experience. The whole process is explored in training and goes smoothly enough (which surprises no one for the simulator is programmed to do exactly what the builder says his airplane will do). And the builder in the beginning convinced the FAA that his product will perform according to the charts and graphs which come with it. In the real world of line flying, things have not invariably gone according to plan, but the book provides the best data available and we went by it religiously. We also knocked on wood now and then.

Before taking the runway it makes sense to recall the immediate actions to be taken if an engine does fail during the roll or initial climb, along with the special engine-out routings suggested at such mountain-surrounded fields as Reno. A typical airline trip leaves at well under its allowable maximum weight but there are every day a good number of memorable departures at maximum gross weight. They are usually observed at the terminals from which the long hauls launch and at high altitude airports. The locals know—and watch. On my first max gross departure from Mexico City I noticed, as we taxied out, that ramp workers were lining up facing the runway. "There must be someone coming in with a problem," I said.

"No, there's someone going out with a problem—us," said the copilot, adding, "It's just a suggestion, but you might want to line up real close to those boundary lights and bring 'em up to max power before you release the brakes." It was good advice.

The best seats for this show were in the cockpit; there we'd be lined up and awaiting the tower's nod. A final glance at the numbers on the take off data card; we're "three bricks shy of a load." "Four more bricks and it won't fly," the engineer might comment on such an occasion. Max gross. But there was little reason to sweat the outcome for we, with considerable expert help, had laid a solid foundation for this flight. Its successful departure would be as assured as science can make it.

I can never forget those times. Cleared to go. Ease the thrust levers forward, wait for all four turbines to spin up and stabilize, then work them right on up to full power. Brakes off. Well, what did you expect—whiplash? We're moving, aren't we? Remember, jet engines are inefficient at low speeds. The airspeed's alive. There's 80 knots, 100—miserable acceleration so far—120. Come one, you big mother, we are using up this airport fast; 130, 135, 140—has the needle stopped its slow advance?—150 . . . V1. Right hand off thrust levers and onto wheel because we are going to fly. Rotate.

Pull it off, not abruptly, not too slowly, but with smooth steady back pressure to get the nose up there about seven degrees. Over-rotation would drag the tail. Now the mains are free so ease the nose on up to 10 or 12 degrees to nail speed on V2 + 10. There is no hurry to get the wheels up; those big doors open first and we don't want extra drag just now. positive rate of climb showing, so now: gear up! It folds into its wells, the doors close and the monster feels more like an airplane and less like a raft being shoved upstream. We slowly labor up to a thousand feet, nose over slightly and gradually accumulate enough knots to begin flap retraction. The last lights go out, the mild shuddering ceases and the airplane assumes its characteristic rock solid slide through space. Climb power. Let speed build up to 285 and forget the 250-knots-below-10,000-feet speed limit. The controllers are aware we require greater speed for maneuvering at this weight.

Leaving 10,000 feet: let speed build up to 340 for the long climb, landing lights off, seat belt sign off and how about a round of coffee? It is a common observation among long distance crews that, after the preparatory ground work and first 30 minutes of flying are completed, most of the hard work has been done. From then on, it is largely a matter of watching the machine operate itself.

It is foolish to imagine that our intensive preflight ritual had no parallel with the operation of a small airplane. Size, number of seats and trip distance do not change the basics of safe operation. Considering the elaborate assistance we enjoyed, there was little excuse for our not doing the job right the first time. The private pilot is on his own. Only through self discipline will he accomplish for himself and his passengers what was done for us. The apparent casualness with which we departed with heavy loads for distant points is deceiving. There was more to it than met the eye. I spent as much time and energy preparing for a Texas to Tennessee hop in the Bonanza than I was later to spend before a Texas—Europe schedule in a 747.

There can be no duller way to spend an afternoon than in class listening to an airline performance lecture—the numbers and how to use them, yet periodically they rubbed our noses in them. Likewise, the least interesting pages in any small airplane's manual are those listing stall speeds, centers of gravity, rates of climb and range, yet no other information in the book is more important. We had to learn performance in the military and on the airline; the private airman should.

A review of accident reports proves that the ingredients for many a disaster were unwittingly mixed on the ground before flight began. Thorough preflight planning, including an honest facing up to the limitations of the pilot and aircraft at hand, would have prevented many a tragedy. What a great experience flying any aircraft can be when a pilot invests his best in preparation. The pilot who starts out right is a credit to his trade. To him I say, as I did to an outbound airline friend, "Have a good trip," because I know he will.

# Landing the Big Ones

Big does not mean more difficult when you get down to those last fifty feet. From there to touch down it's a piece of cake, providing, of course, that you arrive at fifty feet in good shape—"on profile" and well within the "flight envelope," in the parlance of those who would have you think big airplanes require super pilots. True, there is more to do in preparing airplane and crew for arrival in the Boeing 747 than in say, a Cessna 172, but the checklist is normally completed overhead the outer marker, leaving the pilot on the wheel free to maintain attitude and speed right down to the concrete. It's no big deal with practice, no matter how impressive it seems to the layman.

What is "big," anyway? The DC-3 was once considered enormous. Its introduction to schedules in July, 1936, was attended with almost as much fanfare as the maiden voyage of the Queen Mary a month earlier. "It's a flying house," said one awed reporter, but its pilots soon found it could be shoehorned into the smallest municipal airport, providing it arrived over the fence right on speed. Faced with a short strip, the true DC-3 artist learned to three-point and roll to a stop in a few hundred feet.

It was the same hoopla all over again when DC-4's and the early Constellations appeared after World War II - at least with the ex-Three crowd. The Old Man would nail it on approach speed with everything hanging down ten miles out, to the quiet amusement of any copilot with B-24 time under his belt. Nothing was said, of course; the patriarchs had to learn for themselves that four engines and tricycle gear were, while somewhat more demanding, also more fun to fly.

Neither type had reversing pitch props and this made arrivals on short icy runways extremely interesting. The best plan, in fact, the only sensible plan, was to slow way down and plant it firmly on the numbers then get busy with brakes. Rocking the wings could help drive the mains down through slush to the runway surface.

As regular as Christmas, someone in a Four or Connie would land hot or long (or both) at old Chicago Midway each winter, knock over the ILS shack and slide to a stop under the traffic light at 59th and Cicero. If the ceiling dropped below 400 feet before the ILS was fixed (which it invariably did), the field was closed and all crews repaired to the Stevens Hotel for as much of a binge as could be put together on five dollars a day expenses.

Then came the jets and off we went again. The word was that the 707 would eat your lunch on arrivals. Some senior heads breezed through training but others needed fifty hours of dual to qualify. A few gave up and went back to Electras. Years later, when my group's turn came, the 707 had become just another airplane and anyone not ready for the FAA examiner after four periods of instruction was considered slow. Surprisingly enough, the huge 747 was blended into the scheme of things with minimum fuss and bother, pilots finally having learned that bigger usually means different, not more difficult. Today's jumbo trainee can complete training and earn his rating entirely in the simulator. In such cases, his first landing in the airplane itself is made on a routine schedule with passengers on board (and a check airman in the right seat, of course). Who would have believed it?

A sound philosophy of big airplane operation results from prior experience, thorough training and, as the champions of any sport will tell you, practice, practice and more practice. No other aspect of flight captures a pilot's attention and imagination as do those last fifty feet. A safe and sane arrival is the bottom line but there's more to it; he wants to accomplish that as gracefully as possible every time. It's a matter of professional pride, of striving for an above-average performance. While a mature individual works hard to please himself rather than to impress others, audience reaction is something to think about in our end of it. More than once I have played to a gallery of 400-plus who, quite unfairly, of course, judged my entire ten-hour show by its final minute. I preferred to have them think I was hot stuff but it worked out another way now and then.

Several factors work together to make a landing smooth or otherwise. The pilot who disconnects the autopilot when he leaves cruising level and hand flies to touch down has the best shot at a smooth arrival. Like a relief pitcher, he must warm up. Compared with small aircraft, control loads in big airplanes are heavy. A pitcher is said to be "loosening up" whereas he is doing the exact opposite; he is tightening up muscles made slack by inactivity. A few minutes of hand flying does the same for a pilot. And it sharpens the mind as well.

A big airplane, because of its size and weight, cannot alter speed and direction rapidly; its pilot must remain well ahead of it throughout approach, landing and roll out. Minor deviations in course and speed must be immediately noted and corrected. If he begins "chasing the gauges" he's in real trouble. It is sheer hard work in a new type but soon enough becomes second nature. Most pilots feel right at home in a different plane after 200 hours.

The machine itself has certain characteristics to which a pilot must adjust. The DC-3 often rewarded an attentive pilot with a greaser but the old lady brooked few liberties and would quickly slap a careless wrist. The DC-4 had big tires, long struts and was a dream to land. Fly it down to one foot, hold the nose up there and wait; she'd settle like a brood hen on her nest and make you look better than you were. The Six came with high pressure tires and stiff struts; a distinct but not uncomfortable thump was the usual outcome of the most careful approach and flare. Douglas' last recip was the long-range DC-7C, perhaps the finest propeller-driven airliner ever built, a big, barrel-chested airplane even by today's standards.

It was 27 feet longer and 25 tons heavier than the original Six, yet the square footage of elevator was identical. Ask an aerodynamist to explain that one. The result was predictable but we had to learn the hard way. Chop the power at fifty feet and it glided like a sack of sand. With the wheel full back it hit hard on all three wheels. The ticket was to carry a smidgen of extra speed and power into the flare, closing the throttles as the nose rose. Done just right, the big job squatted lightly on its mains with that delicious drag of rubber on asphalt that strokes the ego.

The Electra, for all its good points, was not designed for smooth landings. Small, high pressure tires and rock stiff legs made the grease job a rarity. A soft gear modification reportedly improved matters. None of our Electras got it. Prop-driven equipment, the Electra included, enjoyed a favorable feature not appreciated until it was lost: the braking effect of idling propellers. The jet engine develops considerable shove even when idling, making speed control of critical importance. Every 10 knots of excess velocity over the fence produced 1,000 feet of float, they warned. And, due to the slow spin up of certain engines, it was equally important not to chop power prematurely. The apparent drawbacks when coupled with its somewhat strange control responses, seemed to make the novel 707 a handful of airplane. At first, it was indeed, but we soon adjusted.

Under the loose "707" designation, Boeing issued a variety of models, each with its own personality. We began with the 707-227, a fireball which sizzled down final at 145 knots under load; circling approaches to Runway 36 at old Kansas City Municipal were events to remember. The – 138B was a short fuselage, big wing version designed to stay up almost forever. Short-coupled, it was skittish in chop.

The monstrous intercontinental - 320 was magnificent in all respects, stable down final, stately in the flare. Then there was the 720-227, in reality a medium-range 707 with small engines. We still talk about that one.

Grossly underpowered when compared with its sisters, the 720 in Mexico City at max gross takeoff weight could double your pulse rate on departure, yet was the easiest of the four to land. So we learned to fly the Boeings four ways. None was light on the wheel; you kept them in trim or worked yourself into a lather. The 727 had a much lighter feel and was more forgiving and the 747 was the best of the lot. All three basic types reward the conscientious pilot with a fair share of slick landings.

But I beat around the bush. Is there a secret that always works in big airplanes? No. There are certain ingredients which improve the odds (assuming reasonable wind and runway conditions): a few minutes of hand flying prior to the approach; a track from outer marker to airport flown as accurately as if the ceiling were 200 feet; good tight speed control from 500 feet on down; a properly trimmed airplane. Add a dash of luck and stir well. Good results are almost guaranteed and spectacular results are entirely possible. If, after carefully following this recipe, you arrive like an overload of bricks, you simply didn't add enough luck.

# A Footnote for the Colonel

Y ou won't find Birdville on the map, nor will you find Sam Cody mentioned in Texas histories; it's as if he never existed. Well, there was a Birdville once and Samuel Franklin Cody was born there in 1861, the same year his father joined the Confederates. Few sons of the Lone Star State began with less and accomplished more. None matched his contribution to early aeronautics. Aviation has produced many men and women worth knowing about. I say Cody belongs in the top 25 of that illustrious roster.

The English remember the huge, friendly, flamboyant Texan with affection. "Those of us who knew him loved him best," said one after his death. Others have since unearthed the incredible facts of his life and they read like an Horatio Alger novel. Cody grew up in the saddle, earning at age 12 a man's wages for a man's work—15 dollars a month. Then Indians came, killed his brothers and burned down the farmhouse. Cody escaped with a bullet wound.

He matured on the plains as a cowboy, buffalo hunter and, at 20, trail boss driving 3,200 head of cattle some 1,300 miles to Montana, a feat which paid $125 a month. By then Cody was six three, weighed 195 and could fairly be described as a self-made man.

One episode perfect for a *Gunsmoke* script sums up the man and the times. Eight riders stopped at a railroad construction camp to eat and bed down. In the bar a giant laborer taunted the cowboys, suggesting that young Cody was likely all mouth without his Colt. Cody removed his gun belt and floored him. The outnumbered Texans thought it best to move on and were riding away when the humiliated laborer fired, hitting the tall cowboy in the leg. Cody dismounted, knocked the pistol aside and finished the job. He carried the bullet in his thigh for life.

Always eager for fresh adventure, Cody grabbed a chance to deliver horses from Galveston to London. There he met the buyer's daughter, Lela David, and became her frequent escort on the bridal paths of Hyde Park. On a later trip to England they were married. Back home, he found that cowboy pay did not meet family expenses yet he knew no other trade. Rumor had it that men were becoming rich overnight in Alaska. He caught gold fever, packed Lela and their baby son off to London and set out for the Klondike.

Though he slaved through the bitter winter, the gold he panned scarcely bought passage back to Seattle. He reached home flat broke. In San Antonio he joined a wild west show. Billed as "Captain Cody, King of the Cowboys," he hit pay dirt. The tall, striking figure with shoulder length golden hair and a flowing moustache toured major eastern cities and was an instant success. He loved the life and in two years had saved enough to join Lela in London. He sailed from New York in 1889 and never returned to his native land.

In England Cody put together his own show along the lines of the enormously successful performances staged throughout Europe by Buffalo Bill (William Frederick Cody; no relation though the two became friends.) "The Great Codys" featured Sam's superb horsemanship and "trick shooting" skills, including splitting an apple on his own head by firing at the trigger of a rifle held in a vise across the stage. Lela and sons Leon and Vivian became expert shots under his coaching and joined the show.

When public interest in such entertainment waned, he wrote a five-act play based upon his Yukon misadventure, completing it in a week. He built and painted his own scenery, hired a cast of 40 plus orchestra and launched "Klondike Nugget." It was a roaring success and made the Codys famous during a five-year tour across Europe. Now the big showman had funds for other ideas.

While the details are sketchy, it is known that Cody modified a Winchester to fire 16 rounds a second. British army officials came to a demonstration but dismissed the idea as a matinee stunt. For some reason, no attempt was made to sell it elsewhere, though it was featured in the road show.

With characteristic drive and optimism, Cody plunged into another interest—kites, confident he could improve on existing designs. After hundreds of trials he settled on a triangular double box configuration that remained stable in winds as high as 60 miles an hour. Don't think in balsa-and-tissue terms; his man-carrier spanned 19 feet, had 1,000 square feet of lifting surface and weighed 180 pounds. Cody thought big. A series of smaller "lifters" hauled a steel cable aloft, proving a pull of 2,000 pounds against the winch. The rider ascended in a wicker basket slung from a trolley beneath the monstrous kite, regulating rate of climb and descent with bridle adjustments.

Cody rose to 1,000 feet and surveyed the scene with well deserved satisfaction. Lela had to try it, of course, so up she went, expertly handling the controls. "I never knew fear when I was with him," she said. "He told me it was safe so I knew it must be." Their three sons made many ascents. There were accidents, some serious, but the Cody clan seemed to draw on an endless supply of luck. Two small kites with weather gauges were sent up to 14,000 feet, a new record, and Cody was made a fellow of the Royal Meteorological Society, an honor he cherished.

The Army took little notice, even when Cody promised to train aerial observers for the Boer War. The Navy was interested, however, and towed him up and down the Channel while he telephoned the position of ships beyond the view of deck officers. That use of heavier-than-air craft from a British warship is said to mark the birth of the Royal Navy's Fleet Air Arm.

Cody's appearance must have come as a shock, wearing as he always did a black Stetson, long frock coat and sporting long hair, moustache and goatee, yet the sailors took to the cheerful Texan on sight. His enthusiasm was infectious. Colorful "Colonel" Cody (a stage rank) was accepted for what he was—a big, jovial American who accomplished just about everything he set his mind to. An attempt to span the Irish Sea in a kite-towed boat failed due to uncooperative winds, but he managed an overnight Channel crossing, arriving at Dover in time for breakfast.

At 42, Cody was pleased with his success and popularity, but most of all with his "war kites," as he called them. They represented true adventure, not the pretended risks in the music halls. "I am not much in love with acting," he said in an interview. In a lecture he announced plans for a flying machine, ". . . on the lines of my kite but with an engine." Four months later the Wrights succeeded at Kitty Hawk.

A surprising Army request to serve as an observation kite builder and instructor came as a mixed blessing. It meant full time profitable work in aeronautics but the aeroplane project had to be shelved. Turning his back on a 15-year stage career, he disbanded the wild west show and spent months on kite and airship problems. He built gliders in his spare hours, one of which flew with a tiny gas engine. One glider accident put his son, Vivian, in the hospital for six months.

Spending personal funds and working in a borrowed shed, Cody built a huge pusher biplane with a 52-foot wingspan weighing 1,200 pounds. In his new *All the World's Airships,* Fred Jane observed that the monster was "immensely strong." Size and strength were Cody trademarks. He was often seen tying knots in bracing wires with his bare hands and was the only one able to spin its 50-horsepower V-8 engine into life. A reporter took one look and dubbed the creation the "Flying Cathedral" and the nickname stuck.

While he saw photographs of successful American and French aeroplanes, Cody saw no reason to modify his original concept which, by the way, he carried in his head. There were no blueprints or lists of materials simply because Cody never learned to read and write. He eventually mastered a huge "S. F. Cody" for official paperwork, holding the pen, someone said, like a trowel.

The finished product included a shock-mounted landing gear with steerable tailwheel, ailerons (perhaps their first use) and ground-adjustable wing camber and propeller blade pitch. In the summer of 1908 it was towed to Laffan's Plain, a rough, rolling pasture surrounded by trees. On one *uphill* run to test the controls, there was a gap of 234 feet in tire marks, a greater distance than the Wright's first hop, but Cody dismissed it as "just a jump."

On October 16, with the press watching, he gave it full throttle, rose to 40 feet and flew 1,390 feet, crashing when he attempted to avoid trees. The big man emerged from the wreckage bruised but smiling. The illiterate Texas genius had become the first man to fly in England—or anywhere in the Empire for that matter.

Such was the beginning of the struggle. The Army declined to advance funds for further development of his plane. Reporters derided the feat, pointing out that over in France the Wrights had flown 70 miles. Cody shrugged off the abuse, redesigned his plane and the following years added to Empire firsts—the first passenger carried, the first woman carried (Lela, naturally, who rode weeks before the Wrights invited a lady aboard) and a 40-mile cross-country flight.

A fascinated witness to the events at Laffan's Plain was King George V who always addressed the big Texan as, "Colonel," leading to the mistaken assumption that Army rank had been bestowed. In five short years, the irrepressible Cody built and rebuilt—for there were many mishaps—six machines including a monoplane, a seaplane and a four-seater. He became a British subject in order to qualify in the Military Trials which he won hands down in a two-seater with enclosed cockpit.

That victory erased all remaining doubts. Cody was a national hero. Never one to rest on his laurels, he entered one aviation contest after another, usually capturing the top prize. He flew 185 miles in just over four hours, then 261 in five, climbing to 5,000 feet enroute. At the age of 52, he was the grand old man of the new science and affectionately called "Papa Cody" by the young sports he challenged.

Then, at the peak of success and fame, his luck ran out. Approaching to land at Laffan's Plain, witnesses heard a sharp snap and the wings of his latest plane folded upwards. Leon and his young brother, Frank, rushed to the wreckage but their father was dead. Vivian saw a London headline, CODY KILLED IN AIR CRASH.

General Douglas Haig personally delivered the King's condolences which included, " . . . he did so much for military aviation." Fifty thousand people lined the route from Cody's home to the Military Cemetery where the old cowboy was the first civilian to be buried. Watching, a friend said, "I doubt if he ever had an enemy."

So ended a remarkable and almost forgotten chapter in air history. Lela went into permanent seclusion. Vivian and Leon devoted their lives to aeronautical research in England while Frank became a pilot in the Royal Flying Corps and was killed in action. Laffan's Plain is now part of the sprawling facility known as Farnborough. Its Officers Mess displays a model of Cody's first plane.

Birdville is gone, long since overrun by expanding Ft. Worth. A recent history of the original settlement contains no mention of the Cody family. A dozen miles to the east on the dry prairie where young Sam learned to ride and shoot, is the immense, bustling terminal called the Dallas - Ft. Worth Regional Airport.

"Cody Field" would have been more fitting, don't you think?

# About the PA

It all began with the megaphone. Then some radio wizard rigged a mike to an amplifier to a loudspeaker and gave us the public address system and I for one have never forgiven him. To be fair, it wasn't his fault; it's the way they use it that's galling.

The same can be said of two-way radio in aircraft. Introduced as an aid, the slave became master; we serve it, saying and listening to three times what is necessary simply to get the right words on the tapes. Playing the tapes back is the first step in investigating an "incident." The exchange of useful information is almost secondary to the urgency of covering one's own tail.

Early PAs worked well enough in railroad stations. The announcement of the *Broadway Limited's* impending departure echoed through awesome Pennsylvania Station like a call to worship. Train number —enroute stops—track number—"All aboard!"—period. That was the way to use it.

The young airlines copied railroad format - the *Broadway Limited* became the *Overland Flyer,* Pullman became Skylounge, redcap became skycap and so on—but employed the PA more to advertise than advise. I can hear it now from the scratchy speakers at Bowman Field, "American Airlines announces the departure of its Flight Number 21, the *Sun Country Special,* for (nine stops) and Los Angeles. All passengers holding tickets on Flight 21 should proceed to the boarding gate." There was more about putting out smokes, showing your ticket to the stewardess and so on and they ran through the whole spiel three times, which was rather pointless when there was only one DC-3 on the ramp and three people waiting to board. But we ate it up in 1940.

Never to be outshined, Captain Eddie came up with, "Your attention please. Capt. John Payne of Eastern Air Lines' southbound Flight 7 advises he has the airport in sight and will land in approximately ten minutes," and we'd watch for the running lights. Someone would say, "There he is!" and I'd wait for a close look at Capt. Payne.

It was right off the cob, but right for the times. After the war the airlines matured in most respects but didn't outgrow their PA windiness. By 1950 the speakers at busy terminals were rarely silent. Departure and arrival announcements were interspersed with calls to board limos, the paging of passengers, police, flight crews and skycaps, baggage claim instructions and more, all of it long-winded. A new nomenclature emerged. "All passengers holding tickets on Flight 73 should now be on board" and, "Flight 27 is now in the final boarding process" and, "This is your last and final call for Flight 5" were substituted for, "All aboard!" This was progress in the view of vice presidents who wrote the announcements. Don't imagine ticket agents dream up the witless lines that boom through terminals.

It was a relief to escape the incessant terminal chatter and get on board. Then came DC-6s equipped with PAs. Pilots were instructed to use it. They could order second lieutenants around and expect compliance but it didn't work on the patriarchs who commanded the new wonder. Most ignored the handset ("I'm a pilot, dammit, not a tour guide!") but eventually they fell into line when the shotgun approach was replaced by polite requests. Some mumbled a few words about speed, altitude and ETA and that was it for a three-hour trip. The average captain tried to keep his fares informed about progress and interesting landmarks.

A few fell in love with the PA, much to the anguish of their captive audiences. These frustrated toastmasters launched into detailed preflight briefings, paused long enough to get airborne, then kept the mike hot until arrival. One read off every weather sequence clipped to the clearance, Ogden, Utah, included, as we flew from Dallas to Chicago. Another provided a tedious nuts-and-bolts description of the DC-6, including mention of its 14-cylinder engines. We never reminded him they were 18-cylinder radials. He was a great ad for ear plugs.

We had a history buff who knew something unusual about every place we passed. His brief comments enthralled passengers. A professor who once taught him wrote our boss, "If Capt. Martin had been as keen on history in college, he'd have made better grades. Flying with him is a pleasure!" The PA could be used to good effect.

And it can be, but rarely is. Some of what drives frequent flyers up the walls is unavoidable. The pre-takeoff lecture on seat belts, oxygen masks, emergency exits, upright tray tables and seat backs and all the rest is required by federal regulation, as is the post-takeoff admonition to keep belts fastened whenever seated. Failure to make these announcements can result in fines for crewmembers and the airline. It can be argued that nearly all of this information could be as effectively dispensed in placard form. The recent introduction of pre-recorded tapes for required announcements minimizes the assault on rider ears. No crewmember can match the effect of a trained speaker who, after a dozen tries, gets it said exactly right.

Newspaper columnists like to take pokes at airlines, never failing to ridicule cockpit commentary. Recently one captain was portrayed as a real boob because he gave football scores, a topic which bored the writer. The writer was the boob; he didn't consider the captain's plight.

There is no exactly right announcement. I've been there. In back are 400 people, all kinds and ages. A few are first riders who want to know speed, altitude, the temperature outside, all the details. You could talk for an hour and they'd ask for more. There are businessmen who want to hear, "On time," no more. Many fares are sleeping. Some have a genuine fear of flying. There are vacationers, people going to funerals, others to weddings, workers going to new jobs and others who have just lost jobs. There are overseas visitors who, knowing no English, listen carefully to tone and inflection. What to say and how to phrase it? You can't please everyone.

One of my Convair skippers ordered me to make all announcements. I suggested that he go back and monitor my spiel; he took the bait. I concluded my announcement with, "Our captain is now in the cabin to answer your questions." He got back to the cockpit 20 minutes later. By the end of our four-day trip he had relented; he would not try to get me canned.

During a slump years ago, a 707 departed with one fare aboard. After serving him dinner, the girls sat down to talk. Half an hour later the PA came on, "Your attention, please. This is your passenger speaking. Will someone get me a coffee refill?"

Attempting humor is extremely risky. One of my captains got away with it. We were delayed at the gate. Any irate gentleman opened the door and demanded an explanation. "Sir, are you men on board physicians who just attended the convention here?" The passenger nodded. The captain picked up the mike, made apologies and said, "Perhaps this 30-minute delay will make up for the *hours* I've spent waiting to see my doctor." It worked; we heard them laughing.

Another (not one of ours) came up with, "Ladies and gentlemen, we are over Salt Lake City. Set your watches back 50 years." That didn't come off as hoped, in fact, it earned the humorist an unpaid vacation.

The cleverest yet: an airline 707 with Marines aboard departed Saigon. From the captain, "Gentlemen, we are delighted to have a hand in returning you to your homes and loved ones. As a special treat, our topless cabin attendants will serve lunch." The cockpit door opened and out walked the copilot and engineer to pass out the trays, both stripped to the waist. I wish I'd thought of that.

And I'll never forget the lovely British girl who, when the no smoking light came on, said "All right, chaps. Fags out." That ad lib beats the inane, "Please extinguish all smoking materials," which always makes me look to see if my suit is on fire.

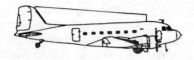

# The Other End of the Line

$A$h yes, the layover, as much a part of airline life as ground school and check rides. In the DC-3 days we stayed in downtown hotels—the Albany in Denver, the Rice in Houston, the huge Stevens in Chicago. If those old walls could talk! (and it's just as well they can't.) Downtown was the place to be when layovers ran from 24 to 36 hours. Then as now, the typical airport restaurant offered dismal food and abominable service at outrageous prices, one exception being Joe Gilbert's wonderful coffee shop at old Kansas City Municipal which did as much for midwestern air travel as Braniff and TWA together. The pin money they gave us for expenses went further downtown. Movies and clubs were close by and, for those of us of cultural bent, the art center, library and museum.

It was two to a room, of course—captain and copilot. The engineer of a DC-6 crew bunked with another engineer or moved in with the copilot and gave the skipper the single. Rank had its privileges. Such togetherness created problems. One captain would want the window open; try that in Minneapolis in January. The next might set the heat on 80, wrap up in a blanket and turn on the late, late movie. The resulting discussions were often heated and always futile. RHIP.

Most hotels treated us well. A few were resentful, particularly in summer when our commercially-priced space could have been sold to tourists at cutthroat rates. In those we got cool treatment at the front desk and rooms next to the elevator or laundry, as if we ourselves had signed the leases. More than one manager was roused from bed at 3:00 a.m. by a hard-nosed old skipper demanding better accommodations.

In the winter we logged much lobby time, criticizing company policy, lying about flying experiences or speculating on the friendliness of the brunette at the check-in counter. Conventions were a real pain with hordes of strangers clogging elevators and restaurants and otherwise infringing on territory already staked out by us regulars.

One of my captains saw profit in convention confusion. A bland little man, Jake looked like—well, anyone he wanted to look like. Brazenly approaching the credentials table, he'd say something—I never knew what—and come back with name tags that opened all doors. "Pin this on, keep quiet and follow me," he'd say, striding into the exhibits hall, not that we had much interest in plumbing supplies or whatever was being pushed. Within the hour and loaded down with colored brochures describing commodes and septic systems, we had invitations to the hospitality rooms upstairs which, of course, was the name of his game. It is still not too late to say, thank you, American Standard. Attorneys were the dullest crowd we worked, morticians and bankers the liveliest, believe it or not.

The Republican Convention at Chicago in 1952 gave us close glimpses of Ike and Dick but we were forever rushing back to our room to keep track of the voting. I should have stayed with Jake that time because there he was, seated with the Montana delegation. Had we laid over in London, that character could have talked his way into Buckingham Palace for lunch.

For some years we put up at the St. Moritz in New York which was plush indeed. It was the Manhattan digs of many names, Walter Winchell, Alexander deSeversky, Mickey Mantle, Charles Laughton and his wife among them. We felt somewhat out of place there.

But all that was way back. New work rules and rising layover expenses forced managements to tighten schedules and give crews minimum turnaround times. Most international crews still enjoyed long layovers downtown, but domestic crews were put up in motels near airports. They got home sooner, which is what we wanted all along, and didn't spend hours each month in cabs. From airport bedrooms in Chicago and Pittsburgh, we'd watch our trips arrive, then walk to operations. It was all quite different.

American motel units apparently come down the same assembly line from identical blueprints. The names—Holiday Inn, Ramada, Travel Lodge—are distributed by lottery. The majority maintained reasonable standards and were clean, comfortable, convenient. Other franchise owners spent fortunes on gleaming facilities then turned them over to college kids to run; we boarded in our share of those. The management pride that once characterized good hotels was too often missing, so we got a window unit that delivered more noise than cool air, a lamp and TV that didn't work, a bathroom not really spotless and a coffee shop that closed just as we checked in—and there we were out in the boondocks, miles from anywhere. Many of us brown-bagged it to insure a bite at the end of the line. While we grew from DC-3s to jets, we retreated from linen tablecloths to stale sandwiches. Progress.

The young bucks and gals of later days made for the sauna, pool and tennis court, diversions rarely found in the old hotels. We had a good time all the same, inventing fun when things got dull. In the late 1940s a series of hotel fires claimed many lives, making some pilots extremely nervous. One captain had a horror of burning in his bed, a phobia well known to all, so what happened to him was inevitable. Get the picture: late Saturday evening in the old King Cotton in Memphis; big dance downstairs in the ballroom; old Charlie sawing logs on the sixth floor.

The phone rang. An obviously high strung "operator" reported a minor fire and requested that he evacuate at once. Walk down stairs, don't use the elevator, leave your belongings and please, please hurry. Panic-stricken, Charlie threw a blanket around his shoulders, raced down the hall and took the stairs three at a time. He dashed through the first door he saw on the ground floor and found himself in the ballroom. He stood there, disheveled and wild-eyed (looking like an Apache chief headed for a big powwow, according to eyewitnesses), the dancers froze and the music stopped. "Don't stand there, you idiots!" he shouted. "This place is on fire. Follow me!" and he led the mob to the street outside where they stood in the snow, looking for smoke and waiting for the fire engines.

Such an outrage begged for revenge. The perpetrator of this humiliation was shortly thereafter asleep in a Texas hotel, having turned in early in anticipation of a 5:30 wake up call. Charlie got a pass key, slipped in and reset his watch. The phone rang minutes later. "Good morning, captain, cab pick up in thirty minutes," said a feminine voice. Nothing suspicious about that. The victim shaved, dressed and went down to the lobby. But where was the rest of the crew? He glanced at the lobby clock. Midnight.

The practical jokers never rested. One extremely correct fellow was the butt of numerous pranks and never caught on. He was awakened at 2:00 in the morning once by the "manager" who ordered him to come down stairs immediately and make good several hot checks he had given the cashier. He stormed down five minutes later, four gold stripes, scrambled eggs, purple with indignation to confront a night clerk who had no idea what he was talking about. When he awoke the next time, there was a note under the door on the manager's letterhead and "signed" by him, offering one last chance to buy back the checks. Would you believe he bit down hard all over again?

And there was the fearful soul who cringed at any hint of scandal. He often discovered empty bottles and lipstick-smeared glasses outside his door in the hallway. What to do? Moving them was risky. Once while carrying a tray of such damning evidence away, it was his rotten luck (he thought) to run smack into two incoming crews who gave him stern looks of disapproval. Intimate items of feminine apparel found their way into his suitcase and his company mailbox was crammed with lurid reading matter that is mailed in plain brown wrappers. The poor devil took on a hunted look and seemed to welcome retirement.

The room numbers on lobby signboards inviting conventioneers up for free drinks were known to be swapped for those of freighter crews resting prior to a midnight wake up call.

One luckless copilot emerged from the shower to find all his clothes missing. Just then his captain walked in. No, he hadn't a clue but did recall passing their stewardess in the hallway and, yes, come to think of it, she was carrying a large Halliburton suitcase which did seem a bit odd. The copilot dialed her room. Fun's fun and we've all had a good laugh, he said, now how about bringing it back? After much pleading she finally agreed to meet him at her door and hand it over; no begging or threats would change her mind.

Oh well, be a good sport. Wrapped in a bed sheet, he glanced outside. The coast was clear. Halfway down the hall, he heard, "Ding dong," the elevator bell. Damn! He took refuge in a linen closet. Through the crack he saw his captain and stew pass, chuckling over something both found amusing, and take the elevator down. They were off to dinner and a movie, a double feature, no less.

Within the week that skipper tried to pick up his flight bag at another airport and found it was nailed to the floor. His companion in crime was at the same time trying to convince the truck drivers at her apartment that she had not ordered five yards of gravel, much less a load of sheep manure.

Those were the days.

# Cruising

Last Sunday's paper carried a feature about airline food preparation headlined, "Dining Out at 30,000 Feet." Thirty thousand feet. Reporters and ad copy writers are for some reason fascinated with that altitude. We are shown the business executive doing paperwork, the handsome couple smiling over martinis, the friendly stewardess pinning junior pilot wings on a little boy, Gramps and Granny snoozing in sleeperette seats—always at 30,000 feet.

If any of these cute little scenes was indeed played out at 30,000 feet, we can only hope someone was hurrying forward to pound on the cockpit door because they weren't supposed to be at 30,000 feet. Normal cruising levels are 29,000, 31,000, 33,000 and so on up through 45,000 feet. Even- and odd-numbered altitudes are assigned from 29,000 on down. Thirty thousand feet is an altitude you go through, climbing or descending.

Forty-five thousand is far more impressive in any event, but you never see it mentioned. That's eight-and-a-half miles up there, not bad for an airplane with 330 souls on board. Of course, you had to have the one airliner legal to fly that high in order to advertise that. We did. So, when enough fuel had been burned off, we occasionally went right to the top simply because we could and—let's own up—to wave the company flag. A position report, which we knew would be overheard by competitors flying less advanced equipment, identified our line and the fact we were operating the latest thing—the Boeing 747SP, that suffix meaning "Special Performance." Needless to add, our promotion people went right on extolling our superlative silver service dinners—as served at 30,000 feet. They didn't have a clue.

Which is not to say other types could not get that high when pushed, even if limited to 41,000 feet by FAA rule. More than one 707 struggled up to 50,000 feet on training or ferry hops when fuel loads were down to landing minimums, and I'm sure the late model DC-8s could match that.

Cruising on long distance runs was a monotonous, time dragging, fatiguing exercise most of the time. It is no exaggeration to say that 75% of the mental effort required to fly a 747 from Texas to Britain had been expended upon reaching initial cruising level. The rest of it was watching, listening, checking, rechecking and checking once again as the huge wonder sniffed its way along the programmed trails leading from the New World to the Old. The 747 was a pure marvel, yet it was a mindless assemblage of parts requiring continuous monitoring, and we never forgot it.

One starlit evening, nearing the end of a seven-hour run from Brussels to Boston in a spanking new 747-200 with all the latest gadgets, our speed began to deteriorate so slowly as to be almost unnoticeable. It was the gradual lessening of wind noise around the cockpit windows which suggested things were not completely right. All four thrust levers were inching back ever so slowly and, of course, the autopilot was easing the nose up to maintain altitude. The cause was a malfunction in the auto-throttle system, a fluke so far-fetched that a groundschool instructor later declared to be an impossibility. Pilots have to cross the t's and dot the i's missed by ground people.

Once in a while something happened to break the almost unbearable monotony of those post-midnight hours of smooth cruising. Or something was made to happen. One old captain of mine would periodically rouse himself, bang his fist down on the glare shield and shout, "We've got to have more money for this night work!" The flight engineer and I would almost jump out of our skins, no matter how many times he'd done it, which was exactly what he intended.

During the early Electra days when their wings were coming unnailed for mysterious reasons (we'd lost one, Northwest another), we were peacefully romping along at the reduced airspeed stipulated by the FAA. It was two a.m. and we were about to cross Nashville when a hostess crept into the cockpit. That misguided woman thought it a grand joke to drop the metal logbook on the cockpit floor. The resulting awful clatter aged me six years. The captain, as nerveless a human as ever lived, didn't flex a muscle. He slowly turned to her and said, "How about a black coffee?" After she left he said more which I will not repeat. Other girls tried the same stunt during those nervous months. It was a bad joke which never drew a laugh.

Thirty thousand feet may come into vogue after all, now that the FAA is considering reducing aircraft separation at high levels. Since major terminals cannot cope with the current traffic flow, the point of stepping up the flow is not readily apparent. If the rules are changed, the cockpit view of converging traffic will take some getting used to.

Many the time we watched a contrail at 12 o'clock and bet beers on whether he'd pass over or under us; at 20 miles he seemed to have us bore-sighted and we knew we would pass within the minute.

At night an approaching flashing beacon was all the more confusing. You could only hope the people down there peering at those big green radar scopes had their act together. Years back a Viscount captain decided that an approaching target was on collision course, though it was, in fact, a thousand feet above him. He began climbing, thereby losing what little visual reference he had to begin with, and increased his rate of climb as the other plane drew closer. He crossed the opposing aircraft by feet, his nose way up there, stalled and spun out. Control was regained near the ground and an emergency landing made. Fortunately, the night was clear for the spin rendered his flight instruments useless.

Cruising, that time between leveling off and starting down which in my logs ran from 12 minutes to 12 hours. It was all of it memorable but I think the best hours were those lazy ones logged in DC-3s on cool autumn evenings down there at five or six thousand, padding along under the stars, watching the familiar lights edge into view and slowly fall away beneath the nose. Those were good times. Yes, I chose to forget the awesome line squalls, the pitching and rolling about in summer chop, the freight train progress in headwinds, the nerve-wracking approaches to slick runways in crosswinds. The copilot's trade back then offered minimum job protection, few fringes and paid off in peanuts. Forget all that. I would not have traded one of those enchanted evenings for any other work.

Did our ads ever crow about, "Dining at 5,000 Feet"? I don't think they did. And those cheese sandwiches weren't all that bad.

# Them and Us

Here's another gadget to save us from ourselves, the "flight phase monitor." The present array of bells, horns, rattles, flashing lights and verbal warnings is not enough, say the experts; we need even more help. The plan is to install sensors all over the airplane which feed data to a computer. If things come unnailed in a big way, this gizmo will review the inflow of bad news and tell the pilot what to do. "He would only have to follow directions," says one preview. There is no mention of a banana if he responds in time.

Is there no way to get these self-important busybodies out of the cockpit before they do more damage? A pilot is already so occupied following their directions that he cannot give full attention to flying. He has to think about legality rather than good sense because of their regulations. Many pilots have met sudden ends while adhering exactly to procedures adopted by these self-appointed experts. Their philosophy isn't working and more bells and horns won't set it right.

The DC-10 crash at O'Hare is cited as proof of the need for more cockpit aids. Simulator tests showed that the captain might have saved the day had he known what had happened to his wing. True, but this is the tip of the iceberg. Had pilots played a decisive role in the Ten's certification the flaps would not have retracted in the first place. Engines have separated from a long list of airplanes in the past. A pod-mounted turbine is, in fact, designed to break free before it damages the wing. No panel of experienced pilots would have approved an airplane that would become uncontrollable if an engine fell off—or an underfloor hatch opened. These things happen sooner or later and you'd better count on it.

But pilots had no say, being expressly excluded from the certification process. Builders claim that "outside" involvement could compromise trade secrets; the FAA concurs. They do not want pilots asking questions much less demanding changes. So, minus such interference, they bet the Ten would never shuck an engine or lose a door, knowing full well what would happen if it did, and the FAA agreed. At Chicago and Paris both bets were lost and their new pride and joy joined the roster of aircraft which, in their original (FAA-approved, that is) configurations, were time bombs. That the production and licensing of a new design is solely in the hands of people willing to take such rash gambles seems incredible but that is how the system works.

A similar low regard for pilot intelligence is apparent in day-to-day operations, the exact techniques for which are laid down by non-flying desk pilots. Their procedures make sense as guides to good practice but are, in fact, rigid requirements, deviations from which are violations of federal law. The point made clear on check rides: you will fly the airplane our way, or else. Knowing that his every word and move are being recorded can hardly enhance a pilot's judgement when he's out on his own.

Slavish obedience to published procedures without regard for other factors can lead to trouble. Example: when surface winds are strong it is standard practice to increase speed on final approach by half the steady wind plus all the gust, this correction never to exceed 20 knots. The pilot who thinks this modest adjustment will keep him out of the trees in every situation has much to learn. It's no use having a taped voice yell, "Pull up, pull up!" in his ear after restricting him to too-slow a speed to begin with. Pray you never ride behind a milquetoast whose fear of authority clouds his better judgement.

Forcing a pilot to wear two hats is absurd, yet he must and everyone knows it. After studying recent accidents, an FAA official has even allowed that ". . . there were instances where the normal procedures don't apply." Good Lord! Orville Wright could have told him that.

Modern training is vastly improved over the nuts-and-bolts schooling of 25 years ago yet it remains too much a Disneyland approach to real life experiences. Pilots know better than the builder, the owner and the FAA combined what information is needed to fly an airplane from here to there. They should write the curriculum. Instead, they must absorb what the ground crowd thinks they should know, much of which is theory useful only in passing tests.

Often heard is the dour comment, "After we play their little simulator game we can go out and learn to fly the airplane." Give the fed a steep turn, an engine out approach, a back course, a no-flap arrival—fill in the squares and get the rating; this is the way it's done. Then go learn for yourself how it handles in chop at 41,000, how the brakes work on ice, how it responds in a cross wind. Learn its peculiarities with a full load of passengers and hope you get a sharp copilot the first month.

The ground experts loom big in the picture until there's an accident and then they are suddenly silent. They built and approved the airplane and dictated training and operation, resisting pilot involvement in any part of it, but now their fingers all point to the cockpit. Before the ashes had cooled at O'Hare an NTSB official was before network cameras voicing his guess that the captain likely could have prevented the disaster. He spoke the truth but not at all in the way he intended. The ground people want all the authority but none of the responsibility.

We all work toward the goal of safety but what strange methods we use to achieve it. The them-and-us syndrome continues, pitting one group against the other. It should at least be worth the try for all of us to sit down together in an atmosphere of mutual respect and realistically explore the problems that need solving. It might be found that instead of installing a new computer we could better utilize the one already on board, the one between the pilot's ears.

# Preflight Musings

The slow night drizzle ran down the windshield and side windows, obscuring the view of airliners creeping past in search of gates. We stuffed paper towels into spaces between the panes of dripping water. Already 20 minutes late, we waited with patience born of experience; the drenched ramp workers were doing their best. The horizon was lit by almost continuous lightning, occasionally dramatic; to the northeast, that is, the direction we would fly.

From my flight engineer perch behind the pedestal I regarded my companions. The copilot had 10 years seniority and soon would upgrade to DC-3 captain. He sat immobile and stared at the distant fireworks. What was he thinking? The captain, a venerable patriarch who in the beginning flew single-engine Vegas along the same route, said nothing. Did he ponder the weather, the options, or was he in the least concerned? He offered no clue.

The outside hustle concluded with the audible slam of a belly bin door and the lead agent held up three fingers. "Turn 'em," said the captain, coming alive. I reached for the four switches, the copilot reached for his mike and we went to work.

Or it was this, 15 years later: I sat to the right of a 25-year captain. The industry in the meantime had mushroomed and to some degree matured; there was far more experience in that cockpit; the airplane was larger, faster, far more complex. Now we knew more about the squall line ominously illuminating the horizon and, with radar and improved communications, were somewhat better equipped. The same cold rain dripped onto our legs, we still plugged the cracks with Kleenex and again we were late. We patiently waited, each lost in his own thoughts. At last, from the overhead speakers, "Hello, cockpit, you are cleared to start," and, from the captain, "Turn Number Three," as I called ground control for taxi clearance.

Or this: now I sat in the left seat of an airplane weighing six times as much as the largest four-engine type I ever copiloted. On the right sat a younger captain who opted for international work rather than the domestic schedules he could have commanded. At the flight engineer's panel sat a 12-year man who had briefly held a captain's bid during the previous summer's travel boom. But, the more things had changed, the more they remained the same. Midnight approached while we waited (we were late, of course), saying little while eyeing the welders' convention on the far horizon—as usual the horizon we must cross—and cold rain ran down the windshield obscuring the outside view. Finally, "Hello, cockpit, we're ready for push back," and I responded, "Brakes off," noting the engineer's thumbs-up signal that the last door light was out.

I remember a thousand such episodes and recall them often. The specifics are hazy—the places, the weather, the types of aircraft and even my rank in the cockpit—but the feeling of mild apprehension remains vivid in memory. Departing on a clear morning to cruise in ideal conditions to a daylight arrival is one thing. A maximum gross weight night takeoff from a marginal runway into lousy weather is something else. You consider the options, basing decisions on data which, to a disquieting degree, is pure guesswork.

A good pilot is a realist. He acknowledges the limits of man and machine which cannot be exceeded with impunity. He knows that the most significant weather from his standpoint is often the most rapidly changing, therefore the picture given him 30 minutes earlier may have dramatically changed since. He balances pleasing probabilities against unpleasant possibilities. He recognizes personal motivations and external pressures and examines them in the light of doing what makes sense. And so, where does he draw the line? When to go, when to wait, how to weigh the risk?

As Eddie Rickenbacker observed, every form of motion involves risk. If you would avoid all of it, stay in bed. There are degrees of risk in all travel from walking to every means of surface, water or air transport. The idea that flying, safety-wise, could match and even surpass most surface travel was preposterous 50 years ago, yet it came to be. Travel by public and private aircraft would never have reached its present state had every pilot insisted on ideal conditions every time. Risk in varying degrees is inherent in all flight and must be accepted. The bottom line: how much is reasonable, all things considered?

The risk equation comprises many factors. Plus factors include meticulous maintenance, adequate airports and navigational aids, favorable weather and—most importantly—experienced, responsible pilots. On the minus side, among other things, are careless repairs, foul weather, marginal fields and—most importantly—inexperience, negligence or complacency in the cockpit.

For all of standardization, no two aircraft, no two crews, no two weather situations are precisely alike, nor will a particular combination be repeated. Recently an expert crew in a well-maintained airplane landed normally followed in minutes by another expert crew in a well-maintained airplane which crashed short of the field. So far as anyone knew, the same weather conditions existed; in fact, they had lethally changed, almost within seconds.

No pilot has seen it all. The surprise in encountering a quirk of weather, mechanics or human behavior never before seen or even imagined—is a factor. Nothing would surprise an experienced pilot more than to fly for a year without something slightly—or grossly—out of the ordinary happening. There is truth in the saw about his work being hours upon hours of monotony punctuated by moments of stark terror.

There can be no comparison here between wartime and peace-time flying. An acquaintance who flew B-17s said his group lost as many crews on an "easy" mission than his airline lost during his entire 35-year career. (He also wondered if the comparatively slight risks of airline flying might be cumulative, an interesting thesis.)

The goal of peacetime civil flying is a perfect safety record. Notwithstanding the recent rash of major accidents, we have come closer to reaching it than most of us would have predicted 25 years ago. Vastly improved technology must be credited for much of it. Today's small private airplane can be fitted with pilot aids undreamed of a few years ago and the modern airliner is a marvel. But both operate in an environment far more demanding than that known 25 years ago—and neither can think for itself. Sharp pilotage in all phases of civil aviation deserves more credit than it receives.

"There can be no compromise with safety," a well-meant maxim, was not conceived by a pilot. Every flight is a compromise between numerous factors, good and bad, known and unknown. It is the continuous balancing of safety factors that gives piloting its challenge and fascination. Responsible decision making is what being a pilot is all about. "There can be no *unreasonable* compromise with safety," reads better.

A layman could mistake the dedicated pilot's outlook as a preoccupation with disaster. This would be to misunderstand him completely. Misjudgement in most ground activity can be set right after work is under way; such may not be the case in flight. Only in the simulator can the action be frozen while corrections are made.

So we sat there often when the flight ahead suggested special problems—and we thought. What we were doing, of course, was shedding the casual approach good enough on the ground and starting once again to think like airmen.

While safe flight requires a pilot's best efforts until brakes are set, the whole business came most sharply into focus for me just prior to a night departure, when rain streaked the windows, dripping onto our legs and lightning revealed the horizon. And we were already 20 minutes late.

# By the Numbers

The final problem was an ADF letdown to a circling approach, with an engine out. I turned off the runway and awaited the verdict. "That's all I need," said the fed. He signed the rating. "Everything was OK except you were five to 10 knots fat on speed now and then. You need to watch that," he said. There is a time to speak and a time to be silent. I nodded.

A similar experience by another pilot didn't end so merrily. The senior skipper flew with cold precision, right on the money, except he was 10 knots "fat" throughout. His fed wouldn't buy it. "I want to see one approach right on bug speed," he said. The captain replied, "Until I know this airplane better, I'll fly it by my numbers." No rating. (After a conference with his boss and FAA higher-ups his ticket was endorsed, however.)

He obviously felt that when you're not completely sure, a little extra speed is insurance. I'm with him. Unthinking adherence to the book in every situation is unrealistic, indeed, foolhardy. A review of accidents in recent years in all types of aircraft proves that many pilots came to grief while operating strictly by the book.

In the beginning there was no book. The first aircraft were built by trial and error and flown by the seat of the pants. Piloting was self-taught. The World War I pilot was schooled in mechanics and theory of flight, then soloed with minimum dual and thereafter mastered the art on his own. Fortunate was he who logged 40 hours before seeing combat.

The increasing complexity and cost of airplanes after the war led to more ground and flight training. Students were lectured on weight-and-balance, performance and tested on their understanding of engine and airframe limitations, but piloting techniques remained a matter of individual judgement for the most part.

There were as many ways to fly a DC-3 as there were DC-3 skippers. This provided excellent training for copilots who learned all the ways, right and wrong, to do the job. It was, in fact, the only way they learned anything, the sole training being three landings. Six of us were thus "qualified" in less than an hour; we flew our first trips that day and thenceforth absorbed wisdom by osmosis. While an experienced DC-3 driver could solve the weight-temperature-elevation-runway riddle at a glance, such eyeballing proved disastrous in high performance types introduced in World War II.

Technicians drew up tables, charts and checklists which, eventually, covered everything from firing up to setting brakes. Despite grumbling by old-timers about this intrusion, there was no arguing its purpose. The operation of advanced types posed problems no pilot could solve without technical aid. A revolution in the art of flying had begun; no one dreamed how far it would go.

From the first, technical data were presented more as gospel than guides to good practice. It was made clear, not that you should fly by the numbers, but that you would. Horn, bells, rattles and taped verbal admonitions were installed to prod the careless who fudged speed or altitude or otherwise veered from the straight and narrow. A recorder was added to tape aircraft performance parameters and another to monitor cockpit sounds.

The new philosophy: a pilot cannot operate safely unless he adheres to procedures laid down by the aircraft builder, as approved by the FAA. He will use his own initiative only on those extremely rare occasions when something malfunctions, and then only to the extent of implementing approved corrective procedures.

In theory, it's a grand concept; in practice, it can provoke as much trouble as it prevents. This was clear to the older heads who, when the occasion demanded, ignored the book and relied on experience and common sense.

When regarded as a machine operating in given conditions, an airplane's performance can be calculated to a fine degree. But it performs in a mysterious environment. Weather is a riddle defying precise measurement on the minute-to-minute basis most interesting to pilots, and is specifically unpredictable. Every landing accident account includes "reported conditions," meaning the last observation made prior to the mishap. What was observed and what a pilot encountered at minimums two miles away and 20 minutes later have been remarkably different. The uncountable combinations of wind, precipitation and cloud cannot be reduced to graph coordinates.

The side effects of weather cannot be accurately calculated. A recent technical study of braking action in rain, ice or snow confirms that no device developed to date can be relied upon for precise friction measurements, concluding, ". . .therefore pilots must rely on experience . . ." Engineers work with absolutes; pilots with variables.

The human condition is frustratingly elastic from a mathematical standpoint. Health, temperament, fatigue, age, experience, confidence, fear, skill, stress—such factors cannot be plotted on graphs. A hydraulic pump switched on during preflighting will displace the same volume of fluid 12 hours later. Deterioration of a pilot's performance during that period depends on immeasurables. He cannot be reduced to numbers and fitted into an equation.

Ideally, from some viewpoints, he would be removed from the picture altogether. With present technology an airplane can be programmed to fly from New York to London, land and, no doubt with another black box in the belly, find its gate, all untouched by human hands. (Adding a cafeteria would eliminate cabin attendants.) Of course, there'd be the matter of selling tickets . . .

Pilots are here to stay. We also can be sure that flight will be further automated. And that the people up front will be portrayed as caretakers of a virtually foolproof machine that flies itself. One line has dropped "captain" in favor of "flight manager." Jumbos can now be ordered with two cockpit seats. The thrust is to substitute computers for brains.

The increasingly encouraged reliance on computed solutions rather than human judgement breeds complacency. The pilot of 30 years ago developed his point of view when airplanes were, comparatively speaking, primitive and prone to breakdown. Suspicious, wary and self reliant, he survived by his wits. His book was based on unpleasant experience.

Today's new hire blossomed in the computer age and cannot remember when a question typed on a keyboard didn't produce an immediate and absolutely correct answer on a TV screen. He is conditioned to rely on computer-directed machinery and computed data. He will adapt to today's glass cockpit much more easily than his seniors and never really appreciate what a pilot's dream it is.

We six vets warmed the engineer's seat for two years and the copilot's for 13 more. We remember those years in terms of line squalls, gusting crosswinds, slick runways, wind shears, sick engines, tripped breakers, gauges inching toward zero, inoperative this or that and all the other problems that from time to time presented themselves in the real world of flying. It was a tiresome and frustrating period in our lives, but what priceless training.

Today's self-flying airplane is a far cry from the plodding old DC-3, but it operates in the same environment and will present similar problems, though less frequently. Its copilot in many cases will advance to the left seat after a fraction of the apprenticeship we endured. I wish for him a long and rewarding career, meaning I hope real trouble seeks him out, the stuff of which nightmares are made, frights that shake him to the core. Then, when he takes the left seat, he will fly strictly by the numbers—but know when it's time to put the book away.

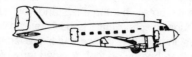

# The Cons of Being A Pro

You think you would like to fly so you enlist in one of the services or go out and buy your own training. At the end of three or four years you've logged 2,000 hours in the right kinds of equipment and meet the requirements for some interesting cockpit employment. You like what you've seen so far and decide on a piloting career.

You find work in whatever corner of the big picture seems most appealing and begin to sell your skill. You are a pro. You've not arrived but you're on your way. Now you will begin to learn what the professional flying life is all about. There are some surprises in store, not all of them pleasant.

First, you become aware that you have chosen one of the most visible of vocations. Your performance is conducted right out in the open where all the world can watch. You realize that all the world *is* watching and wonder why this never struck you before. The most trivial incident involving an aircraft is grist to the media mill. It's life in a goldfish bowl.

Recently a corporate jet arriving at our local field blew a tire and skidded off the runway into the mud. No damage, no injuries, but there it was surrounded by fire engines on page one captioned, "Close Call," while a four-car pileup claiming two lives five miles from the airport was described—but not shown—on page three.

Unfair? Certainly, but such an appalling sense of newsworthiness and a tendency to wild exaggeration about flying incidents extend into the highest media levels. When the Eastern 1011 lost all power near Miami, TV news heavyweights excitedly reported the "near disaster" as the jumbo "plunged" toward the sea. Neither term was reasonable. Powerless, the 1011 glided, completely under control; the event was a near ditching. This brand of reporting hurts everyone in aviation for it perpetuates the notion that "flying" and "dangerous" have much the same meaning, a notion that remains widely held. Of course it's unfair, but there it is and you must live with it.

You were taught in school that it is the American way to presume that an individual in trouble is innocent until proven otherwise. You will learn not to lean heavily on that. A video tape of the highlights of a typical accident investigation hearing would produce more cautious pilots than a week of groundschool lectures.

You have to appreciate the aura of machine worship that pervades aviation and the reasons for it. We are not far from the time when few people accepted flying as sensible and safe. Fear of flying is still widespread. Every one of us wants the system to work and all of us are saddened and frustrated when it doesn't. And all of us, pilots included, are apt to conclude, upon hearing of an accident, that it probably resulted from a cockpit mistake. There is immediate suspicion that we have been let down by one of our own.

Any pilot involved in an incident warranting a full-fledged investigation is in for a grim time. The proceedings may require 30 days to explore in minute detail the 30 minutes leading up to the event. The thrust will be to determine what happened, rather than why; mitigating factors and underlying causes will scarcely receive the attention we pilots think they deserve.

An example: the landing gear and flap handles on a certain post-World War II airliner were on the rear of the control pedestal, side by side, out of sight in the dark. You felt for the flap lever after landing and it was all too easy to grab its mate. A number of luckless copilots did and of course the subsequent belly slides were laid to "pilot error" which, technically, they were. The more sensible shape and location of these controls in modern airliners is proof that poor design was a contributing factor though it was never mentioned. Many similar examples can be cited.

Seemingly arrayed against a pilot on trial (which does not overstate his plight) is a small army of "expert witnesses"—the builders of the aircraft and its engines and component parts, its owners, weathermen, various local and federal officials, insurance adjusters and so on and on. The opposition (a fair description) is formidable. Each has a special interest to protect; the legal and financial repercussions of an unfavorable verdict can be staggering, amounting to hundreds of millions of dollars in an airline case. Understandably, sidestepping blame is the real name of the game. Interestingly, it is unlikely that any of these witnesses will have firsthand knowledge of the pilot's specialty, much less have experienced the particular dilemma that called him to the carpet. In fact, few will even be pilots.

All of which leads to another surprise: you needn't be a pilot to know all about what a pilot does. You will be both amused and amazed at what laymen say about you. They will make your work sound so simple, so one-two-three. So much has been made of technological advance that in the popular view you have been reduced to a button-pushing robot who follows procedures in a book and instructions radioed from the ground. Your aircraft is the star performer, not you. You are but another player on a big team of technicians, and teamwork is what makes the system work. This premise is continuously stressed—until things go badly. At a hearing, all those good teammates point fingers at you. You were there. You dropped the ball. It's all your fault.

Among your most vocal critics will be pilots themselves, and what clannish, self-important snobs some of them are. There's the military jock who looks down his nose at all civil flying, the corporate type who snorts at airline flying, the private pilot who imagines the military, corporate and airline people want all of the sky for themselves and the airline fellow who thinks he knows more about everything than all the rest put together. These self-appointed experts are not typical by a long shot, but there are more than enough to go around. They make a lot of noise and it is best ignored.

Their distorted views will nettle if you pay attention. During a recent discussion with a general aviation pilot of considerable experience, he sized up all airline flying like this, "We all know flying those push-button airplanes under the direction of controllers becomes quite routine." He really believed that; I think he expected me to nod in agreement. I wished I could arrange some airline jumpseat passes for him. Let me pick the routes and weather. The most irksome is the fellow who, after an accident, puts himself in a cockpit he never occupied and immediately knows what happened and why.

The system is far from perfect. It steadily increases cockpit responsibility while steadily reducing cockpit authority. It unfairly and unrealistically places blame. But it's the only system we have and it works well enough. To contentedly perform within it, the pro must fully understand the system, why it works as it does and appreciate his unusual role in it. The chances available in most other pursuits to hide or minimize blunders are simply not there for him.

The high visibility of his performance serves a worthwhile purpose. It makes him very, very careful. And that's very, very good.

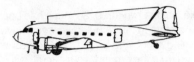

# The Feds

To paraphase Will Rogers, I never met a fed I didn't like. Right off, "fed" carries no derogatory connotation in airline parlance; it's inevitable slang in an industry with an affinity for long-winded titles. I did not continue liking two of them, however, one an eager young inspector who wanted everything exactly by the book. He rode our Convair trip into Chicago Midway Airport. It was my leg to fly. Strong, gusting surface winds. We landed on 31L, right beside a large hangar known (to us, anyway) to produce freakish conditions at the flare, so I carried extra speed to touch down. The inspector did not approve; my captain did and they got into it somewhat heatedly, but nothing came of it. We guessed his superiors squashed his report.

The other was an utter misfit, a pain to every pilot he examined. His disdain for airline pilots was well known. Shortly after our trivial brush (two questions into my 707 oral exam he declared me completely unprepared; another inspector passed me the next day), he was transferred to another region and soon thereafter given early retirement. Two out of all of them was not bad. The rest were fair, reasonable, often helpful. We got along, got the job done right and that's the name of the game.

If you're going to do much with piloting you must understand and accept the rules by which this somewhat strange game is played, otherwise you will only make yourself miserable. All pilots are licensed and regulated by the Federal Aviation Administration; all must meet and maintain FAA standards. The more deeply we became involved, the more stringent the requirements. It's this simple: the FAA giveth and, when sufficiently provoked, the FAA taketh away. If this is too Big Brother for an individual or strikes him as a violation of his rights, he should try of the professions that polices itself, which is most of the rest of them. A professional pilot is more closely watched than a paroled convict. And he can forget the military; service flying is even more regimented. The cockpit is not the place to do your own thing.

I knew a pilot who fought the system until the day he retired. He saw himself as a professional who had long since proven his skills. He bitterly resented the never-ending monitoring and recurrent checks that are part of airline life. A fed on the jump seat made him livid, yet his seething was apparent only to those who knew him well. When thus infuriated, he flew with cold precision. I can see him now, taut as a banjo string, tight-lipped, his cockpit deportment so correct as to poke fun at the whole business. I really don't think the FAA bothered him unduly, no matter how he raged. He simply used his resentment to work himself into a lather because he did best when angry. It wouldn't work for most.

It makes more sense to learn the rules and play by them. In this contest you are pitted against yourself, not the FAA. The typical fed is on your side. He derives no pleasure from a busted check ride. I see it this way: we pilots belong to a very nice club. Unless you can qualify for membership as we did, the feds won't give you a card and the rest of us don't want you to have one. A good solid performance along will pay the dues.

Think of a fed as a pro for he most certainly is. He has already earned the license or rating you want and don't imagine it was handed to him. Our airline trained scores of FAA air carrier inspectors and I've watched them sweat just as we did. Most were ex-military, some with impressive backgrounds. The fact that a fed with 50 hours in a 737 may monitor the simulator check of a captain with 5,000 hours in that type makes him none the less able to tell good work from bad. I have never ridden cockpit in a 737 but I could tell in the first 10 minutes if its crew was competent—and so can a fed.

The typical FAA agent is conscientious; he works at his job and expects you to work at yours. He is also an individual who approaches things in his own way and you have got to please the particular inspector you draw. If you fail, you may get him or another on the second try. Two of us took the Convair oral exam together. Eager to display our knowledge, we made the classic mistake of volunteering more information than was required to answer his questions. Our examiner let us chatter on, as feds are prone to do, and we both flew up blind canyons before it was over. We passed, but not without some embarrassment. A fed may privately agree with you that a particular rule is inane but, as the FAA's representative, he is required to enforce it.

I learned beforehand that my Lockheed Electra examiner was ex-Navy and had flown the huge Martin Mars flying boat during World War II. We spent 20 minutes talking about flying boats, then he said, "When we finish talking about my military career, we can get on with the test". I swear I was not trying to snow him. He was a numbers man—weights, speeds, pressures, limits, the works. I remembered enough to get by and we were through in 45 minutes. He was back for the airplane check the next day. Mine was a poor performance, the worst rating ride I ever flew, in fact, but it drew a pass. He was more than fair and recognized that it wasn't one of my best days.

The (second) 707 fed liked essay questions, such as, "What can you tell me about the anti-skid brake system?" That oral lasted all afternoon and even included the flush toilets. The flight test was a breeze, surprising no one more than me for I had really sweated that one. After the 707, the 727 was child's play, being one of the nicest and easiest airliners to fly ever built. On the rating ride at a strange and smoggy California field, I would have lost the runway on the circling approach but for landmarks pointed out by the fed. He could have sat there and said nothing, thus requiring another approach, but he didn't. I remember him. Good type.

The 747 inspector was somewhat nitpicking on the oral and in the simulator. I was his first candidate in the jumbo which probably explains it. My instructor and I played it the only smart way—his way. The follow up approaches and landings in the airplane itself were observed by an FAA old-timer of long acquaintance. That was a fun ride.

It was not always sweetness and light. There were "discussions" along the way, usually with feds riding jumpseat out on the line, some of whom felt that unless they criticized they weren't doing their job. That type is like the magazine editor who thinks he's not editing if he doesn't do heavy rewriting of every piece that crosses his desk.

The main difference between writing and flying is that the FAA edits the only magazine in town.

# "The Holder Shall Wear..."

To one reared in the thirties, it came as a shock that some pilots actually wore glasses. My heroes in *Wings, Lilac Time, Hell's Angels, Devildogs of the Air* and all the other screen epics (you name it, I saw it) were supermen of extraordinary vision. Jack Holt and Errol Flynn in glasses? You might as well have put Betty Grable in army boots.

Magazine writers insisted that anyone less than a perfect physical specimen could forget being an Air Corps cadet which bothered me no end. Mild astigmatism had required my use of lenses in high school, an item of personal history I neglected to mention at enlistment.

After transferring from the RCAF, the Army sent me to fly as copilot with airline veterans recruited to establish the trans-African supply route, the first being a crusty old bird colonel straight from the chief pilot office of Pan Am. He carried several pairs of specs—one for VFR, another for instrument flying, a third for night flying and so on. "Hold her, son," he'd say on downwind while he fished for his landing glasses. The old boy could fly, his impairment nothwithstanding.

Several of my Army skippers wore glasses, bifocals even, and why not? They spotted traffic I missed and flew the gauges with uncanny precision. Welcome to the real world of flying.

Perhaps a third of my airline captains wore glasses and the percentage increased as the years rolled by. I admit to having felt a little sorry for them in that they had no choice; it was on their tickets, a pointed reminder of the "aging process." One developed cataracts on both sides and was grounded. A relatively minor problem had robbed us of another familiar face; it happened in our game with disturbing frequency.

But that was not the end of him. The operations were successful and, fitted with lenses like the bottoms of beer bottles, he asked to be relicensed. A year and a lot of expense later he made it, to become the first double cataract case to regain an FAA First Class Medical Certificate. I was his copilot during his first month back on the line. Within two weeks you would never have guessed that he'd missed a day's work. He flew another ten years and finished up on jet equipment.

I was thankful for continued good vision and smug in the conviction that I would never need glasses. My turn came, however. A copilot made the point gently—"Hey, Dad, you gonna take us home the scenic route?" I turned up the lights and read 238 degrees in the window instead of the correct 268 degrees. In recent months 3s, 6s, 8s and 9s had become fuzzy at night. And all the gauges seemed to shrink in the dark.

The eye man said, yes, a "slight correction" was in order. Clear glass on top; nothing amiss with the long range look. Oh well, what the hell. Wear 'em at night until things improved. But you don't improve; you go right on downhill to thicker lenses. My FAA physician soon noticed that without help I could not read the fine print and added to the ticket, the holder "shall have corrective lenses in his possession while exercising the privileges of his license." I was hooked.

Pilot reader, if or when you sink this far, have them run the reading lens all the way across the frame. The little inserts have insufficient lateral range to take in the panel without rapid head swinging which will convince your copilot you have a nervous disorder to boot. Or, you can get half frames if you don't mind looking like a librarian.

Needless to add, trouble with distance followed ("I've lost that 747; you still got him?"), meaning corrections up and down plus the new limitation: "Holder shall wear . . ." It wasn't all that bad, actually. An update every year or two pulled everything back into focus and on you fly almost as good as new. One stew of much seniority said glasses made me look distinguished. I picked up her dinner check for that.

Then, about a year later, a new headache. Near and distant vision remained adequate, but the panel blurred enough to make close work a problem. Try shooting a Cat II with the flight director slightly out of focus. An outdated pair of glasses proved perfect for instruments, but too weak for reading. I carried both and the swapping back and forth during a holding/approach sequence was exasperating.

Back to the eye man. You bet we can make trifocals, he said—distance on top, reading on the bottom and a new correction in between that would keep the instrument panel in focus. The result was wonderful. One small problem: the center glass was 7mm (about 1/4") from top to bottom and that is not enough. I got one row of flight gauges but there are two rows to scan. With continuous nodding I get it all but my copilots were prone to stare.

These are great, I told the man, and I'll keep them as spares. Now build another set with the center part 12mm deep and trim the other lenses accordingly. He shook his head. The center lens was available only in the 7mm size. Come on, I said, we put men on the moon and gave them a car to ride around in; you mean we cannot cut a sliver of glass 12mm wide? Sorry, but all lenses are ground by two outfits, Bausch & Lomb and American Optical, and we can only assemble what they grind. Your trifocals are the only possible combination, he claimed.

I eventually discovered he was talking only about the lenses he handled. Center lenses wider than 7mm were available on special order as he should have known. But by then I was accustomed to what I had and I flew until retirement with them, in fact, I'm wearing them now.

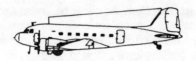

# Deadheading

The total in Column 11 of my log is now 2,014:40. That column is headed, "Passenger." What's the point in logging riding time? None, I suppose, but it's there and I kept it going from the beginning. This is the Royal Air Force format designed in the 1930s and issued to all Empire pilots during the war. Indeed, the diarist is sternly advised that "This book is an official document and the property of His Majesty's Government," a reminder that the several copies in my care are not really mine at all and that the next post could bring an order · from His Majesty's daughter's Government to return them to London immediately. I rather think she wants me to keep them. God save the Queen!

In the beginning, a ride in an airplane was an adventure excitedly anticipated, to be relived and related, with much embellishment, long after and, of course, to be carefully recorded. The first two hops were a birthday gift from my parents, a round trip ticket from Louisville to Cincinnati on American Airlines. Recollections of that day are more vivid than memories of most flying days since. It was not without some apprehension that I boarded DC-2 NC14275 and took a front seat next to the left engine, but whatever doubts about flying remaining were forever swept away as we lifted from the grass and roared at incredible speed across the toy houses below. It was an awesome moment. NC14924 brought me home and the tail numbers and day's flying (1:30) were duly noted.

The same year, Clarence Chamberlin came to town in his monstrous Curtiss Condor, offering hops at three dollars. Two weeks after Lindbergh's triumph, Chamberlin had flown nonstop to Germany in 42 hours. Such a man must have more than luck going for him, my father agreed, providing ticket money. If memory serves, 28 fares rode sideways on benches, their backs to the windows. Chamberlin could be seen up front with his wife riding as copilot. Their pet Scotty lay on the cockpit floor between them, sound asleep. The big V-12 water-cooled *Conquerors* came to life with irregular crackling and popping that raised goose bumps. At full throttle—well, it was like sitting between two giant theater organs. I'd give a hundred times the price to ride that ship again. NC727K—20 minutes.

Upon high school graduation I was given a choice: a wrist watch or a trip to the New York World's Fair. That was in 1940. A friend and I left Kentucky by bus, each with fifty dollars (and warnings not to talk with strange women); we spent five days there and had enough left over to ride a Douglas DST sleeper from LaGuardia to Philadelphia on the trip home. Money went far in those days. NC25686—50 minutes.

Local hops brought the grand total to 4:10 by the day of enlistment, all of which was transferred to the new blue logbook. During the war Column 11 began to look silly, not worth the bother, but entries were made all the same. Most are meaningless today. Here's one I remember—a ride from the desert to Cairo in a Martin Baltimore. Its pilot, a thin, foppish type, told me to sit in the nose and "fasten my lap strap securely." He rolled the bomber into a tight vertical bank before the wheels were up and headed out ten feet above the sand. It was like riding a 200 mile-an-hour dune buggy. We shot across a P-40 field right on the deck, then he racked it around for a second pass that caused a number of mechanics to drop their tools and lie flat.

A fatherly wing commander whose ribbons were earned during the first war offered a lift back in a Blenheim, a maidenly bomber relegated to training. Off we went in safe and sane flight—until we neared the P-40 base. "I wonder what those fighter chaps are up to," he said, sticking the nose straight down for a closer look. With speed well past the red line, we rocketed between hangars and under phone lines, leaving a trail of spread-eagled observers. "And they insist I'm too old for ops," he shouted as we climbed straight up. Such rides are easily remembered, recorded or not.

Most of the time we rode C-47s and I cannot explain why all that deadheading was necessary. Yet, here they are, flights all across Africa for forgotten purposes. It was hardly air travel as we know it today, sharing the confines of a stripped Douglas with freight and too many other people, some of whom invariably got sick during the hot bumpy ride. When regular transport was unavailable, we were shipped off in B-17s, B-24s, B-25s or anything else headed in the general direction.

Back in the States, the assignment was to a ferrying outfit. Compared with overseas flying, it was miserable duty. The work involved as much riding as piloting. Each of us carried chits good for travel by bus, train, or plane, the priority of which exceeded that awarded most other wartime travellers. The necessity of our rushing back to base (where the routine was parades and VD lectures) was questionable. Complying with orders to "return via the first available . . ." led to interesting situations. I had the distinction of bumping an admiral from the last TWA eastbound from Burbank. The old salt was livid, even after reviewing my orders, hinted that he could arrange my transfer to the uttermost parts of the earth. I appropriated his seat anyway, hoping the Army took care of its own, which it did. I heard no more of it.

How slowly we flew in those days. Consider this: Chicago to Reno on United Air Lines via Moline, Omaha, Denver, Rock Springs and Elko (11:55); and St. Louis to New Orleans on Chicago & Southern through Memphis and Jackson (4:45).

Braniff, the line which hired me, sent a pass to ride from Chicago to its base in Dallas. After takeoff the DC-6 headed toward as mean a line of storms as I'd ever seen. I cinched my belt and wondered how airline fellows solved such riddles. We drew close to the ominous cloud, slowed and plunged right in. It was immediately apparent that a DC-6 wing was as limber as a DC-3's. After 15 minutes of thought-provoking travel, we suddenly burst into sunshine. Dinner was served and we blocked in on time.

Deadheading was part of airline life then and there was no pay for riding to pick up a trip. At the end of the month, four or five copilots, each an hour or so short of 85, would work a nonstop to New York, one actually up front and the rest "flying" out their remaining minutes in back. You rode home as empty seats became available, a problem during a period like Christmas week.

Multiple crews complied with time limitations on international schedules, one in the cockpit, one "resting" in the cabin. On DC-6 sleeper runs we'd grab unsold upper berths and try to sleep. It was not easy when you appreciated the takeoff situation—a short gravel runway with hills at the end and visibility almost zero in a tropical downpour. By the time power was reduced to climb, adrenalin flow was a pint a minute. Then, seemingly minutes later, you'd suddenly awake in a horrifying silence and look through the little window. Havana. Time to go to work.

The total in Column 11 climbed to hundreds of hours. Annual interline passes made possible such trips as New York—Bermuda on a Colonial DC-4 in 1955 (3:40). On the return trip I noticed fuel streaming from the left wing. The captain came back, took one look and hightailed it back to Hamilton. The next day we flew back to New York in 4:40.

Noteworthy (that is, if any of these entries are) was New York to Pittsburgh in a TWA Stratoliner (2:05). A big brute with four engines and conventional gear, it was the first pressurized airliner. That "Sky Coach" (N19309) had the British railway car cabin arrangement with an aisle down one side opening into compartments in which passengers sat facing one another. Very nice.

In 1965 we flew from Kennedy to Brussels on a Sabena 707 (OO-SJH-7:05), touching down exactly on the minute estimated in the captain's post-takeoff announcement. I wondered how he did it. In Europe, travel was accomplished in three interesting types: the Caravelle (delightfully smooth and quiet), Vanguard (built like a battleship, rode like a tank) and Trident (looked like a 727 but the nose gear folded sideways). The bearded Trident skipper invited me to the cockpit to watch a coupled approach to touchdown, the arrival routinely used in zero-zero weather at Heathrow (G-ARPG- :45).

During the 1960s ours was among the lines flying contract schedules for Military Airlift Command. These normally originated at Travis AFB and operated through to Vietnam and other Far Eastern points. Considerable deadheading was involved in the work. We were forever crossing the bay from San Francisco to Oakland in S-61s, my first helicopter rides (interesting, but how to relax in an aircraft that has to be landed at full power?) One bay crossing was flown in a UAL 737, memorable in that we flew for five minutes, then sat on the ramp for 25, waiting for a gate. Another involved a TWA 707 bound for Paris. "Let me get this straight," said the agent. "You want to get off in Oakland?" The stews led me, the sole fare aboard, to the best seat and brought the complete kit for long distance travel—eyeshade, slippers, maps, toiletries. Total time, gate to gate—:10.

Most leg times out there ran from five to 11 hours: Manila—Tokyo on Air France; the reverse on KLM; Manila—Honolulu on Continental; Guam through Wake Island and Hawaii to San Francisco on Pan Am (a trip with superlative meal service) and Tokyo—Tacoma in a Braniff freighter (9:05). Getting to and from home in Texas added much time to Column 11, though I make no claims as a commuter. Compared to that logged by some—crewmen who live in Colorado and are based in Florida, for example—my total is modest. A stewardess friend for years flew 60 hours a month going to and from work. She was based in Texas and lived in Honolulu.

Many business people have impressive air travel records. A gem salesman told me he routinely made two round trips a week between New York and Europe and had more than once made four. It is guessed that Lowell Thomas held the all-time record for non-pilot hours.

One of my brothers has made it a hobby to "collect" airlines, airliners and airports doing his business travels, often waiting extra hours in some remote place to catch a type plane not in his log. You name it and he's probably flown (in) it, from the Ford TriMotor to the Concorde. His 52 airliner types (on 55 lines to 176 places) do not include the DC-2 and Stratoliner, I remind him.

Some European lines provide passenger trip logs with spaces for aircraft, distance, time, crew names and so on. One such travel souvenir sent to our cockpit contained five globe-circling trips, travel adventures well worth recording.

Years back a newsman set out to span the nation, riding feeders only. Later the papers reported that one Fred Erdman was so enraptured by flying that he bought a $322 excursion ticket allowing three weeks of unlimited riding on Delta Air Lines. He intended to get his money's worth, saying he would land at every Delta stop from Bangor to Miami to San Francisco during 130 flights covering 100,000 miles. Not surprisingly, he would pass through Atlanta three times a day. (Delta pilots say that when they die, all routes to the final resting place, whichever it is, pass through ATL.) I wonder how Fred came out.

Air travel is in some ways the dullest, most unrewarding means of public transit yet devised. It is, perhaps, a reflection of these hectic times; it lacks the appeal of a crossing on the Queen Mary or a night run on the Broadway Limited. The Mary's foghorn blast no longer echoes through Manhattan's canyons at high noon to signal high adventure; the Hudson piers stand empty, deserted, filled with memories. No longer does the heartbreaking wail of a racing steam locomotive sift into the farm lad's dreams to taunt with hints of wondrous places beyond the horizon. Those sounds are gone and with them the more relaxed and gracious day they represented. And we wouldn't go back, would we? So we sit strapped in the magic silver tube, mindful of its blazing speed, counting the blessings of time saved, glancing at our watches. It's altogether marvelous, but it's not half the fun.

And yet . . . there are those enchanting moments in air travel which surpass anything experienced by sea or rail. These passenger times and accompanying notes remind me of a few and that's why I'm glad I kept Column 11 going. I remember a long ago ride in a TWA Connie, reaching New York just after dark. Heavy traffic dictated a landing delay so the captain gave us a low level tour of the city with running commentary, skillfully converting an annoyance into a treat. I remember sweeping across the Golden Gate at dawn and turning to watch the first light of day reflect from the beautiful hills of San Francisco.

I remember circling tiny Ascension Island at dusk, waiting for a flight of bone dry P-38s to land after their long hop from Brazil, amused that such a barren rock looked so wonderful to us all. I remember gazing down at map names—Paris, Cairo, Saipan, the Nile, the Dead Sea, Greenland, the Aleutians, the Panama Canal, Khartoum, Berlin, Saigon and a thousand more—and believing for the first time that each is, after all, a real place. I remember the always thrilling first glimpse of our own shores following a long homeward dash. And of course I remember the unknown crewmen who made possible these two thousand passenger hours. Gentlemen, thank you each and every one for your good work.

Most of all I remember those first two DC-2s on those first rides. A little book, put together by British historians, gives the service life of each of the 200 14-passenger DC-2s built. I dug out the registrations of my pair and looked them up. NC14725 in which I rode to Cincinnati was sold to the RAF. It crashed in India in 1942. NC14924 which flew me home was also sold to the RAF. Three Me. 110s jumped it over Iraq on Christmas Day, 1941, and shot it down.

I would have been happier not learning that.

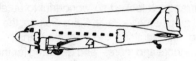

# LAX - GUM

It was a Saturday night, 2230 local time. Poised on Runway 24L at Los Angeles International, we awaited the tower's nod and once more rechecked the big ticket items—fuel, flaps, controls, trim, pitot heat. We had checked them twice or more during the preflight ritual but once more was cheap insurance. One weakness of the checklist theory is that everything is in the same size type. Large, red, underlined caps should emphasize the potential killers. All else is foam on the beer.

Cleared to go. Landing lights on, ease the handles off the stops and flip the switch. A black box somewhere took over and worked them forward to the exactly right takeoff settings. The JT9s, almost inaudible until now, took up their familiar deep growl and the 747SP rolled ponderously, gathering itself for flight. The airspeed needle eventually left the peg, crept through 100 knots and casually advanced toward the velocity which would, if the paperwork was right, insure lift.

Heavily we galloped along between the white lights, regarding with mounting interest the red ones ahead. Rotate. We rose a few feet, all 348 tons of us, swept across the beach and plunged into absolute darkness. Trip 505 was airborne.

Thirty-three minutes later we leveled at Flight Level 350, slowly built speed to Mach .85 and punched the "CRZ" button. The thrust levers inched back individually, automatically. Fuel burn thus far—23,600 lbs, right on schedule. The dim glow of San Francisco appeared over the nose. True, the great circle route lay somewhat to the west but upper winds and traffic flow that evening dictated a more northern track. This was the night's best road to Guam, so we began on 310 deg, swung westward later and flew the last segment on 210 deg. Computer theory would be compared with actual progress throughout the run, with adjustments being made as necessary.

We left land 100 miles beyond San Fran, eased left to 282 deg, making a final match of inertial navigation gear with radial/DME fixes and added fuel readings. We were 1:10 into the trip and had burned off 36,000 lbs. of fuel; 254,000 remained, 3,000 more than shown on the yellow print out. Well and good. Ahead lay 5,004 n.m. to be flown, which mileage we would span in 10:14, predicted the computer flight plan.

Such numbers gave me pause for most of my time had been logged on short to medium range domestic schedules. Total hours divided by legs comes out at 1:45. When compared with a Houston—O'Hare hop, this LAX-GUM run was something else. It was a different world.

Different, that is, not more difficult. For all the mystery and romance surrounding long overwater runs to faraway places (an aura which global crews do nothing to dispel), that duty demanded no special breed. The work was more mental than physical. A DC-9 driver might do more manual flying in an afternoon of thunderstorm weather than his transocean senior did in an average month. The international end of it was for the most part—watch, wait, think, plan and, on occasion, sweat.

Waypoint 6, roughly 1,000 miles north of Hawaii and 900 south of Alaska, fell behind 15 minutes late, an annoyance more than a worry. After repeated calls to Anchorage and Honolulu, San Francisco broke through the static to copy our position and read the latest Guam weather sequence. We were now at FL 390 with 150,000 remaining in the tanks, 5,500 behind flight plan. That would bear close watching.

Waypoint 8 was 430 miles north of Midway. The 379 kc homer was unidentifiable but the nervous ADF needles pointed in the general direction. Elapsed flying time so far—6:37; 3,105 miles lay behind, 2,317 ahead. We typed in the remaining positions as new Waypoints 1 through 4. So far we had not seen a single light—ship, aircraft, anything—or heard a word from another trip. Consumption was down to 20,000 lbs an hour which was remarkable; the largest 707 burned 13,000 in cruise.

We pressed on through the dark, now thinking of Ellen, a smallish typhoon which for two days has twiddled her thumbs 250 miles west of Guam. Should she decide to move east, her peripheral gusts could make our target unpleasant, even unuseable. Ellen was growing, we learn, but had yet to make her move.

Should things go sour, Wake Island was our ace in the hole. Our only out, that is, and we must divert to it no later than (new) Waypoint 2, 2:20 short of Guam. There was nearby Andersen Air Force Base on Guam, or Saipan, but typhonic winds often reach them simultaneously. Fact: if we continue, we would have to land for there wouldn't be fuel enough for a retreat to Wake. Also to be kept in mind was that our ship will need an hour of ground time before it could escape the area.

Waypoint 2 found us cruising at FL 430 and running 18 minutes behind flight plan with 59,000 lbs of fuel remaining. The computer sheet suggested diversion to Wake by the time fuel was 56,000 lbs. Check the weather again. Guam was now reporting occasional rain showers, winds gusting to 20 knots, no change expected for at least four hours. We'd go for Guam.

Waypoint 3. We're 436 miles out, having been in the air 10:19. Ellen was now moving north at 10 knots. No sweat. We had it made. Twenty minutes later the VOR flags fell away and we picked up the GUM 035 radial. The INS sets had done their jobs faultlessly and positioned us within three degrees and 12 miles of where we should be. The Marianas came into view on the 300-mile scopes and we identified Saipan, Tinian, Rota and dead ahead, the large greenish lump that was Guam. Approach control welcomed us on 119.3, vectored us clear of a rain shower and onto the Runway 6L ILS. It was still pitch dark.

We landed, carefully taxied down the narrow exit to the glistening ramp, set brakes and shut down. The fuel gauges totalled 21,500 lbs. Block-to-block time: 12:02. Back in L.A. it was ten o'clock Sunday morning. In Guam it was 2:00 a.m. Monday. We talked with the outbound crew, mentioning several minor squawks. Then we rode along dark roads lined with lush dripping jungle growth to the hotel, signed in and ordered steaks.

# One In A Thousand

My dictionary defines *air-minded* as, "interested in aviation; favoring increased use of aircraft." If we modify that to include pilots only, leaving out passengers and all others who buy flying services, how "air-minded" is your state? Where are most of the pilots?

Before looking at the figures, make a guess. Obviously, Alaska must be way up there. (In fact, it tops the list.) How about the next four? California? Texas? New York? Illinois? Those were my guesses. Surprisingly, none is among the top 15; New York ranks 48th, believe it or not.

The FAA defines an active airman as one who holds both an airman's certificate and a valid medical certificate. Included in the official count are seven categories—Student, Private, Commercial, Airline Transport, Helicopter (only), Glider and Lighter-than-Air.

The accompanying roster is based on the 1980 census and the FAA's pilot records for that year. Men and women are included, of course, but not military airmen. The "Airmen" column shows the number of pilots per 100,000 people, rounded off to the nearest whole number.

"Go west, young man," said John Soule in 1851 and, if amended to include young women, it remains good advice for the budding pilot who wonders where the flying is; all but two of the top 20 air-minded states are west of the Mississippi. Nearly 45% of all active airmen live in those 18 states. Alaska has well over three times the pilots of its nearest competitor, and as many as the lowest dozen states combined. Would you have thought that Nevada ranks Number 2?

But, the more you consider the distribution, the more sense it makes. Generally speaking, most pilots live in broad, sparsely populated areas with relatively few major highways and infrequent—or nonexistent—public surface transportation. The high pilot populations of such states as Nevada, Montana, Idaho and Wyoming clearly indicate the working nature of much general aviation and refute the notion that most small aircraft are playthings of the wealthy. New Hampshire is a strange exception; the 44th state in area, it ranks 18th for whatever reasons.

If private flying was mainly a sport of the affluent, most pilots would live in the wealthiest states. Yet, of the ten states with the highest per capita income—again using 1980 data—six are in the lower half of the rankings. The District of Columbia ranks second in personal income, for example, but look where it stands in active airmen (last).

The 1980 certificate breakdown is revealing: Student—24%, Private—43%, Commercial—22%, ATP—8%, Helicopter, Glider and LTA—2%. While an unknown percentage of Private tickets are put to business use, piloting-for-hire is performed by less than a third of all active airmen. The low helicopter count is of airmen not licensed to operate other aircraft; Private, Commercial and ATP pilots with helicopter ratings raise it to 4% of the grand total. For all of the publicity accorded rotary-wings, particularly on television, they occupy a small corner of the arena.

And where do the ladies fit in? They were 5% of the total in 1975; this rose to 6.4% in 1980 and dipped to 6.1% in 1983. Commercials or ATPs were held by 7% of them in 1974, 12% in 1983. While women are certainly in the game to stay, their penetration of the pilot job market is less dramatic than media attention suggests.

In passing, the most Student Certificates in 1980 were issued in September, the least in December. No surprise there.

The young man or woman thinking of an aviation career should note that while the total number of active airmen dropped from 827,071 in 1980 to 718,004 in 1983, the number of *nonpilot* licenses rose from 393,486 to 432,890 during the same period. These categories—mechanic, parachute rigger, ground instructor, dispatcher and flight engineer—show steady annual increases. Despite the introduction of two-pilot transports, there were more flight engineers (38,546 of them) in 1983 than in any previous year, interestingly enough.

Women shared in the nonpilot rise, in fact, the number of women mechanics rose dramatically from 890 to 1,493 in just three years. Since mechanics in certain areas earn excellent pay, and since the most ambitious have advanced into top supervisory and administration positions—all of which sharp young women are sure to notice—it's probable that their invasion of this traditionally male-dominated field will continue at a rapid pace.

Back to pilots. If you're old enough, you will remember that near the end of World War II there was much talk about an-airplane-in every-garage when the boys came home. Euphoric nonsense? Of course, but considering the astounding strides made in flight during the previous five years, it seemed to make sense. More than one wartime pilot who didn't spend five minutes thinking it through invested everything in Aeronca, Porterfield and Rearwin stocks. I'm not laughing; had there been any spare cash, I'd have bought Waco. Considering his or her demonstrated driving skills, imagine the average American wheeling out his own plane and flying off to work!

Four decades later, we pilots remain a small, indeed tiny, segment of modern society. If you held any sort of ticket to fly in 1980, even as a student, you were among 365 out of every 100,000 Americans. If you held a Commercial or ATP, you were among 112 so privileged. Our numbers have since decreased; by the end of 1983 they were 305 and 100, respectively, based on the FAA's count and estimated population growth. Thus, if you are rated to fly for hire, you're one in a thousand. It's a select group.

The largest decline has been among student pilots which is disheartening in many quarters, but an encouraging fact for young men and women bent of flying careers. Each passing day sees ATP and Commercial holders leaving the list due to retirement and other factors, and Private holders moving up to take their seats. The former supply of ex-military airmen has meanwhile dwindled along with civilian students. No crystal ball is needed to foretell the future awaiting the youngster who hangs in there and logs those first important hours.

The FAA's records tell where pilots are now, not where they came from. Pilots are nomadic; they go where the work is and follow it when it moves. Of all the pilots who flew with my Dallas-based airline, I'd guess no more than 15% were native Texans. So, while a number of states do not appear very air-minded, all have produced notable airmen. West Virginia, for one example, was the birthplace of one of the most remarkable pilots in history.

Charles Edward Yeager.

**Licensed pilots per 100,000 population (1980)**

| | | | | | |
|---|---|---|---|---|---|
| 1 | AK | 2,716 | 10 | ND | 620 |
| 2 | NV | 816 | 11 | OR | 585 |
| 3 | MT | 734 | 12 | SD | 556 |
| 4 | CO | 699 | 13 | NM | 537 |
| 5 | WY | 687 | 14 | FL | 523 |
| 6 | ID | 647 | 15 | NE | 517 |
| 7 | WA | 629 | 16 | CA | 512 |
| 8 | AZ | 626 | 17 | OK | 511 |
| 9 | KS | 621 | 18 | NH | 476 |

| 19 | MN | 469 | | 35 | MI | 276 |
|-----|------|-----|--|----|----|-----|
| 20 | TX | 448 | | 36 | TN | 275 |
| 21 | UT | 436 | | 37 | OH | 273 |
| 22 | IA | 415 | | 38 | AL | 272 |
| 23 | HI | 409 | | 39 | LA | 271 |
| Nat'l | Avg | 365 | | 40 | MS | 248 |
| 24 | ME | 354 | | 41 | MD | 245 |
| 25 | VT | 332 | | 42 | MA | 238 |
| 26 | GA | 331 | | 43 | NC | 237 |
| 27 | CT | 326 | | 44 | SC | 230 |
| 28 | MO | 325 | | 45 | NJ | 229 |
| 29 | AR | 317 | | 46 | PA | 194 |
| 30 | WI | 316 | | 47 | RI | 191 |
| 31 | DE | 315 | | 48 | NY | 179 |
| 32 | IL | 304 | | 49 | KY | 177 |
| 33 | VA | 302 | | 50 | WV | 160 |
| 34 | IN | 281 | | 51 | DC | 126 |

# Alternate Airport

Every pilot lives with the specter of "busting a physical." No matter how fit he feels or how much attention he pays to maintaining good health, the picture could change overnight and he knows it. He's seen it happen. The phantom assumes sizeable dimensions for the professional who must gamble everything against physical well-being. The permanent loss of his license would be disastrous unless he has considerable savings, loss-of-license insurance or another skill to fall back on.

Each pilot deals with the dreadful possibility in his own way. At the one extreme is the blind optimist who gives it no thought, at the other the worrier who thinks of little else. Neither viewpoint is reasonable. The optimist lives for today; if it happens, it happens, and he'll worry about it when it does. The pessimist so frets over the aches and pains of increasing age that he threatens his own physical and mental well being. He cannot appreciate the vast difference between reasonable concern and corrosive worry or understand that undue apprehension itself can damage mental and physical health. He is prone to ulcers and nervous breakdown. I've seen it happen.

The average pro buys loss-of-license coverage, lives sensibly and finds something to occupy himself on days off. There are two schools of thought on the right use of leisure time. One is that outside pursuits should be purely diversionary. Sports, boating, private flying, hobbies and home upkeep are acceptable; active involvement in another business is not. Long ago I thought about a productive, that is, moneymaking sideline, not because I harbored great fear of flunking a physical, but to see if I could turn a dollar at something beside flying an airplane.

Some of my seniors were adamantly against such schemes, insisting that our profession demanded undivided attention. "An airline pilot should not run a business," said one. "It takes his mind off

the profession and that's wrong. Invest in real estate or the market."
Another saw it differently. In his small machine shop were racks of
spark plugs which he cleaned and tested under subcontract. Few
knew that every engine in our fleet ran with plugs inspected by one
of our DC-3 captains. "The extra income equals the night money I'd
make flying the freighter," he said. And, I thought, you've got something here that would be a godsend if you lost your ticket. His way
made sense to me.

Some pilots are sharp with investments. They have the mysterious knack of doubling and redoubling money until they have achieved
financial independence. Some, that is. The passive road to security
was too risky for one of my inexperience, even if I'd had significant
funds to invest.

Collecting aviation books was my hobby. Going through cata-
logues, I noticed that prices here were twice to four times those of
overseas booksellers. It took no genius to see the possibilities. I put
my modest library up for sale, bought a classified ad in an air magazine and plunged into the mail order business—or, rather, timidly stuck
my toe into the water.

The mail order idea was sound. It required no front or regular
business hours, minimum start up money and could be put on the
shelf when I flew. But the product was completely wrong. It was un-
believably difficult developing a market for such specialty items. After
all, how many individuals out of a thousand will buy any sort of book,
much less one dealing with aviation? That, and the fact that profits
were the sole source of new capital, made growth painfully slow. But
it was an enjoyable and constructive pastime. Unlike many friends,
I no longer took the airline home with me. It was good to get away
from flying and equally good to return to it and forget business problems. The totally dissimilar vocations nicely offset each other.

I found even modest success to be immensely satisfying and
there was the comfortable awareness that another trade was being
learned. No job insurance could match that in potential long term
benefits. The enterprise, unlikely though it was, eventually grew into
a family enterprise making possible many good things we could not
have afforded otherwise. At the end of five years, had we expanded
into broader fields of reader interest, we could have survived on what
it brought in. Our success became a problem, however. We no longer
owned the business; it owned us. Its demands on time and energy
were more than my regular work allowed. The airline came first,
always.

We sold out and tried publishing, leaning on what had been
learned selling books published by others. This was more easily
managed, tripled the return per hour invested and offered a tantaliz-

ing, if remote, chance at a killing. A book is one of the few legal monopolies remaining; a publisher controls the sole source of supply and that's as good as share of the mint—if a title catches on. We tried a little book on the famous P-51 Mustang fighter, including in it some novel illustrations not found in the typical "airplane book," and rather timidly ordered 2,500 copies. That was back in 1963. The title is still in print and has sold nearly 50,000 copies. Needless to say, we tried others and eventually authored and/or produced 34 books which have sold more than 700,000 copies. I quote these figures not to parade accomplishments but to show what can be done through hard work, which it was, believe me, even with a project as questionable as the one we chose.

As mail order sales led to publishing, so it led to profitable ideas far removed from book sales and publishing. I passed the physicals and retired on schedule so you might guess I needn't have done any of it, that the thousands of hours logged at a desk might as well have been spent on the golf course.

You'd get an argument on that from a lot of pilots I know, this one included. Shortly after my retirement our airline collapsed. The panic sale of big homes, expensive cars, cruisers, private aircraft and the like told the sad story in many cases. The adjustment was easier for moonlighters. While a good number of our people eventually found employment with other airlines or in different kinds of flying, others turned attention to expanding sideline businesses. "I'm not going to chase a flying job all over the world," said one. Another comment heard often was, "Even if I find another job this good, never again will I depend on it as I did before."

Do not assume that we retirees escaped unscathed. With a stroke of his pen the bankruptcy judge slashed pension pay by 70% in some cases. In my situation, the continuing modest income that began with a tiny enterprise founded 25 years earlier suddenly assumed a significance never anticipated when I bought that first three-line classified ad.

Until a few years ago an airline pilot with ten years seniority could relax. His future was almost a sure thing—if his health remained good. Early retirement for medical reasons after age 50 did not equal financial disaster, considering improved insurance and pension funds. Deregulation changed all that; suddenly, wages were reduced, in some cases by 50%, and bankruptcy became a threat. Meanwhile, pilots in their 40s and 50s with first class physicals found themselves on the street. Their seniors were shocked to learn that pension funds had been milked (with federal approval) by faltering managements desperate to cut expenses.

Two grandfather lines folded. Their names fly on and some of their pilots, but to all purposes they are as novel as the "upstarts" who forced them to the wall. The fate of other long-established trunks—and no less that of newcomers—is in doubt. We are yet in the early stages of an industry revolution. Continued upheaval is the only sure forecast of the future.

My greatest mistake was not starting a sideline business sooner. A secondary pursuit, though established as a hedge against disaster, is certain to provide more than profit dollars if enough hard work is invested. Mine was great fun from the first and produced opportunities I never would have had without it. One idea logically followed another in a strange way that altered our direction and purpose many times and led to things never foreseen at the beginning. And, as a well known financial advisor said recently, "Your own business is the best possible tax shelter."

The lesson in all this—for me, at least—is one of those taught during the first days of flight training: no matter how familiar the route, how fair the weather or how smoothly things seem to be going, always keep the nearest alternate airport in mind. You just might need it.

# One of Those Days

You could fly between Texas and New York during the cold months with few weather problems—if you were in phase with the fronts. Be at home when it went sour on the route. Other crews always seemed to get there just as the roof fell in and for them it was a longish winter. It was all luck. For several weeks that winter our Dallas—Ft. Worth to LaGuardia to Hartford to LGA to DFW schedule went smoothly. We held a time or two at Robbinsville and did a few turns at Carmel coming back but nothing more. One February day our luck ran out.

A strong cold front curved from Quebec to Georgia, its leading edge lying across our route at Baltimore. The same line, if plotted from Omaha to Houston, could be expected to plod steadily eastward, but strange things happen when advancing cold air reaches coastal waters. The whole mess sometimes floats right on out to sea, which is what the weather people predicted that day, but it can stagnate for no apparent reasons and make real mischief. We thought the forecaster too optimistic this time. Events proved he had this time made a bad guess.

We pushed back with twice the usual fuel, taxied to a vacant ramp and shut down, next to two other eastbound trips. New York was saturated; expect release in an hour, the controller said. "It's going to be one of those days," said the copilot. While it was unpardonable to comment on how well things were going, a prediction of hard times ahead was allowed. I had a gut feeling he was right.

Three hours later we crossed Charleston, West Virginia, at Flight Level 370, in the clear. On the horizon, extending from left to right, squatted the mass of gray cloud. Washington had an amended clearance. Were we ready to copy? (a question that says more than it asks.) After Casanova, fly 025 degrees until receiving Harrisburg, then via Victors 31 and 6 to Snowy, to hold as published. Harrisburg? Snowy? We never go that way. We had charts all over the cockpit; there's

Harrisburg, tune in 112.5, and there's Snowy, 23 DME west of Allentown. We refolded the maps. Then Washington was back with a new clearance: fly-Victor 106 and Victor 232 to Frebe and hold there, left turns. Frebe? Washington pronounced it, "Freeb." Who dreamed up these stupid checkpoint names anyway? We found Frebe and remarked the charts. New York took over, told us to overfly "Frebe" and hold at Beers. We found Beers, set up the radios and were cleared down to FL 250.

Then it got choppy, uncomfortably so. Plenty of ice on the wipers. We wished for a inertial navigation system to learn the wind and finally figured a 30 degree correction would maintain the pattern. After nine trips around the oval we asked the obvious. The controller could supply no expected approach clearance time but guessed we'd be there for another hour and maybe longer. Some problem with the computer, he said. Our engineer was meanwhile fiddling with the pressurization, an electronic marvel which, like FAA's computers, requires no human attention—when it works. Ours was so screwed up a stew came up to ask about the ear popping. He was also concerned about No. 3 generator whose voltage and frequency were fluctuating beyond limits.

Half an hour later we were recleared to Sweet, descended to 18,000 and advised we'd be there at least an hour. It was downright rough at Sweet. Through a rift we caught sight of a Delta L1011 in the stack 1,000 feet lower and could see him wallowing as we were. New York called back to add 30 minutes to our EAC time and that did it, fuelwise. Give us a clearance to Hartford, we said, and were shortly on the way.

The remaining short distance paralleled the front and was flown at turbulence penetration speed—280 knots indicated. The turbulence could be described as moderate to "extremely moderate." (We need an official adjective that means worse than moderate, but not as bad as severe. If you say severe there's a big flap involving written reports and an inspection of the airframe.) Bradley approach control vectored us toward the Runway 24 ILS. The ATIS tape was interesting: the ceiling was 200 variable to 300 with half mile visibility; rain; surface wind from 260 to 300 degrees at 25 gusting to 45; wind sheer reported at 600 feet on final approach by the last arrival.

The approach itself was pure calisthenics; full throw of the wheel and thrust levers back and forth from full power to idle, trying to keep speed within a 50-knot arc on the gauge.

(An interesting indication of the broad gulf existing between the theoretical world of ground experts and the real world of flying is to be found in the riddle of approach speeds when surface winds are strong. According to the manual, half of the reported steady wind and all of the gust should be added to the calculated approach speed, this correction never to exceed 20 knots. I fervently hope I never ride with a pilot who adheres to that restriction when he runs into the approach conditions we found that day at Bradley Field.)

There was one thing going for us—the wind down final was steady and with the nose slewed left 25 degrees, the localizer remained centered. As advertised, the cloud base was at 250 feet; we crammed it on, forced it to follow the centerline and taxied to the gate. Fifteen minutes later the wind gusted to 70 knots and the rain came down in buckets. The front had arrived.

An hour later things picked up down at LGA so we headed south, now running three hours late. Of the 106 fare who bought DFW-LGA tickets, all reboarded the flight. I would have taken the train had there been a choice. It was still rough, though not quite as bad as before, and we were immediately accepted by LGA Approach. LGA's Runway 13 ILS is unique in that the localizer is for some reason offset and crosses the runway 2751 feet from the threshold. Nevertheless it is listed as a precision approach and with a decision height of 250 feet. That is exactly what we needed—250 feet. Landing on that strip is akin to coming aboard a carrier—you'd better not be low.

A surprising total of 82 souls filed aboard our long-delayed return to Texas and we blocked out exactly three hours late. It was the usual routing—the Ringoes 9 departure with Westminster transition and, as we banked westward across glistening Manhattan, it was obvious we would soon ascend into clear skies. But that long day was not yet finished with us. The New York Center man said we must hold at Solberg, right turns, at 14,000. Come on, come on! But there we sat and bounced for ten minutes. Then we were cleared to climb and continued toward home. At 19,000 we were suddenly clear of all cloud and climbing smoothly through clear moonlit air. For the first time in hours we could turn off the Fasten Seat Belt sign.

According to the timetable our flight arrives DFW at 8:20 p.m. That evening we set brakes at 11:27. Our actual flying time—11:43 for the day.

"When I get home I just may take a short nap," said the copilot.

"That was a bummer," said the engineer.

I'm getting too old for days like this, I thought. But I didn't admit it to either of them.

# Trust

In the fifty years following Kitty Hawk, flying an airplane was conceived as one-man work within the trade and by the public. The use of second pilots and mechanics aboard large World War I machines and the addition of copilots on airlines in the 1930s changed nothing. One pilot flew the ship, made all decisions and was solely held to account if something went wrong. "Commissioned ballast" was how World War II copilots described themselves and the postwar airline copilot was an underpaid apprentice, there mainly to learn. Newspaper stories about accidents always mentioned "the pilot" as if the DC-6 had one chair up front. In the early 1950s I sat through a lengthy accident investigation during which the copilot's testimony lasted 15 minutes.

The check pilot of that time reflected the philosophy by playing the role of an incredibly stupid assistant. Call for flaps and he might drop the gear; ask him to tune the radio and he'd pick a range forty miles away—things like that. He bore careful watching. On a C-47 check ride I let down to minimums on one engine and was told to go around. I called for gear up, crammed on full power, retrimmed and watched from the corner of my eye as the check rider unlatched the floor lock and yanked the long handle. The ship mushed along, refusing to climb more than 50 feet a minute and I couldn't figure a reason for it. We slowly struggled up to 1,500 feet. "You're asking for real trouble trusting your copilot like that, " growled the instructor, pointing at the hydraulic controls. He had lifted the flap handle; the wheels were still down. On the next try, I raised the gear myself and was complimented. Such was the thinking then.

As the skies filled with faster, more complex equipment, the copilot and flight engineer gradually came into their own as necessary members of the cockpit team. Today's big airplane crew is trained as a unit with each member sharing responsibility for safe operation. While teaching a pilot-in-command to do it all himself as though his copilot and flight engineer were complete dummies seems idiotic in retrospect, the underlying philosophy was based on a sound maxim: *Don't trust anyone!* Modified, it remains good advice.

We are taught from infancy to believe certain ideas, trust certain people, have faith in certain precepts and by nature we want to believe. Joining the real world of adults is somewhat of a jolt. Certain "truths" are revealed to be questionable and certain people prove untrustworthy so we seek the blend of hope and caution that insures a happy life. One main difference between a pilot and ordinary people is that a pilot must quickly learn that suspicion and distrust are imperative hedges against disaster.

We pilots have to trust many people whether we like it or not—those who designed and built our planes, their engines and components, those who keep them in repair and service them and the federal people who regulate and monitor their work. We cannot personally check map and chart accuracy; we must have faith in traffic controllers, we have to believe that weather reports reflect actual conditions; weight and balance data is supplied by people we never see, but upon whom we must depend. An unseen army of experts has a hand in every flight and we must depend on all those people.

True, ground mistakes have been costly. A lengthy list of designs bearing official approval proved anything but safe to begin with. Old-timers tell tales involving slip shod maintenance, fueling mistakes, incomplete weather information, traffic confusion and so on but there is no profit in dwelling on such history. These factors are beyond our control.

The overwhelming odds are that the system will not betray me. The big question is my performance as pilot. The chances are a thousand-to-one that any problems I encounter will be in small or large degree of my own making. Even in the thousandth case I'll likely be blamed. The ground army takes care of its own and rarely has difficulty "proving" pilot error, no matter what the mitigating circumstances. These being the game rules, I regard the overall picture—my role in it not excluded—with sharp suspicion, for to do otherwise is unrealistic.

Some of the airliners I flew had logged 30,000 to 50,000 hours. That's a lot of stretching and twisting and many firm arrivals. Yes, I know all about 100-hour inspections and metal x-raying. I also know that well-maintained airplanes have shed wings, doors, engines, flaps and other vitals for no apparent reasons. A new design may contain an undiscovered flaw; a proven one may have undetected cracks. Flying well within published limits made good sense to me.

Likewise the engines. Those turbojets were wonderful, so much more dependable than the finest recips, yet I reminded myself of their failings. On rare occasions they flamed out, seized, surged, stalled, froze or ground themselves to scrap metal, leaving a crew with an interesting situation to salvage if they could.

I regarded all performance figures with reservation. In the beginning, a factory test pilot proved to the FAA's satisfaction that my airplane, at maximum takeoff weight, could be accelerated to a certain speed then brought to a safe stop on the runway, should an engine pack up at that speed. He accomplished this on a deserted runway, knowing beforehand what would happen. I was told to depend upon his results. I could not match his feat if I lost one at V1 on a Kennedy washboard runway, driving through heavy rain in the turbulent wake of another jumbo. In fact, I once had a chance to try it in ideal conditions—smooth dry runway, clear afternoon. When an engine blew up at V1, I used full reverse (the test pilot was allowed brakes only) and still ran 600 feet off the far end. Carefully rehearsed demonstrations are to real life flying as Disneyland is to Times Square.

Weather data topped my list of questionable information. It's the state of the art, not the people who practice it. Today's pilot knows more about what's already happened than the airman of thirty years ago, but little more about what's going to happen. I accepted a terminal forecast for what it is—an educated guess—and planned accordingly. Winds aloft data was always distrusted on fuel-tight flights, being wildly inaccurate on occasion. It's the way winds are recorded and the lapse between readings.

I'd put my fellow crewmembers up against those of any other airline anywhere yet I watched every move they made and I expected them to watch me. As one wag put it, "I wouldn't trust my mother to tune in a VOR." Non-pilots, even those closely involved in our work, never quite appreciated that mutual distrust aloft contributed to safety more than all the warning bells and lights in the cockpit. The blunt questions exchanged between pilots without any offense being taken would surely have ruffled feathers if tried with ground people. The pilot of whom dispatchers, mechanics and managers spoke highly was skilled in diplomacy, an invaluable asset.

While the pilot in command of today's big airplane cannot possibly do it all, he can watch it all. He is keenly aware of psychological "set," the insidious tendency to assume that a normal and right situation will continue so. Many the old captain who jogged me with trickery, pretending to misunderstand a clearance or dropping a comment that should ring a bell. It kept me alert and made me wary; it was excellent training. Young pilots are too ready to expect the best from man and machine. Faith can move mountains—and get a pilot into big trouble. You have to disbelieve.

In the total pilot/airplane equation there is one individual I distrusted more than anyone else. Me. At first it was ignorance and cockiness that led me into jams and pure luck that got me out. "Luck is a commodity," theorized an old hand long ago. "I don't know how much I had to start with, or how much I've already used." My own account was surely overdrawn. It was complacency I must dread. Eternal vigilance is the price of safety, read the signs in flying schools. No human is capable of eternal vigilance, of course, nor need he be, even to fly a complex aircraft. The secret of safe flying lies in focusing complete attention in the right direction at the right time. In most regimes of flight the subconscious (if instilled with the right habits) can easily cope with routine monitoring, leaving the conscious free to plan ahead and simply enjoy the ride.

It was important to know airplane limits and to operate well within them. It was important to recognize the limits of the system—traffic control, weather reporting, maintenance, airports and the many other factors beyond pilot control, to anticipate problems and be ready with answers. Not be completely surprised, that is.

Most important of all was a frank admission of personal limits. Most of us were average types who could only hope to be reasonably competent in a small corner of the total piloting picture. I watched an ag pilot at work the other day, racing along the rows, expertly laying dust in the tight corner of a V-shaped field. He probably couldn't fly my airliner around the pattern; I know I couldn't do what he does. The would-be flying jack of all trades and master of none invariably makes the front page.

Continual suspicion and distrust, unless tempered with common sense, can lead to paranoia. The occasional pilot carried it too far, convincing himself that his copilot, forecaster, mechanics and the entire FAA were in league to do him in. He would not trust his mother to darn socks and why he didn't quit was a mystery.

The typical professional pilot is neither a pessimist nor an optimist but a realist. He is the round pin the ground army keeps right on trying to hammer into a square hole and their efforts amuse him. The variables and combinations of variables confronting him are beyond number and this indeed is the fascination of piloting. He expects them, sorts them and adjusts himself to them, knowing it can never be the other way around.

Someone has said that flying is like playing bridge; though the same 52 cards are used, you never get the same hand twice. A pilot must play with the cards that are dealt. And know when to throw them in.

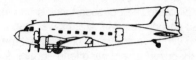

# St. Louis, You Are Mine

It was midnight and one of those evenings of awesome peace and beauty that settle as a benediction upon the land after savage storms have washed the air clean and moved on. We could see the towering anvil heads away to the east, marching shoulder to shoulder across the plains, aflame with continuous lightning, proclaiming their inexorable advance with window-rattling thunder. Their immensity and awesome power appeared on the radar as a green scar which paralleled our track and posed no threat to us.

Above the invisible horizon stood in their appointed places a treasury of stars made all the more vast by our lofty station. How many stars are there, an astronomer was asked. More than there are grains of sand on all the beaches on earth, he replied. And how many can be counted through a bug-stained plate glass windshield from seven miles up? A tiny fraction, but enough to touch the heart.

Below in random patterns were spread the lights of man—that thin line of weak specks being late traffic on a freeway, the small clusters being sleeping villages strung along it like dewdrops on a moonlit cobweb, that dim glow a city a hundred miles distant. Scattered in every direction were the farms, each with its pinpoints of light twinkling against the darkness. Man's defacements of his planet are as brush strokes on a canvas—coarse and meaningless close up, sensible and even beautiful from afar and all the more so at night.

Then a familiar dazzling spectacle slowly drifted into view on my side, looking as if every precious stone unearthed had been strewn across miles of black velvet, ten million multicolored lights neatly framed in my side window, frozen there once again for my inspection: St. Louis. I peered down at one of the tiny diamonds. You there, resting behind that tiny lamp that marks your part of the whole, the flyspeck of our globe you struggle to hold, listen—your light and all the rest are mine in a way you cannot imagine. I'd never say something like that out loud but I often thought it when passing St. Louis and a thousand other hamlets, towns and cities.

The grand spectacle inched from view; I gave St. Louis back to the slumbering souls who imagined they owned it, having disturbed not one with my musings. The dimly lit dials said we were vaulting hill and dale at ten times the highway limit yet we seemed motionless in space while the dark blanket beneath slipped toward us and inched away under our feet. We dreamed of our own tiny lights far ahead, those winking proofs of our own existence, lights which before dawn might themselves be seized by night raiders peering down.

Routinely and subconsciously we scanned the instruments which told why we were up there and how long we could remain. Though beguiled by the night, we were aware of its treachery. But all was well and we raced on through the dark.

Night flying. What memories the hours in that column of the log book evoke. I recall my first night flight more vividly than most of the thousands made since. At full throttle the Pratt's yellow exhaust lit up the right wing alarmingly; I correctly guessed the takeoff flame was always there, though unseen by day. The last runway lights whipped past and we plunged into the black void beyond. The flight gauges said we were in a climbing turn. Level at 3,000 feet, I tried to make sense of the view outside. Towns were obvious, with cars marking the roads between, but what towns were they? The few scattered farm lights were no help. I drank it all in, entranced and confused and had to confess, when the instructor said, "Take us home," to being hopelessly lost, the answer he fully expected.

The airman works in the twin worlds of day and night, each requiring its own techniques. The differences are at once apparent while the similarities appear later. The beginner must immediately recognize that visual clues are to be distrusted after dark, that departure and arrival in particular involve some degree of instrument flying. The night pilot must forever remind himself of this. Many pilots, including some of considerable experience, have flown into the ground after takeoff or during approach simply because they didn't glance at altimeters. The view through the windshield can be deceptive; it can be dangerously so at isolated fields and in mountainous areas. Airline crews are urged to monitor glide slope and/or VASI lights on all approaches, regardless of weather and the surface lighting available for visual reference.

What you don't see can kill you. Many pilots, experienced ones again included, have flown into hills, trees, antennas, buildings and other obstacles they obviously would have avoided had they seen them. Darkness can obscure the terrain as completely as cloud. A thorough knowledge of enroute conditions and the hazards near terminals is essential whether flying at night over the Florida swamps or between Nevada mountains. For every hazard to air navigation marked with lights there are ten thousand unlit perils awaiting the unwary.

"Sur by mtns" was the note beside the western field from which we flew lumbering C-46s in World War II. Of the six possible departures, five required a turn immediately after takeoff to avoid rising terrain. When the "mtns" were snow-covered and the moon was full, it was like taking candy from a baby. On moonless nights we paid as close attention to range signals as when the ceiling was 400 feet and stayed at minimum enroute altitude until we saw lights in the narrow valley. Blackened smudges on mountain sides were pointed out to our students as evidence of carelessness.

A departure across unlit terrain is fraught with unpleasant possibilities. Wake Island got our keenest attention. Upon becoming airborne you plunged into black nothingness with not a light to be seen ahead. It was an instrument takeoff in every sense. On landing it was impossible to determine with the eye if the approach profile was reasonable. Many domestic airports are nearly as bad, with approach paths so poorly lit that outside clues are best disregarded.

Imagination and common sense will solve most night flying riddles before they become problems. Flying at night is different, not more difficult. The unavoidable investment in training, preparation and thought are far out-weighed by the rewards. There is immense satisfaction in as safely completing a flight after dark as if it were flown by day. Who'd buy a car with no headlights?

Night flying is a term of many meanings for there are nights—and there are other nights. I remember short nights as when we left Japan at dusk and saw the first glimmer of dawn soon after midnight. And nights that never ended as when leaving Hawaii westbound in mid-evening, flying west for 11 hours to the Philippines where the clocks read four a.m.

And nights tinged with mystery. We flew an eastbound 747 over the North Atlantic once in moonlight bright enough to read by, the lingering contrails of other flights clearly visible. In the early hours we noticed a vapor trail obviously left minutes earlier by an aircraft flying due south on a track, that if continued, would take it between the hemispheres to Antartica. The Scotland controller said he had no flight plan for such a flight. A military mission—yours, ours, theirs? He wouldn't guess.

And nights of surprise, harmless and otherwise. I got quite a shock on my first hop from Japan to California. We were supposedly three hundred miles offshore when I looked down and saw hundreds of lights spread out in every direction. My crew, old hands on that division, let me sweat with nav gear and charts for long minutes before they laughed. It's a traditional Pacific joke; I was looking down on the huge Japanese fishing fleet. On another evening while flying an L.A.—Texas schedule, we listened in on unusual air-ground chatter. All lighting and communications at Albuquerque International Airport were out, the backup system had failed and no one knew when service would be restored. Then the lights of one runway were back on, then back off again. The resulting conversations with planes heading there were interesting.

And the mean nights when nothing went right. Wind and cloud could do it to you, contriving as they would to reduce speed, rough up every altitude and fold terminals just as you arrived. Toss in a radar that painted a line squall ahead, then went blank, and you'd not have to worry about dozing off. You emerged from such nights sorry you ever heard of flying. The pilot who regularly stays with it after sundown remembers plenty of them.

But most of all he remembers the good nights. The atmosphere of perfect tranquility experienced when flying on a fine evening is unmatched by anything known on earth, even by the serenity known to the sailor on a starlit tropic sea. It is what the pilot sees from his seat in the lofty black void, or perhaps it is what he cannot see, that makes the magic. He cannot explain it to anyone who has not felt it anymore than the astronauts could describe their view of us, a strange bluish orb poised there in space. They alone remember that and I envy them that vision.

I satisfied myself with the royal treasure of priceless stones displayed beneath my feet, each fortune sliding from view to reveal another as priceless. Soon a familiar glow resembling the embers of a monstrous campfire would rise from the dark ahead and we would leave our magic world and drift down toward it, toward the lights of home. While we awaited that welcoming sign, I was enchanted and prone to rhapsodize and even to be seized by the insane notion that I owned St. Louis and all the other lights slowly slipping beneath my feet.

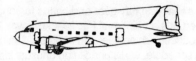

# The Killers

There were 96 preflight items on my 747 checklist, arranged like this:

|                     |    |
|---------------------|----|
| Cockpit Preparation - | 35 |
| Before Start - | 17 |
| Before Push Back - | 6 |
| Ready for Start - | 5 |
| After Start - | 3 |
| Taxi - | 20 |
| Before Takeoff - | 10 |

The Cockpit Prep items varied with the seats and were accomplished by each crewman on his own; the rest were read aloud by the engineer who had been taught to repeat a challenge until he heard the right response and in fact to monitor each response. If each of us adhered exactly to the ritual, we arrived at the runway all set to go. Traffic permitting, we took off at once.

In theory it was a splendid way to do business. In practice, it was a headache with no guarantees. The problem was distraction. At the gate the cockpit was usually crowded with ground people, each with questions or information. In this parrot cage I ran through my 58 pre-start checks, the other two did theirs and between us we copied ATIS information, the clearance and load data. During push back and taxying there was plenty outside to occupy our attention, yet I was supposed to insure that the remaining 38 inside items were carefully checked.

A checklist can provoke as much trouble as it is designed to avoid. Intent on every inane preflight detail, pilots have taxied into other airplanes, off concrete into the mud and onto active runways. Yet the pilot whose priorities are sensibly arranged is apt to hear, "Pitot heaters," reply, "On," and never look to see if indeed they are turned on. I did it more than once. So we'd reach the runway and I'd wonder if we've done it all. Flying was ever a fun business to me and I would not allow nagging uneasiness to diminish the pleasure. Immediately before launching was the time for a quick hard review of basics, a drill requiring no more than 15 seconds that made me feel comfortable about everything.

Mine went like this: Power. Our 727 drivers were encouraged to taxi out on the outboards and start No. 2 just prior to takeoff. Most airlines adopted some form of this practice (and of killing the same engine following the landing roll), within which worthy fuel-saving motive lurked a lethal possibility. More than one airliner, jumbos included, staggered into flight with a dead engine, according to rumors. It was also said that more than one Cessna Skymaster has tried it with a stationary rear prop.

To an outsider, such a blunder seems incredible, but an experienced pilot can understand it. When a dead engine becomes normal in the preflight environment, it is insidiously easy to accept that "look" as normal for departure. The same sort of oversight has led pilots to cram on power with the red ribbons of control locks draped over their knees and luckless Navy types to roar off with folded wings. So, a final glance verified that engine readings were in the green and —yes, *all* the fires were lit.

The control pedestal. Speed brake handle forward, flaps extended, stabilizer trim set. If any of these critical items was not properly positioned a warning horn sounded when power was advanced. At least, it was supposed to. Some years ago a freighter attempted takeoff from an Alaskan field on a bitterly cold night—with flaps retracted. In the frigid air, full power was attained before the thrust levers were advanced far enough to close the takeoff warning horn switch. It became airborne, but in such a nose-high attitude an engine stalled for lack of ram air, inducing a roll the pilots were unable to counter, the outboard ailerons being locked in neutral with flaps up. I'd as soon depend on a railroad crossing flasher as on that throttle switch.

Pitot heaters. There were two little switches on the overhead panel which looked no more important than all the rest. But they were and they were not wired into the takeoff warning horn circuit for reasons I could never understand. A large jet is believed to have crashed due to loss of control caused by pilot response to wildly inaccurate flight instrument readings provided by frozen pitot heads. Minutes after take-off on a warm day we might be climbing through freezing moisture.

Fluids. We couldn't go far without fuel. Experienced pros have in fact departed with whatever was left in the tanks upon arrival, only to hurry back minutes later, miserable with embarrassment. Who needed that? In three seconds I could scan the fuel gauges, check that the flight engineer had us set up tank-to-engine with a crossfeed open and confirm oil and hydraulic fluid levels.

Controls. Ailerons, rudder and elevator, full throw. "Wring 'em out, man," as one old-timer admonished long ago. He flew the mail in DH-4s and retired on 707s with more than 30,000 hours. I still hear him loud and clear. A large four-engine jet took off, climbed at an impossible angle, stalled and crashed. A stone picked up during taxying had lodged itself against an elevator hinge, causing an entirely preventable disaster.

Lights. None of the panel data was worth anything if you couldn't see it. I only experienced complete electrical failure once and that was on an approach to Wichita in a DC-3 on a sunny morning when it was of no consequence—but you never know. Today's typical airliner has battery powered back-up instrument lighting that remains on even if all generators fall off the line. The next line in the manual says the battery should last for 20 minutes. Was my flashlight within easy reach?

Operating from busy terminals has evolved into a devilishly complicated exercise even for those who do so routinely. It is all too easy to become lost in detail and lose sight of the overall picture. Each item on a checklist is important or it wouldn't be there; it is not good to lift off with incorrectly set altimeters and clocks, mistuned nav radios, the rotating beacon off, screwed up pressurization or the APU still running but such silly mistakes can be set right later. They won't kill you.

The same quick review of basics immediately prior to takeoff can be modified to fit any airplane, regardless of size or complexity. In my little Cessna I can quickly confirm that tanks are full, flaps are up, the carb heat is full cold and so on. It takes only seconds.

Cleared for takeoff. One last look around before releasing brakes and a glance back up the final approach path. The tower man is subject to considerable distractions himself. I just might save us both from embarrassment. Or worse.

# History Lesson

Every pilot with significant time in his log remembers hairy moments that still make him sweat. Thinking on them, he shakes his head. "Had I known then what I know now . . . " It is often said that aviation is terribly unforgiving; it can also be incredibly forgiving. The fact that many pilots are willing to relate their blunders speaks well of them. Through the monthly "I Learned About Flying From That" feature in FLYING magazine, more than 550 good people have said "Listen to how I screwed up. Don't let it happen to you!" My hat is off to every one of them.

Without question, many disasters have been prevented by such candid confessions. It is my theory that every accident, no matter what the circumstances, has a constructive lesson, for at least a few of those who learn of it, and it is a sharp reminder which prevents someone somewhere from repeating the same mistake.

For many years I read every CAB accident report in my corner of the picture—air carrier operations. Reading between the lines often revealed mitigating factors given scant notice and a tendency to focus attention on consequences rather than underlying causes. While I did not agree with every pilot error verdict, it was usually clear that, if the unfortunate crew had it to do over again, the situation would be handled differently. That reading made this pilot clean up his act more than once.

A bad crash hurts and embarrasses the rest of us. Aside from the loss of life, it causes economic damage beyond the destruction of another aircraft. In one way or another we all pay the bill. And it is discouraging that, even after making allowances for unusual human, technical and weather problems, most accidents are preventable.

Consider the causes repeatedly cited: slapdash preparation, stalls at low altitude, fuel starvation or exhaustion, collisions, structural over-stressing, flight into towers and hillsides, buzzing, operation under the influence of drink or drugs, disregard of limitations. They translate into pilot ignorance, over-confidence, complacency and, often, sheer stupidity.

The sure-fire ways a pilot can eliminate himself, his passengers, and perhaps a few innocents on the ground, were demonstrated at the first of the century when ignorance and inexperience were valid excuses. The pioneers simply didn't know any better. To ignore the hard lessons they learned is madness, yet they are shrugged off every day.

"Nothing can stop the Army Air Corps!" was the rousing conclusion of the World War II song. "Through these portals pass the best damned fighter (bomber, glider, helicopter, transport, whatever) pilots in the world" hung over the operations door of many outfits. The cadets of wartime air forces were assured that because they got the world's finest training they were better than the enemy. I poke no fun. Considering the duty, the stakes and the level of experience, self confidence had to be fostered and maintained.

(Similar pep talks were once heard at a major airline which told its new hires, "Americans are the world's best pilots and you are the cream of the crop." Some actually believed it. Most chief pilots understood that company loyalty cannot be bestowed; it must be earned.)

A sense of responsibility cannot be drilled into a student pilot. Flying nearly always attracts bright individuals who needn't be told that it can be hazardous to their health. The dire possibilities are all too obvious. Unfortunately, a self-important and/or unimaginative few don't get the picture or learn it. If they stay long enough they make the news.

The enthusiasm flying generates has led to false notions of what it involves. It is still seen as adventurous and exciting. If you can fly an airplane you raise eyebrows. The old mystique has not entirely vanished. Come on, pilots, you're not reluctant to tell laymen about that FAA card in your wallet, are you?

Certainly, flying is all the good things outsiders imagine. It's not only great fun but a skill that can be productively used in a thousand ways. Sensibly employed, an airplane can be a valuable tool in many businesses. But too much is made of rewards and not enough of demands. As a result there are people driving more airplanes around than they can handle if things go sour and attempting things no true expert would dare.

Another theory of mine is that if history was made a required course in every flying school, the accident rate would dip remarkably. History? Hear me out: a would-be pilot ought to know something about how this art developed. Man's envy of birds can be traced back to 3,500 B.C. It is often mentioned in ancient writings, including the Bible (Psalms 55:6). Human flight was wistfully envisioned as a wonderful escape; indeed, there were religious overtones—the devout praying they would ascend into heaven and not plunge into the other place.

In 1783 a balloon rose in France. At long last, the bonds of earth were broken. That momentous first hop almost ended disastrously due to fuel exhaustion. Its "pilot," overwhelmed by the view, grew careless and found himself rapidly sinking toward buildings. He hastily piled the last of the damp straw onto the grate, climbed again and drifted into open country. Ballooning was a grand but chancy sport. The aeronaut painstaking with construction and repairs and who kept a wary eye on the sky usually survived. There was a time to gas up and a time to go back home. So what's changed?

The Wrights' invention opened a new avenue of research and led hundreds to take up the challenge of controlled flight. Santos-Dumont, Bleriot, Farman, Cody, the Voisin brothers, Cornu, Curtiss, Latham, Grade, Rodgers, Roe, Sopwith and Chavez were the Chuck Yeagers 75 years ago. We should know something of them, don't you think? We fly because of them and what they discovered.

Think of the tens of thousands since who gambled their lives and fortunes in advancing the science, sometimes losing both. Consider today's airplane—the B-1, 767, 182, Learjet—any modern type of any size. It has emerged from an incredibly costly struggle and embodies uncounted lessons learned the hard way. It is a legacy beyond price. To use it as anything less is a betrayal of those who gave it to us. When a pilot runs his tanks dry and crashes, brave Pilatre de Rozier must once again turn over in his grave. The irresponsible among us give the Frenchman little rest.

Modern air history deserves close study. It reveals that an alarming number of nice aircraft are converted to scrap metal every year by the same stupid mistakes that caused crashes in the beginning. The right and wrong ways to fly were determined decades ago.

Santayana said, "Those who cannot remember the past are condemned to repeat it." How can a student remember things he or she was never told? A history of the past 200 years of piloting would seem as important a subject as weather or weight-and-balance. Airplane salesmen might be annoyed with an instructor heard telling his student about all the things he should not attempt without extensive training and experience. But, if such advice produced safer pilots, the accident rate would decline and with it the number of absurd suits brought against our industry—and often won—by survivors of irresponsible pilots.

On the other hand, a lecture on say, flight into cloud, illustrated with pictures of aircraft whose pilots thought they could manage without IFR training, might not be worthwhile. A detailed study of the specifics of past mistakes might be time wasted, but I'd like to see it tried. I'm convinced we cannot fly in the face of history.

# Courtesy

My parents stressed manners and consideration for others. So did most of my skippers, military and airline. My folks said courtesy meant civilized behavior in a society which remains savage in many respects, of being "well bred." In the cockpit it meant appreciating that the courteous way was also the safest way.

One old-timer comes to mind. In social exchanges he was brusque, often abrasive. On the job he was affable and cooperative. His power changes were smoothly made and well within limits; his reversing and braking were sparing; in chop he nailed it on the limiting speed and he insisted that copilots and engineers treat the machinery with identical respect.

"This ship is pushing 45,000 hours," he'd say. "That's a lot of twisting and stretching and hard landings. What's going on down there under the floor—corrosion, loose rivets, cracks, metal fatigue? We don't know, maybe nobody does. If I am rough and the next crew runs into a big problem, maybe something they can't handle, I would always wonder, wouldn't I?" His consideration for others improved his own chances, of course.

He knew airplanes. Older equipment sometimes develops weaknesses that escape notice during the most careful checks. Years ago, ominous spar cracks were found in a widely-used four-engine type when fuel cells were removed for cleaning. The word went out; other carriers took closer looks and more cracks were found. Reinforced, the airliner continued in safe service for years. Few of its passengers —or pilots, for that matter—heard anything of it. Numerous such cases can be cited.

It happens to all types and ages of aircraft. Design errors have had lethal consequences in new aircraft and, obviously, attrition can affect the airworthiness of a type of splendid reputation. While the private owner answers to himself for handling abuse, we had to depend on each other. Fifty crews might fly a given ship in a month of domestic service. We thought of the next crew and expected the inbound crew to think of us. We covered one another.

A considerate pilot is interested in the other fellow's neck as well as in preserving his own. Much has been said about the cozy atmosphere prior to deregulation, with each carrier exploiting monoply routes for whatever the market would bear. Hogwash. There was fierce rivalry between us—but we left it at the gate. When we noticed something wrong with another airliner—an open cargo door, a fluid drip, smoking engines or brakes—we picked up the mike and said so, period. The other fellow's logo didn't matter. To keep quiet and let him find out for himself was unthinkable. In-flight radio exchanges between competitors regarding weather, traffic and runway conditions was routine, indeed expected. Sharing vital information was the right way to do business, the courteous way, the only way. It was for the most part a gentleman's profession.

I say *was* because the recent turmoil produced by deregulation has produced instances of "dirty tricks" including rude radio remarks and other interference with competitors, some of it infringing on safety. The perpetrators are beneath contempt; their conduct is reprehensible. Certainly, we had a handful of selfish characters who flew as though they owned the sky, but I never saw one stoop that low.

Fortunately, the inconsiderate pilot is in the minority. In my new corner of the picture (private flying), he's the self-centered, undisciplined boor who runs-up with no regard for anyone behind, blocks the taxiway when others are ready to go, barges into the pattern without announcing himself, drives around as though he were up there alone, is a nuisance in busy airspaces with his long-winded chatter and caps his jaunt by blocking the gas pumps. He's an embarrassment whose parents didn't teach him much. And he certainly didn't serve the stern apprenticeship I remember.

A pilot who ventures far from home must do business with a host of ground people—weathermen, fuelers, weight-and-balance experts, mechanics, FAA controllers, local and federal officials and others, seen and unseen. If he flies for hire, he has owners to satisfy and perhaps fares to please and schedules to meet. He is deluged with information, advice, suggestion and instruction, some of it questionable, some irrelevant. The courteous pilot graciously accepts all assistance, keeping private opinions of its worth to himself. Arguing with or belittling anyone in the supporting team proves nothing and only makes the job tougher for everyone else. Besides, it's rude.

The demands of certain weather/traffic combinations are extreme. The atmosphere becomes tense, confusing, occasionally frightening. It's all too easy to blame someone else for trouble. The fellow who snaps back at a tower controller or vents his frustration on fellow crew members doesn't have it all together. He's lost his cool. Composure under stress is the trademark of the topnotch. He remains calm and civil no matter what. When the chips are down he simply talks faster.

Flying is very much an individual effort. Even in two-pilot equipment each performs separate duties and smoothly blends his work into the overall exercise. It is silly to get carried away by that, however, for the interdependent nature of modern piloting is all too obvious. We depend upon ground people for support. They perform work we could not if we tried. They deserve respect and courteous treatment at all times. We pilots depend upon each other to adhere to clearances and otherwise observe the rules.

A lack of common courtesy in the cockpit is inexcusable and can be deadly. Pray you never ride behind a pair of stiff-necks who will not leave their petty differences on the ground and work together like the professionals they are supposed to be. We pilots measure one another in terms of training and experience. Common courtesy is never mentioned yet I can recall few really good pilots who were not considerate human beings. Now . . . if you have stayed with me this far, there's only one thing left for me to say:

Thank you.

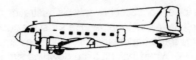

# The Final Prize

In the beginning, flying seemed to make wonderful promises, not the least of them being a release from the bondage of school. Then, after offering to teach us to fly, the RCAF marched the surprised lot of us off to class, six no-nonsense weeks of it—algebra, trig, physics— to weed out the inept. You could wash out without ever seeing an airport, much less one of their "aeroplanes."

We subdued survivors were posted to No. 9 Elementary Flying Training School and marched in quick step right past the flight line to another school. Theory of flight, engines, navigation, weather, Morse code and ignore the barking Kinner engines outside. Oh, we flew all right, but at what an inflated price. For every glorious hour aloft we paid with eight at books and blackboards.

You had to pass. Performance in the yellow Fleet trainer meant nothing unless matched by good test scores. There was no second chance, indoors or out; the class roster dwindled at a chilling rate.

So it has ever been in the military, during wartime at least. I chanced upon the thick notebook of a forgotten fighter pilot and thumbed through pages of the numbers he memorized before realizing he had been lectured seventy years ago, as a Royal Flying Corps cadet. Some things never change. The airlines must, for economic reasons, employ the same grueling, fast-paced training. It has been said that a month of it spans the same sum of new knowledge included in an average college semester. Having tried both, I call that an understatement. The kid at State doesn't know he's born.

By rough count, the types in my log were earned by attendance in twenty-five concentrated courses, not counting scores of refresher schools and checkrides. They left their mark. The older you get the more carefully you consider new opportunities. Is the reward really worth the effort? More than a few pilots nearing retirement have elected to wrap it up on a comfortable DC-9 run rather than transition to, say, a junior 1011 schedule, the better money notwithstanding. It is not difficult to convince yourself that the increase, after the tax bite, simply isn't worth the ordeal.

Three years prior to retirement my number came up again: did I want to upgrade? Take it or leave it. For once my ingrained hatred of school was no factor for I badly wanted this final prize. I could do it one more time. I hoped.

"Gentlemen," said the ground school instructor the first morning, "I strongly urge you to dismiss everything from your thinking except this airplane during the next two weeks. Successful completion will demand your undivided attention." In the room sat eight engineers, five copilots and seven grandpas, all old heads representing 250,000 hours of piloting, not a minute of which would affect the outcome. It was start all over again.

Three instructors rotated at shoveling out huge scoops of new facts and figures. They spoke of static inverters, bus ties, feathering pumps, fuse plugs and second segment climb as though we could instantly recall all previous training. A familiar pattern emerged: the young engineers sopped it up like sponges, the copilots took copious notes and we captains read into the wee hours and asked many questions. Old dogs can be taught new tricks, given enough time.

After endless days of it, the final exam. Does the ACM overtemp at 180 degrees C? 185? 175? 158? Maximum TR load after equipment cooling failure must be limited to 45 amps? 54? 74? None of these? The engineers were done and gone in 30 minutes, the copilots in an hour, leaving the captains to their miseries. Surprisingly, everyone made the required grade of 80 or better.

The cockpit procedures trainer, a simulator that doesn't move, came next: start the engines, put out fires, extend flaps electrically, it does everything but "fly." The CPT reduces fumbling in the simulator later on. (The simulator itself cost 10 dollars a minute to operate.)

Next, the oral exam in a tiny room with full scale color photos of the panels arranged as in the cockpit—forward, overhead, pedestal, engineer's. The federal examiner was cordial and strictly business: what's this light? . . . that one? . . . when would you expect? . . . how could you tell? . . . what limits apply if? . . . show me . . . explain how . . . if this light flashes amber? . . . goes steady red? . . . goes out? Like previous orals, it was thorough but fair. Mine took 90 minutes. There are nicer ways to spend that time.

The simulator: the first two-hour session went quite well, the second poorly and the third was pure disaster. Lurching and slopping through imaginary space, my speed and altitude control was appallingly bad, demolishing my self-confidence. Don't worry, said the check pilot, it often goes this way. Outside I looked at the huge beast crouching on its hydraulic legs and thought, you bastard, I'll whip you yet. Three more rides with some improvement, then the FAA check.

The checklist was read and engines started, though not without incident. One engine tried to burn itself off the wing and another refused to accelerate. The examiner issued a departure clearance to a fix via an arc, with holding to be spelled out enroute. Then it was off down the Disneyland runway at full bore. Not unexpectedly, the stabilizer trim ran away at 10 knots less than rotate speed, requiring an abort: thrust levers closed, speed brake pulled, full reverse, hard brakes.

Everything went normally the next try, around the arc and into the hold. The turn inbound was interrupted by a bell and light—wheelwell fire. I recited the procedure. So far so good. Let's see a steep turn each way through 180 degrees, said the examiner. Next the stalls; he settled for two of the series, then issued clearance for an ADF approach. There was nothing to see at the minimum descent altitude so it was climb away and around again for a back course ILS, with an engine failure along the way. I got it on the runway that time. I asked the instructor to hold it while I wiped the sweat from my glasses.

And again—full power, dashing down the strip and, not surprisingly, an engine quit cold at lift off into a 100-foot cloud base. I got it around the pattern in good shape but screwed up the approach; the runway was off to the left; no safe way to make it; go around and do it again. Broke out at minimums on that try with the lights nicely centered but the man said there was a plane still on the runway so go around which, again, was no surprise. Half way through the clean up another engine caught fire. That called for all the rudder trim plus a lot of leg and flying with a watchmaker's touch—and, of course, an entirely different approach to another runway. Ten sweating minutes later we touched down, braked hard and got it stopped with the nose hanging over the boundary lights.

I mopped my face and wondered what came next. That's all I need, said the fed, you did a nice job. I hadn't, really; I should have done better. But I'd passed the rating ride and enjoyed the partial satisfaction of a med student who completes a successful appendectomy on a cadaver.

Finally, the new airplane itself. We departed at dawn and flew to a field reserved for airline training. I did three practice instrument arrivals then the fed came up to watch for the record. First, a four-engine ILS to 100 feet with a touch-and-go, then one with an engine out followed by a go-around and VFR pattern with flight director failed. The others did their turns and we flew home, logging 4:30 for the flight.

In Operations the examiner signed our tickets and there was much hand shaking and exchanges of good wishes. And all of it to get a number added to my Air Transport Pilot license.

B747.

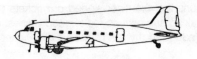

# Now Hear This

It sneaks up on your ever so slowly, evidencing itself in annoying little ways. About fifteen years ago I noticed that, though right-handed, I was holding the phone to my right ear and, with passing time, pressing it harder against my head. Even then people had to repeat things. There were days when everyone mumbled.

It came and went. Most of the time I heard normally; then, as if by prearranged signal, everyone would speak softly and slur words. Most frustrating was the occasional inability to zero in on a speaker, to block out background noice. These lapses gradually grew in frequency and duration.

All right, so my hearing wasn't quite what it was in high school. To verify that the impairment was minor I went to a hearing clinic. "Don't tell me anything about your employment," said the doctor. His examination of ears, nose and throat was exhaustive. Then an hour in the sound-proof cell, pressing the button when squeals were heard and trying to repeat his whispered words. He was a nice man but a chronic mumbler.

Finally, the readout. "You're a career pilot, aren't you?" he asked, pointing to the graphs. I nodded. The lines started high on the left (low frequencies) side, then plunged steeply through the high notes to the bottom of the sheet. I resisted asking, "How long have I got?"

"It's irreparable damage due to prolonged exposure to noise," he said, adding that the left side was the worst. A small reward for the copilot years spent with headset worn on the right side? How about surgery—go in and clean the points and plugs, so to speak? No way, he said, pointing to a colored picture of an ear two feet tall. It was something to do with microscopic hair-like sensors damaged by abuse. The specifics of the human machine's component systems do not fascinate me: I'd as soon not know.

"We can slow further deterioration with plugs," he said, "or design a hearing aid." The plugs were out, of course, and an airline pilot with a wire hanging down from his ear?! And, that's where we left it. The problem did not affect my job, in fact, the volume level set by most of my copilots was too high for my liking and they said, "Say again?" more often. Credit that to concentration and experience; it's easy to "hear" when you know what's going to be said.

Maybe I should sue those responsible, but where to start? Kinner? They're gone, aren't they? Pratt & Whitney, Wright, Rolls-Royce, Allison? How about Ham Standard? Props, not engines, made most of the racket, they said. Silly notion; I'd have to confess the sheer enjoyment those ear-piercing sounds afforded for so many years. Many the time I stood unnecessarily close while a Kinner Fleet clattered past or a short-stacked R-2800 came to life or a 707 rumbled overhead, its JT-3DS singing at full thrust. Such was the glorious music of flight and I loved every note of it.

Cockpit exchanges were sometimes humorous. A hostess would come up and say, "Do you mind if I smoke?" and I'd respond, "You bet, with cream and sugar," but the ensuing laugh was at my expense so no harm done. In the early days I'd served hard-of-hearing skippers; it was part of the job. Now let the youngsters indulge my little problem—which they all did with good humor.

The real frustration came in social situations, my loss of discrimination often making it impossible to understand speech in ordinary noisy surroundings. I heard overall sound but could not block out background noise to understand words spoken across a restaurant table. The result is that the victim becomes reclusive, avoiding situations potentially embarrassing. He slowly withdraws from normal life. It was happening to me.

Retirement solved nothing. The job's demands were gone but not those of family life. My wife was not as patient as my copilots. She said, "Why don't you get one of those aids like President Reagan uses before I lose my voice?" It was selfish to expect others to continue making allowances.

Back to the little chamber, the faint tones, the mumbled phrases, the telltale graphs. The lines now began lower on the left, then fell sharply almost to zero. A real ski slope, eh, Doc? "Yes, but we may be able to give you some help," he said. Help? I wanted complete restoration, like with glasses. He shook his head, "That's not possible, but we should gain some improvement."

The thought of an ear device was repugnant. Glasses? Lots of pilots wear them, this one included. Dentures and hair pieces have taken years off others (this one excluded), being improvements over original equipment in many cases. But "hearing aid" and "old man" go together. That thing in the ear was evidence of decay, like the cardboard window in a tired old car.

The options: one fit over the ear with a little tube curving around to the inside, the first good argument for long hair yet. But me with a Prince Valiant cut? Then there's one that fits inside a temple of your specs, but with that same tube into the ear. And the presidential model which is entirely self-contained. It is a miracle of modern science. Due to its size, amplification is limited but it was worth a try.

"I'll make impressions," he said. Both sides, you mean? "Oh yes, you need help both sides." He sent them off to the lab where the charted data was fed into a computer which dictated the exact circuitry needed "to amplify the high frequencies where you are, er . . . somewhat deficient." The acorn-size, almost weightless gadgets arrived. Each contains a battery the diameter of a pencil and about an eighth of an inch thick which lasts two weeks. There are tiny knobs to regulate volume.

They are not uncomfortable, in fact, you soon forget them. Volume control is tricky; the tendency is to turn them up too high. This raises high pitched sounds (kids squealing at play, dishes clattering, car doors slamming) to an unbearable level and produces a shrill whistle if anything is brought near an ear, as when phoning. I've learned to keep them low, and off when in my shop or out flying the Cessna.

They are not the complete answer, but they do help and are well worth the bother and expense. My wife is speaking normally again and now complains that I don't speak up. Obviously, I don't need to anymore in order to hear myself. Loud talk can be an indication of hearing loss.

During all this I learned that a few professional pilots are required to use hearing aids. The FAA figures: out of 98,735 First Class physicals in force at the beginning of 1984, 33 carried a hearing aid requirement on their medical certificates; more than a third (34,278) required glasses. Interesting.

Another thing goes with failing sight and hearing, falling hair, loose teeth and all the rest. Memory. Like right now: if I could remember where I left my glasses, I could start looking for my hearing aids.

# How Long Can You Fly?

One thing that keeps a professional airman awake at night is the question; will I make it to retirement? The notion of job hunting in mid-life with a worthless license as the main credential has led to ulcers. The majority, it may be said to their credit, face the possibility without alarm and try to prepare for it. Contrary to what their non-flying friends often assume, it is not greed but apprehension that leads the pro into moonlighting. Watching one contemporary after another drop by the wayside gives pause to the most optimistic.

What is the truth of the matter? What are the odds against going the distance? A look at my airline's record is interesting.

In mid-1949 eight of us World War II vets hired on as DC-6 flight engineer trainees. It was a brand new airline position, a necessary stepping stone to copiloting. The seniority list numbered 213, four of whom flew desks, so we are talking about 209 active line pilots ranging in age from about 25 to 45, all hoping to enjoy long flying careers. (Interestingly, mergers and expansion swelled the list to 2,204 names in 31 years, so the future was in 1949 brighter than we thought.)

In 1980 I made a casual survey. Of the original 209, 46% were dead. Ten died in flying accidents; nine on the line, one in a military crash. Most of the rest died of natural causes, though I recall two highway fatalities and one suicide. Two died while in flight out on the line.

At the end of my 31 years with the airline, 34 (16%) were still flying and all seemed in good health. All were within five years of mandatory age 60 retirement and most would retire within two years. Should we all have made it to age 60, which would certainly not be the case if the record said anything, we would have joined the 86 pilots who had already flown until normal retirement. Even with this unlikely outcome, only 120 (57%) would have gone the full distance with active flying. Does this say that in the beginning we eight had less than six chances out of 10 of making it? Not quite.

It is necessary to review the 89 (43%) who dropped out early to get the full picture. Though I once knew all of the other 208 personally or by sight, thirty years strained the memory. A number of pilot friends helped pinpoint individual cases. As far as we could remember between us at that late date, 11 quit voluntarily, three to accept office positions, eight to pursue outside interests. Fourteen more left the scene for a variety of reasons other than health.

This aspect was clouded. A certain pilot was there one week and gone the next and no one seemed to know why. He was usually a relatively new man. You heard he'd quit, been asked to resign or was simply canned, but you never got the details. It was a private matter between him and management. Those 14 were let go for whatever reasons.

That left 64 (31%) who quit involuntarily due to injuries (two in line accidents) or deteriorating health so it may be said that pilots employed 31 years ago had about seven chances out of 10 of completing full careers. These fairly decent odds put to rest the notion still popular in 1949 that "flying is a young man's game."

While considerable research would have been needed to pin it down exactly, it was my recollection that at least half of the unlucky 64 flew until age 45 before being grounded. Some were well into their fifties and others within months of normal retirement at age 60. And there is no question that in certain cases careers could have been extended had individuals listened to their doctors and taken better care of themselves.

Had our chief pilot known all this when he initialed our applications, he could have said, "You run a five percent chance of being killed on the job. Twelve percent of you will quit or leave the line for some reason not related to health. Your chances of retiring normally are about seven in 10, and you can improve these odds somewhat if you live sensibly."

He could have predicted that those who went the full distance would survive well into retirement. The happy fact is that, of the 86 who made it to date, 80 (93%) were still alive, most of them as hale and hearty as when they flew the line. A number were well into their seventies in 1980.

I wondered whether or not these trends reflected industry averages. A friend on Delta Air Lines conducted a similar casual survey and came up with almost the same percentages. Our line operated a variety of feeder and trunk routes plus an international network; job demands were as typical as those on any other line. Some pilots went for the long overwater runs, others for stateside schedules, many for some combination of the two. A cursory run down of the 209 names suggested no domestic/international ratio of longevity, though this conclusion was but an educated guess.

And whether or not these trends will continue over the next three decades no one can say. The accident fatality rate will decrease, of course, though it was not a major factor to begin with.

Airline flying has become a far more involved and complex business than it was 31 years back. The life is more regimented, demanding, restrictive, unforgiving and frustrating in every respect. How well today's new hires will absorb the increased pressures will be revealed in due time. I believe they will take them in stride and hang up a record better than ours.

Incidentally, of my original group of eight, one left for personal reasons in the first year, one died in a crash, three retired normally and three were still flying the line when the airline collapsed in early 1982.

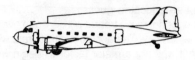

# Harvard Reunion

The yen to fly an AT-6 again stemmed from my Harvard training. The airplane, that is, not the university. American university names were given U.S. trainers used by the Royal Canadian Air Force, thus the U.S. Army's AT-6 airplane became the Harvard aeroplane you learned to fly after "elementary" instruction in a Fleet or Tiger Moth. When he heard of my interest, Glen Hyde, an airline friend, said, "I know just the fellow," and introduced me to George Ceshker, a Frontier Airlines retiree who owned an AT-6. I called him. The immediate response was, "You bet, name the day," and so we went flying.

George's sparking beauty is in fact neither AT-6 nor Harvard but a Navy SNJ-5 which is 99% an AT-6G. The differences between either and a Harvard are cosmetic. Our ships had the British circular stick grip wrapped in cord stained brown by sweating student palms. And the huge face-up compass on the right, seemingly swiped from a dreadnaught. It's funny the things you remember. Everything else in George's N3666F was vaguely familiar and located more or less as I remembered. The only marking on the ship is a large 72 on each side. That rang a bell. It had raced at Reno in 1973 and won the AT-6/SNJ event at 206.6 mph with Bill Turnbull on the stick. So that's where I had seen it before.

I climbed into the back seat. Did the Harvard also have shoulder straps? It must have, probably the old Sutton harness. George fired up by lifting a switch. I missed the whine and screech of the inertia starter. We taxied out, ess-turning for a proper forward view. The pre-takeoff checks—flaps, trim, fuel, controls—and the runup—prop exercise, carb heat, engine readings, mags (100 rpm max drop, wasn't it?) were completed up front in the deliberate manner that would have pleased, Sgt. Campbell, my Harvard instructor.

Brakes off. He eased power up to 36 inches, the Pratt howled and we tracked down the asphalt with little rudder correction. The tail came up and we were almost immediately off and flying. The gear came up with none of the wind noise and door shuddering common to large aircraft and, with power reduced to 30 inches and 2,000 rpm, we climbed nicely at 115 indicated—and I mean 115 good old miles per hour.

The converters are pests. We put together the world's mightiest air power with airplanes measured in feet, fueled with gallons and flown at miles per hour to all corners of the globe. So why change? Gallons to pounds of fuel makes sense, but knots?

We cruised at 165, about DC-3 speed, and I thought about instrument training, the only times we students rode in back. A spring-loaded canvas hood unfolded forward to a catch; push the release and it snapped back should a quick exit become desirable. It was back there we learned to ignore engine noise and chop and to concentrate on attitude, altitude and speed, not as individual readings but for the overall mental picture they gave when continuously scanned. When thoughtfully handled, the Harvard could be flown with considerable precision and quickly restored to normal flight when handed to you in an unusual position or a full blown spin.

Late in the war an intensive course for instrument instructors was conducted by the Army at Bryan, Texas, using AT-6s. A retired Braniff pilot, Clyde Haggard, taught there. "Our students routinely shot low freq and ADF approaches to 200 feet," he recalls, "and to 50 feet on the ILS, in fact, to touch down in most cases." If you could hack it in the back seat of an AT-6, you could learn to fly the gauges in anything else. That is no less true today, come to think of it.

We landed, hangared the silver beauty, and went for coffee. "George, if you're game for a little dual, a couple of landings some time, I'll come right over." I was mostly joking but the phone rang a week later and he said, "Let's go fly some more." It was 41 years to the month since I had first sat in that front seat. George is a sporting type.

He leaned in for a thorough review of procedures and I asked a lot of questions. Most of it came right back but I had forgotten the settings of elevator and rudder trims—11 and 2 o'clock. The wobble pump brought fuel pressure up for several shots of prime. Then, with master switch on and mixture forward, I lifted the switch and the engine came to life at once. Pressure, temperatures and vacuum all normal. George strapped into the back seat with more nonchalance than I could have mustered had our roles been reversed.

The forward view is better than I remembered but ess-turning is necessary during ground travel. The tail wheel steered with the rudders a few degrees each way and was unlocked, as in the P-51, by shoving the stick forward past neutral, a vast improvement over the

RCAF Harvard setup. Its tail wheel was also coupled to the rudder, but unlocked with anything more than a mild correction, leaving many the clumsy student (this one once included) with a free-castoring rear wheel at 75 mph during roll out. Instant opposite brake in exactly the right dose would save it, otherwise there was nothing to do but hang on tight until the big demon completed its groundloop, cartwheel or whatever else it elected to do.

After much double checking, I eased on the coal and away we went. Directional control was easily maintained and the ship flew itself off after a short run. Gear up, back to 30 inches and 2,000 rpm, trim for climb. The ship has a good solid feel all three ways and much inherent stability, but you must fly it every minute, one reason it was a superb trainer. In cruise, trimmed out, the nose is well down affording excellent visibility, better than I remembered. So I just sat there and reveled in the nine-cylinder din, the vibrations felt through hands and feet and watched the landscape disappear under the blunt nose. Lovely! Don't believe them when they say you can't go back.

Though I am right handed—I have always worn my watch on that wrist for reasons long forgotten. On the first downwind leg when lowering the gear, I remembered. Inept fumbling with the lever resulted in a sharp rap on the left wrist and I recalled smashing two crystals in Harvard days. Haste in the P-51 was equally rough on watches. When the wheels fall out there is a slight slowing due to drag but no effect on pitch. The SNJ has a small window in each wing through which a down lock can be seen. If one fails to appear, you shove the gear handle into a second notch and force it into place. Green lights and mechanical indicators are the inside checks.

I tried half flaps on base, full on final, carried 95 over the fence and wheeled it on. The result was a not good, not bad arrival, all things considered. The second try was better, the third passable. The nose stayed in place with little ruddering. Give me five hours of circuits-and-bumps (touch-and-gos to you Yanks) and I'd be completely at home again. Flying back I tried a couple of steep turns then showed George where I lived. It was easy to spot. On our blacktop driveway was painted the British World War II roundel, 28 feet in diameter. It required $60 worth of paint, red, white, blue and yellow, and beats giving directions to friends with airplanes. It was the same insignia used on our Harvards way back.

The final landing on the very narrow strip where the ship is based concerned me. With the tail down you can only see the grass on each side but there was no problem in keeping it straight while slowing. We shut down and I took a last look around inside. By modern standards the old cockpit is crude. Today's engineers would replace the wobble handle and primer with an electric pump, discard artificial horizon and directional gyro in favor of a flight director, swap the big trim wheels for pickle switches and stuff boxes into every corner. The new product would cost ten times as much, require three hours of maintenance for every hour of flight and not serve any better the purpose of teaching the art of flying. We put the SNJ away and went for coffee.

Dean Henry, another airline friend, joined us and listened with open envy at my account of the hop. He said he went into Army cadets later than us, when the AT-6 was the first type flown, the primary trainer. "Eighteen hours was average for soloing," he said, "though some went longer. If you weren't ready by 30 you were in trouble." The ship was—and remains—no weekend toy ready to forgive gross errors. It must have been a big bite the first time around. More than a few luckless students, even among those with a background in less demanding trainers, bought the farm, often by pulling the last turn onto final a hair too tight. Then it was a sudden flick and splash before the student realized his blunder.

Dean remembers an AT-6 mounted on a concrete base at his school which students actually fired up and "flew" until they had the drills down cold. The gear and flaps operated as in actual flight in that odd forerunner of the modern simulator. We talked of AT-6s and other good airplanes, stretching the facts now and then as pilots are known to do, embellishing incidents from the past but never far from the truth with any of it.

It was a nice way to spend a morning.

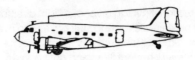

# Old Ways and New

When an old pilot talks about his early days, take him with a grain of salt. I've heard fellow airline captains regale their copilots with wildly exaggerated accounts of flying 40 years ago. Some of what they related was pure bunk. Make that read, "we," for I may have stretched the truth now and then. My generation is no more guilty in this respect, however, than the patriarchs who taught us the ropes, and you can bet old-timers 40 years hence will tell equally outrageous tales.

Take initial flight training, a topic of never-ending discussion: did we really get off to a good start or does today's student emerge as good or better? My cohorts look down their noses at any trainer that cannot be flung about the sky with reckless abandon. They are convinced that only by inducing hairy situations can a student truly appreciate the limits of man and machine and that such experiments should be encouraged. I go along with all of this, but there's no denying that some of my sharpest copilots were products of modern civilian training who never had an airplane upside down. Did we really learn from our wild antics or were they just fun and games?

Fifty years ago almost everyone learned to fly in an open cockpit biplane robust enough for aerobatics. Reuben Fleet's Consolidated Aircraft supplied 60% of the primary trainers used by the Army Air Corps prior to World War II and sold many civilian models. His Ontario subsidiary delivered more than 600 trainers to the Royal Canadian Air Force. Fleet's trim little biplanes were the first steps for thousands of military and civilian airmen and all reveled in the sport it invited, this writer included. So why not fly one again and compare it with a modern trainer?

Surprisingly, there were five Fleets based near our Texas home, one a Canadian-built Finch Mk.II nicely restored in RCAF colors (colours?). This example had open cockpits whereas ours had canopies, otherwise it was just like the ones we flew. Jess Shryack, a retired airline fellow who instructed during the war—our war, that is, agreed to resume my dual training in the Fleet. He would ride in back; airplanes are not always like bicycles. We pushed it out into the winter sunshine. I felt the taut waxy skin, gazed at the finned cylinders, varnished prop, struts and wires. None of it stirred a sense of familiarity but then, it had been 30-odd years. It looked good sitting there, waiting. Rather a plain Jane of an airplane, the Fleet remains a doll in my book.

The front cockpit was spartan, comfortable enough with the right cushions and exuded that once familiar aroma of dope, leather and gasoline. The five-cylinder Kinner came to life right away and we taxied out. You can roll along without swinging the nose except for that top cylinder. Heel brakes. Visibility was unrestricted in most directions. Check the mags, oil gauges, fuel, controls and . . . what else? "Checklist complete. You've got it," yelled Jess while I looked around for more to do. I suspected he was laughing, but I ask you, what kind of airplane is ready to fly after four simple checks? And I thought it so complex during that last peaceful summer of 1941.

Full throttle. Off we went across the grass, wandering a bit because I was late with rudder, came unstuck (as the British used to say) at 60 and climbed away at 70 with minimum attention. So this is what it had been like. No wonder those days are so fondly remembered for it was all over again a most delightful little flying machine. The Kinner's bark was nothing like the awful roar I recalled, but then I heard a bit more then. The small windshield did its job so well I raised the goggles which didn't properly fit over my trifocals. (Don't laugh, young pilot reader; your day will come.)

The controls were heavier than I remembered, the response more sluggish. Memory is a poor reference. I tried a stall, a few turns then went back to shoot landings. I held the top cylinder up there and the old trainer settled gently onto its tires and with little tendency to swing on roll out. Bearing in mind that it was stout enough for aerobatics and can endure the abuse inflicted by a neophyte with more nerve than knowledge, I still see it as a good primary trainer.

But I'm prejudiced. The Fleet revived memories of good times and good friends. You have to understand that the boy who said he wanted to be a pilot in those days raised the eyebrows of his elders. He was supposed to get over such notions by high school and start preparing himself for something solid and sensible that could be accomplished while flying a desk. The war changed all that, of course, and by 1950 everyone had a cousin who flew for TWA. The service opened the door and I joined young men who saw in flying what I did and older men who wanted to teach us how. We talked flying until late every night while outside in neat rows waited the yellow airplanes, the Fleets. Of course the reunion was fun; it could not have been otherwise. So much for nostalgia. I wondered how they did it today.

Sandy Barrows learned to fly in 1974 and had logged 2,000 hours since, mostly instructing, when we flew together. Sandy had soloed 30 students. We walked out to a white Cessna 152T trimmed in red and blue. All metal, high wing, tricycle gear, side-by-side seating in enclosed cabin, raked rudder. It's sharp, businesslike and pleasing to the eye, this modern counterpart of the Fleet. Close inspection revealed a pride in workmanship. I guessed there was muscle beneath the styling. "It's put together, believe me," said Barrows with a grin that hinted at firsthand proof.

The young instructor's preflighting was extremely thorough. "I've been laughed at for my walkarounds," said Sandy. "I'm not laughing," I said. The 152's cowling is screwed down tight. You can see a little of the engine through the front scoops, a bit more when you pull the oil stick. "On the 150 you can raise the cowling and see everything," said Barrows. I said I also liked to look at all the wires and plumbing. When they hide things you get the impression its not important to look.

I climbed in, closed the door and felt half dressed without a tie. That's the feeling after the knockabout quarters of the Fleet. The 152 is deliberately car-like which could suggest that it is a sort of automobile that flies. "Sometimes it has that effect on a student," said Sandy. This is no plus for a trainer. The well-arranged panel contains 10 controls, 10 switches, 18 gauges and an impressive stack of radios. It must seem a bewildering array at first blush, yet I reminded myself that today's student has a much more technical background than we did and doubtless adapts more readily. There's no question that side-by-side seating makes more sense for initial dual instruction than tandem cockpits; a student can better watch demonstrations and be more closely monitored with this arrangement, a decided plus. An intercom system is installed but, at Barrow's suggestion, we put the headsets away. Conversation worked well though the in-flight noises are somewhat higher than I expected.

Ground travel is a snap with easy turning and sure braking. Cockpit visibility is excellent but you must turn down wind to inspect base leg and final before taking the runway. Pour on the coals, lighten the nose at 50 and off you go at 60. Your grandma could do it. Aloft it is light on the controls and sprightly for its power. It's 15 lbs lighter (empty) than the Fleet and its Lycoming is rated at 15 hp less than the Kinner. It's cleaner and scoots along at a better clip. And it's fun to fly. Barrows said the enclosed cabin and cluttered panel tend to concentrate student attention inside and makes the point that the airplane can and should be flown visually by draping a cloth over the gauges, "otherwise they never look outside and that's bad."

Landing is easy and there's no reason to wander if you can remember your left foot from your right, and let's not get into the silly tail dragger vs. tricycle debate. Any good student can master either landing gear arrangement. Since nearly everything built now is a trike, learning to fly in one makes sense. The 152 needs flaps the way a bulldozer needs a drag chute but there they are and why not? A student might as well learn about them from the start, along with flight gauges, radio work, radials, and transponder codes. Their proper use should be taught early in the game. Considering the complex world a student enters today—that is, if he plans to do anything significant with his skill—the 152 is superior to the old Fleet in many respects.

Sandy and I talked at length about training then and now. "What is your opinion of training today?" I asked.

"It doesn't go far enough. There is too little stress on basics. Your training was better in that respect," said Barrows. "After I'd flown 600 hours I enrolled in an aerobatics course to find out if I had missed something. I had missed plenty. Now I try to talk a student into two or three hours of true basics. If he will buy the gas and oil I'll show him."

It was not the answer I had expected. "In what?" I asked. We walked through the hangar to a sparkling Pitts S-2A which, it turns out, Sandy owns and has successfully flown in competition. Well! The Pitts time is not intended to turn out aerobatic experts but to show how careless handling can induce far more horrifying situations than those seen in the usual syllabus. Small and large aircraft have, for example, been flipped upside down by wake turbulence or wind shear, not often, but it's happened. The best chance of resuming normal flight with minimum airframe stress and altitude loss lies with the pilot who has been there before, obviously.

And so the training question was settled once and for all, at least, to our mutual satisfaction. "I give a course in the Pitts," added Sandy. "Ground school, 10 hours of flight training. After sitting there all those years straight and level, maybe you'd like to . . ."

"You think a refresher is in order?"

"It couldn't hurt."

I think she's right.

# The Ten Best

"What are the ten best airplanes ever flown?" asked a friend. The ten best? That's a tough one. Ask a hundred pilots and you'll get a hundred lists. My choices are historically significant, at least, inasmuch as they are typical of airplanes of their times. Each left its mark in aviation (and on me, which admits to personal favoritism.) Some have been the subjects of books; others are forgotten except by those who flew them, read about them—or watched them from behind the airport fence.

The *Bleriot XI*—this quaint little monoplane with semi-enclosed cockpit was a hint of things to come later; biplanes would reign supreme for the next quarter century. Louis Bleriot's cross-Channel hop in it in 1909 was a hint of events to come.

The *Sopwith Camel*—vicious with a novice, deadly in the hands of an experienced pilot, the Camel scrambled to 15,000 feet in 16 minutes. It claimed 1,294 victories, a World War I record. Ten times that many boys fell under its spell in Hollywood epics of the 1930s.

The *Boeing P-12E*—when this scrappy little job peeled off on the silver screen, 10,000 eighth graders dreamed of Randolph Field, the "West Point of the Air." Then they watched its colorful Navy twin, the F4B-4, roar from the Saratoga's deck—and went home humming "Anchors Aweigh."

The *Fleet Finch*—one of the last of a long line of biplane trainers going back to the fabled Jenny of the Great War. Rugged, honest and unspectacular, it was the perfect trainer, a logical first step, the make-believe Spad that fulfilled boyhood dreams.

The *AT-6 Harvard*—a leap forward, a hefty no-nonsense trainer for a new generation of faster, heavier aircraft, it quickly developed the knack. Fly this one well, they said, and you can fly anything else we've got. Its successful candidates proved that to be true.

The *P-51 Mustang*—this appropriate mating of British engine to

American airframe was, in the view of most historians, the best fighter of World War II. It was later modified into a pretty fair racer. Lean, lethal, lovely to fly.

The *DC-3*—the near-perfect design, the airplane that won't wear out, the airplane that taught the world to fly. The acceptance of aviation it brought about directly accounts for much else we enjoy in flying now. The most important airplane ever built, no question about it.

The *DC-7C*—large, luxurious, long-legged, it represented the peak of piston-engine airliner development, set new standards for long-distance air travel and marked the end of a colorful era. Superb lines, in flight or parked. An excellent instrument airplane with delightful control response.

The *707-320*—the "Intercontinental," the long-range model of the fabulous Boeing that introduced Americans to the jet age. A magnificent machine in every respect. Rugged, reliable and comfortable, it was a favorite with passengers world wide and with every pilot who flew it.

The *Concorde*—where the Russians failed and we shamefully refused to try, the British and French made it work. Think on it: supersonic air travel by a timetable! Forget practicality. There was nothing "practical" about the Bleriot hop, but he pointed the way—just as the Concorde has.

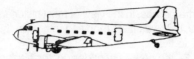

# What Happened
# To KAL Flight 7?

It's a different world out there where Korean Air Lines' Flight 7 was blasted from the sky by a Russian fighter. Long distance overwater flying is vastly different from anything known to domestic airline crews. When the horrifying truth became known, every pilot who had ever skirted that mysterious coast was immediately in the cockpit with Captain Chun, trying to visualize the final hours of flight. As is usual after an airline disaster, newsmen dwelled on what happened; pilots as usual asked why. Some of them would fly that route long after Flight 7 was forgotten. They wanted answers.

It seemed that we might get them but the flight recorders were never recovered —or, if they were by them or us, their contents were kept secret. We had to settle for what was released to the press, which was not much.

Anyone who had navigated that backstretch of the globe regarded the tragedy with special interest. Some 50 crews of us came to know it well during the Vietnam War when our company was contracted by Military Airlift Command to transport people and cargo from California to Pacific destinations. That adventure was known as the PAC/MAC ("Pack Mack") operation. We flew Boeing 707-327Cs which were convertible from passenger to freight work, navigating with Loran and Doppler when beyond the range of shore stations, which was most of the time. The military had more sophisticated navigation gear but the Loran/Doppler setup was the best available for airline use. It served well enough once you became familiar with it and understood its weaknesses. As in all flying, you did your best with what they gave you.

Ground school classes in both devices only compounded their mysteries. An experienced navigator rode along on the first 25 to 50 hours for hands-on tutoring and to verify whereabouts meanwhile. Then a check airman observed a trip leg to see if you had it down cold. No matter what he reported, you didn't and couldn't after such brief experience. So you headed out on your own, hoping for an experienced copilot and flight engineer, and learned on the job.

Loran was a radio device which picked up emissions from distant transmitters and displayed them on a screen. There were sky waves and ground waves to be seen; the problem was to decide which was which, match the right signals, and plot the results on a chart. Where the lines of two stations crossed was supposedly your position. Ideally, this fix fell on the desired line of flight at a point agreeable with predicted speed. If it didn't, you adjusted heading and revised ETA—if you had faith in the fix. Otherwise you waited a few minutes and tried again.

Dual Dopplers confirmed with reasonable exactness that you were making good a desired track and measured your groundspeed. Each radiated four signals to earth, analyzed their reflections and provided course and speed. The autopilot could be coupled to either receiver.

So much for theory. The Loran performed beautifully between California and Hawaii, nice crisp identifiable signals appearing on the screen from Alaska, Hawaii and the mainland. You could plot position to a fine point (which led pilots who shuttled back and forth like streetcar drivers to imagine they were ready for any ocean. In fact, they required additional training and flight checks if assigned to the more difficult PAC/MAC division.)

West of Hawaii it was another ball game. The waves transmitted by Japanese and other Far Eastern stations were weaker and not as readily interpreted. A clear distinction between ground and sky waves, without which a plot was worthless, was not always possible. On one Tokyo—Tacoma hop we flew six hours without a plot that we'd bet money on and were considerably off course when actual position was determined.

The Doppler's main failing was that its radiations would not reflect off smooth surfaces. The Pacific is well named; broad stretches are calm for long periods. At such times a little light marked, ''Memory,'' came on. This was Doppler lingo for, ''I'm no longer receiving good returns so I've locked in the last reliable data. Press on using that course and speed until we fly across rougher seas.'' Those little lights (they usually lit at the same time) often remained on for two frustrating hours or longer during which upper wind direction and velocity could change significantly. Needless to add, indecipherable Loran signals and non-functioning Dopplers went hand in hand more often than not.

It made you think: if we cannot get a decent Loran fix and both Dopplers are loafing, everyone else out here must have the same problem. We would hear another PAC/MAC or military trip report a position on our route; sometimes we'd see him way off to the right or left, leaving both of us to wonder who was closest to the assigned route. The lateral separation of airways was sufficient to preclude collisions but the necessary tolerances limited the number of slots available. It was not unusual to sit at Yakota Air Base near Tokyo for an hour waiting for takeoff clearance.

The game became deadly serious when nearing anyone's coastline. We were expected to cross an ADIZ (Air Defense Identification Zone) on course and close to the ETA given on our last position report. It was usually possible to get a solid Vortac/DME fix in time to update shore-based air traffic controllers, otherwise it was wise to report that position was "believed to be" so-and-so and explain your uncertainty. If you busted the "green fence" (the line on the charts was green) without warning say, 20 minutes early and 80 miles off course, unsmiling young men in crash helmets would crowd your wing in cold silver F-106s and there would be holy hell to pay upon arrival.

That was an interview to be avoided, but it was only that—an embarrassment. The possibility of being shot down for busting an ADIZ, even the Chinese or Russian, seemed remote. Flying along the coast of eastern Asia was accomplished with extreme caution all the same. The charts depicting the Russian land mass warned that infringing aircraft "may be fired without warning." How literally was that to be taken? The same question could be asked about China. President Nixon had yet to reestablish communications with Peking. An American airliner had been forced to land on one of the Russian-held Kurile Islands and we knew that a Korean Air Lines 707 had been damaged by gunfire and forced to land in Russia. Surely that had been a colossal mistake the Russians would not repeat. The general feeling among airline crews was that penetration of Russian air space would probably result in being forced to land in Russia. The distance from Saigon to the Aleutians is roughly 5,000 miles. Much of that offshore travel is only minutes from Russia when flying at Mach .80.

Our PAC/MAC routes did not hug the coast quite as closely as present airways, due to the state of navigation then, though they took us within 75 miles of land. A close eye was kept on the ragged green coast line painted on our radar screen. An operating radar was one no-go item on which there was no fudging whatsoever. Vapor trails were occasionally seen over the western horizon and there were occasional ineffective attempts to jam radio voice channels.

We wondered why a few Russian airfields were not shown on our maps, with homing frequencies, for use in dire emergencies. If an immediate landing became necessary, we would opt to head for one and take our chances with the reception rather than to ditch in the Pacific at night, perhaps 1,500 miles from the nearest friendly air-sea rescue outfit, but such information was never provided.

Our 747s came equipped with the Inertial Navigation System, a big step forward. Compared with the Loran/Doppler rig, the INS was amazingly accurate and trouble free. An error of more than one nautical mile for every hour of flight was considered excessive. (Reporters covering the KAL disaster wrote of *the* INS whereas the 747 had three systems working independently. Two were required for dispatch; the third was a "hot spare," used on every flight.)

The INS is entirely mechanical with no reliance on compasses or radio signals. Waypoints—positions over which you wish to fly—are typed in prior to departure, much in the way a number is selected on a push button phone. Like a telephone, it is a wonderful but mindless device which will do exactly what you ask of it. If you want to call your sister but absentmindedly punch in your brother's number, he will answer. Type in the wrong coordinates and the INS would fly you to the wrong waypoint. The checking and doublechecking necessary to prevent mistakes was tiresome and never-ending, but absolutely essential.

Most INS installations were wired so that the three units could be merged for programming, meaning the coordinates typed into one would be inserted into the other two computers. While this saved time, any mistake was twice repeated. Every captain developed his own system of checks and cross checks during preflight programming and for frequent rechecking in flight.

Additional verification that the desired route was being maintained was provided through position reports radioed from a trip once an hour. During each report, a crew gives its position and the time over, forwards an estimated time over the next waypoint and reads off the name of the one to follow. These were read back by a ground station, word for word. Theoretically, a cockpit error would be noticed by a ground controller before it became a problem. Waypoints could be changed enroute to permit flying an amended route—or to correct mistakes.

Every departing flight was under radar observation for the first 250 miles. Any early deviation would be immediately questioned by ground controllers. Once beyond radar range, however, a crew was on its own. During those dragging times after midnight it was all too easy to relax and await the dawn. I remember those dreary hours flying the 747 from Anchorage to Seoul with passengers. You had to rouse yourselves no less than twice an hour, turn up the cockpit lights, get out the flight plan and once again verify the remaining waypoints. You read them to the copilot and he read them back, looking to see that all three INS readings agreed. Then the flight engineer would read them back to both of us. Turn down the lights and peer into the blackness beyond. Study the radar: does the projection of Russian coastline match the chart? Are we the proper mileage from it? Looking to the mysterious west, we'd wonder who was watching us, listening for our next report. As our blip inched across his screen, what was that Russian thinking?

Were all three of Korean 7's independent INSs giving incorrect course data? The odds against it are overwhelming. Could all three units have been influenced by an on-board or surface force? Theoretically, there is no chance of that. Did the crew commit a gross programming mistake that went undetected for two hours? A possibility, certainly, but it doesn't fit. Radar—the 747 had two—would have revealed the error within minutes, long before the aircraft penetrated Soviet air space.

The crew was Korean, products of one of the most regimented free societies, subject most of their lives to curfews and other restrictions few Americans appreciate. Their land is bordered to the north by a trigger-happy former enemy. Proceeding for ten minutes straight out from Runway 32 at Seoul's Kimpo International Airport can draw hostile gunfire. The nearest friendly neighbor, Japan, is extremely sensitive about unauthorized intrusions of its air space. Sloppy navigation is not tolerated in that tense arena. You stay on course, or else. Capt. Chun was highly regarded and was said to have flown the president of Korea. Gross pilot error is hard to accept.

Was it a hijacking? An interesting possibility considering the last 25 years of airline history. With a madman aboard, Capt. Chun would likely have flown any course demanded to keep his airplane intact. What captain wouldn't?

But all of it is pure conjecture. After an accident laymen ask airline pilots, "What do you think happened?" as though we had access to information not mentioned in the press. True, we can imagine ourselves in a perilous situation and, leaning on personal experience, list some of the possibilities that might not occur to outsiders, but we can only guess at the actual cause.

Our question was not only why did Korean 7 penetrate Russian air space, but why was it shot down? Russia's paranoid obsession with security was no secret yet it was generally, and mistakenly, assumed that an easily identifiable civil aircraft invading their precious territory would be escorted out of it or forced to land—in other words, to be accorded the same firm but civilized handling their accidental (or deliberate) strays had received from free nations on numerous occasions.

It was also generally, and again mistakenly, assumed that a tacit understanding had been reached with Kremlin leaders regarding penetrations by civil aircraft. No matter how sophisticated the navigation equipment or how professional the flying, sooner or later a planeload of innocents is going to wander into someone else's backyard, perhaps with a plausible excuse. It has happened before and it will happen again. That our leaders had not reached such agreement was surprising; that they had not told us—and the flying public—that there was no such agreement was shocking. Only after Korean 7 fell did we learn that the international radio emergency channel (121.5 mc) is deliberately omitted from the receivers aboard Russian interceptors.

In the aftermath came a proposal to halt grain shipments to Russia. Several senators argued that this would be unfair to American farmers. "Why should they bear the brunt of our outrage?" one asked. No indeed. We must take care of the farmers.

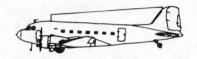

# So Long, Texas

After landing at Love Field, I asked the tower about Braniff Airways and was directed to a row of Army barracks next to a small brick building. In a small hangar were two DC-3's; a DC-4 and DC-6 sat outside. The scene was hardly impressive but in those days you couldn't be choosy. You didn't fiddle around when work was offered. The letter inviting me to an interview came at 7:00 a.m. I shut down my National Guard P-51 just before noon at Dallas, 800 miles away. I wanted the job no matter whose name was painted on the airplanes.

That was in mid-1949. For 34 years our family was as Texan as most people we met, meaning they too were transplants. We lived the Texan way, took great pride in regional progress and bragged like natives. You moved in and were accepted simply because you had the good sense to leave wherever you came from. We soon learned that the average Texan is not arrogant, no matter how he comes across. He's simply convinced that everything in Texas is bigger and better, period—and he's more often right than wrong.

One of our airline divisions, dubbed the South End, operated entirely within the state. We new-hires flew it in summer, wallowing along in the chop, sweat soaked, cockpit windows open, engine roar slowly ruining our hearing. In October the seniors took over, booting us off to the Chicago and Denver-Memphis runs. After the ice and snow were gone—and, of course, the mean spring weeks when Thunderstorm Alley earned its reputation—they'd go back and again we'd struggle up to 8,000 in 105-degree air enroute to "San Antone" and have to start right back down.

I looked down on the parched prairie, the stunted vegetation, the dusty river beds and wondered why people chose to live in such a desolate region. My skippers bristled at such doubts. I reminded one of a comment made by an early visitor, General Sherman, I think it was, "If I owned Texas and hell, I'd rent Texas and live in hell," to which he snapped, "For what he could have got renting Texas he could have air-conditioned hell."

Another took me through the Alamo. On the walls are the names of the heroic defenders and their native states; few were Texans by birth. My kidding suggestion that the shrine ought to be moved to Nashville drew an icy stare. "They came here, they fought here, they died here. They were Texans!" And of course they were, just as we became. Texas doesn't get under your skin, it gets into your bones. You belong. You put down roots. It is a great place.

It is, in some degree, the challenge of making things work in spite of terrain and climate that produces the Texas spirit, of not merely surviving but prospering—and that is as far as I will go, for the Texas frame of mind defies precise explanation. Dallas would have made more geographical sense almost anywhere but where it is, yet we watched it explode into the eighth largest American city, an experience worth sharing. Where we first rented a tiny frame house on the edge of town now stand high rise offices and the north edge of the city has been shoved 20 miles beyond.

It is a land of extremes, weatherwise and otherwise. Oddly, the airline itself was an example. Growth was painfully slow due to the replacement of old types by larger and faster equipment and an exasperatingly cautious management which displayed little of the aggressiveness common to local enterprise. It was two paces forward and one back time and again. After 15 years of it, a new boss took over and began ordering jets by the gross. The shift in corporate mood was astounding. I advanced from Electra copilot to 707 captain in 23 months. The laurels accorded the new team were not entirely deserved, however, as much of the expansion was long overdue. Braniff was a plum ripe for the picking. Great leadership was not displayed by taking advantage of the obvious, but the Ivory Tower crowd came to believe its own publicity, a failing with eventual bitter consequence for all of us.

But what fun while it lasted! We saw our modest midwestern operation grow into a global network. Our pilot seniority list grew from 1,200 to 2,200, the total employee roster to 15,000. Our multi-colored fleet was seen in London, Paris, Hong Kong, Tokyo, all over South America, not bad for a little outfit headquartered in surplus wood buildings when I hired on. We were proud of our outfit and that a Lone Star State airline had pulled it off.

All of which comes to mind when I think back on our Texas years, along with specific events—two mergers, new route awards, our first turbojet, the 707-227, a hot rod that for months left the competition in its smoke, the private airplane crash that claimed Tom Braniff, line accidents which claimed good friends, lean years, fat years, furloughs, hirings, training and, underlining it all, the priceless association with fellow pilots and the grand ground people who served faithfully to the end.

And the family milestones—a daughter born who is a native Texan and proud of it, school and college graduations, homes bought and sold, marriages, grandkids, two critical illnesses, wonderful vacations, very merry Christmases, friends by the score and those perfect spring and fall southwestern days that almost made you forget blistering July and August and the treacherous ice storms of winter.

I remember with special fondness that unique period when five of us—father, son and his wife, daughter and her husband—flew the good old B-line, an unmatched family record, on our line at least. I'd be walking to my airplane at Chicago or Honolulu or Saigon and hear, "Hey, Dad!" You cannot put a price on that.

I remember with sadness the unbelievable external reaction to the Kennedy assassination, when suddenly we were, "Dallas—City of Hate," in major papers and on network TV. In retrospect, that deplorable response reflected the depth of resentment long brewing in less progressive areas. It was pure sour grapes, but it hurt. Texans were not above rubbing it in when out of state, though no real harm was intended. They can dish it out and they can take it, but for Dallas-ites to hear themselves called a city of hate? That stung. It was grossly untrue, an unforgivable slanting of the obvious that has not been forgotten.

So, though the collapse of our airline did not give our Lone Star story a happy ending, we think back on the book and not the final chapter. Texas was a great place to work, raise a family and, yes, a good place to live, all things considered. Texas was good to us and I believe we were good for it. Our name is still there on a little part of its incredible progress.

We got off to a good start a thousand miles to the northeast where the people are as friendly and genuine as Texans. They don't brag as much over here although there is much they could brag about. I registered the car and noticed an airplane on the license plate. I took that as a good omen.

# Twice Highway Speed

We looked down at the traffic on Interstate 64. Yes, we were slowly gaining on the cars and not wandering off to the left and right as they must do to reach the target straight ahead. "How fast are we going?" asked Margaret. "More than twice as fast as they are," I said. I was to repeat that more than once—for my benefit as much as hers.

After a lengthy and frustrating search, we had found an airplane, a 1976 Cessna 172, which seemed to fill the bill. It's a little red and white beauty with blue upholstery, a solid nine-plus inside and out. Its appearance and log entries reflect tender loving care above and beyond required maintenance.

Admittedly, we had vague notions about what airplane would be right for us in retirement. Our grasp of the problems and possibilities of private aviation was poor. Modern aviation involves specialists performing within specialties in ways few outsiders understand. "Pilot" is no more descriptive than "doctor" or "teacher." The average airline pilot is as out of place in a lightplane as a truck driver on a skate board, and he is wise to recognize it.

We simply wanted to fly again. I asked a lot of questions and got as many suggestions. A Ryan Navion beautifully restored in U. S. Army L-17 colors was offered and proved roomy, stable, surprisingly quiet and a delight to handle. The several Navion owners consulted, an intensely loyal bunch, convinced me the "poor man's P-51" has an undeserved reputation as a maintenance nightmare. We were impressed and came within an ace of buying.

Yet, after much soul-searching, a 172 appeared to be the most sensible choice for our purposes, so we wrote a check and were flying it home. Ozark Air Lines had whisked us from Greensboro to St. Louis in less than two hours. "We won't go back this fast," I warned as we walked into the terminal. "My guess is four to five hours with a little wind help." But there was wind harm, not help, and the two legs back required 6:10 of flying. The average groundspeed—106 mph (knots were required in airline work but this is our airplane and 106 sounds better than 92).

After two years on the ground there was more to it than crank up and go. There was a physical to renew, a biennial flight review and I wanted some time in whatever we bought. A young instructor went along for an hour and saw me through several landings. He seemed amused at my questions. Little airplanes can bite as quickly as big ones. Hours were spent with Sectionals, navigation charts, airport plates and the Airman's Information Manual, and it was time well spent. I think I could have picked up where I left off out on the line but this was a much different do-it-yourself world, barely understood by the average pro.

Finally, the moment of truth: following an extended run up and enough checklist reviewing to exasperate an experienced 172 driver, we were off into the wild blue and heading east. The yonder proved to be anything but blue, however, being choked with enough dirty brown smudge to meet the Los Angeles notion of clear skies. Forward visibility was three miles in places, no matter what they were reporting. The Cessna has rather more avionics than I'd sought— dual nav/comms, an ADF, DME and encoding transponder—but before we'd leveled at 7,500, I was glad to have all of them.

Evansville slowly fell behind, then Louisville, though we scarcely saw either through the haze. The Standiford controller pointed out traffic we never spotted and advised we were 98 knots groundspeed which I translated into 113 for Margaret. She agreed that was twice highway speed. I pointed out that considering the meandering track of even the most direct interstate, and the slowed flow through cities like Louisville, we were likely doing two-and-a-half times automobile speed. She said, "This is a nice airplane," pointing to the vanity mirror on her sun shade.

We picked up the Lexington ATIS (the old routines were recalled, one by one) and were vectored to Runway 22 at Blue Grass Field. What an attractive airport that is, bounded on one side by a picture book race horse farm owned by Nelson Hunt. "Really?" said Margaret, "We're ex-Dallasites ourselves," in a way that suggested we had been neighbors. Well, we once lived just seven miles from his place. The tanks took 22 gallons which made consumption a most reasonable 7.8 gallons per hour. Or, about 14 miles to the gallon. So far so good.

The weatherman on the phone was pessimistic about the rest of the route. Scattered thunderstorms were forming over the mountains ahead, he warned, and threatening to form a line we could avoid only by going 200 miles south, a considerable diversion in a 172.

Since Lexington would remain clear, there was no reason not to continue for a look. We put London, Kentucky, on the nose and climbed to 9,500. That didn't quite clear the haze and minor chop so we struggled on up to 11,500, the last 2,000 feet of climb requiring nine minutes. We sidestepped a few building cus and crossed London with no problem. The view to the southeast and the sequences politely provided to us overhead Tri-City Airport included nothing ominous so we tuned in Holston Mountain VOR and pressed on. Two hours after takeoff it was obvious the trip could be completed without diversions.

It was cool, clear and smooth up there with the four-cylinder Lycoming merrily chattering away as though it could run forever. My initial apprehensions melted and I began to enjoy the ride. I detest car travel; an automobile is good for one thing, to get me to where the airplanes are. This was the way to go, the only way.

I flew some very nice military and airline equipment in my time, but it belonged to other people and I flew as they directed. They decided when I'd go, what I'd haul and the route I'd follow. The strategy was their's, the tactics, and those only to a degree, were mine. There was never any flying just for the sake of flying, purely for the fun of it. The average private pilot cannot appreciate the sense of freedom a pro enjoys at the controls of his own airplane, no matter how its performance differs from what he usually flies—or flew.

For me there's no longer any hurry, no more schedule to maintain and the pressures of that hectic life are not missed. True, plodding along at two miles a minute and being confined to the low levels takes some getting used to. I have to remind myself now and then that we are doing better than twice highway speed.

We started down through the smog in late afternoon, found neat little Causey Field where we are now based just south of Greensboro, and arrived. My landings need work. We put the bags into the car and pushed the Cessna into the hangar. Looking back, Margaret said, "that is a very nice plane."

The next day we took one of our grandsons for a ride. He agreed it is a neat airplane, then fell sound asleep on the back seat.

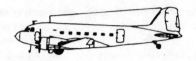

# Forty-five Years Later

It was much different then. You have to understand the backdrop to appreciate what the war did to—and for—young Americans. The Depression left its mark and remains indelible in their memories. A personal recollection: hobos waving from passing freights. How many kids today know about hobos and the hopelessness they reflected? Another: a thin farm boy reading while the rest of us third-graders ate lunch.

"Willie, didn't you bring anything?" asked the teacher.

"No, ma'am."

"Willie . . . did you have any breakfast this morning?"

"No, ma'am."

When I mentioned that at home, my mother said, "You bring that boy home with you after school tomorrow." Willie went through two helpings of hash and biscuits as though half starved, which he was. The next spring a threadbare woman brought a bushel of corn. "Things are a little better for us now," she said. Those were grim days.

By 1939, when Germany invaded Poland, there was reason for hope. Roosevelt's bold recovery schemes helped, but it was the war that changed everything. Most Americans left lean times to enlist; for some it was the first guarantee of "three squares and a flop." Products of strict upbringing and a much simpler existence, they readily adapted to service life. Their outlook was vastly different from that of today's high schooler. The 1937 freshman faced a meager future; he had little chance of college, but by graduation the picture had dramatically changed.

For airminded youngsters it was a dream come true. They filled many cockpits, though the majority of cadets came for other reasons —to escape the walking army, to earn a commission, to join something exciting, indeed glamorous. Flying was novel and adventurous; if you had to serve, it seemed the way to go. Few knew what was involved. It's a fair guess that the average student's first ride was also his first dual.

Few worried about the price. True, it was considered a "one-mistake" game and wartime flying would be even riskier, but the other fellow would pay the bill. Youthful optimism is wondrous—and, in war, tragic.

The bills came due. A high school classmate spun his BT-13 into a Kansas field, eventually recovered and thereafter flew a desk. Another vanished in an A-20 between Brazil and Ascension Island. A third completed 30 missions, only to collide with another B-25.

Some Americans went to Canada, and attach no Lafayette Escadrille aura to that; more than 8,000 of us did. My group was on a troopship at Halifax when we heard about Pearl Harbor. Our first question: where is Pearl Harbor? The following year saw the class decimated. Though trained for fighters, most went to Bomber Command. A loaded Wellington could reach 11,000 feet; its average life was 40 hours, a fraction of the flying required in an RAF combat tour.

Like all the rest in uniform on both sides, we went where we were sent and did what we were told, without question. Three of us ended up in Cairo. We transferred to the Army and were assigned to Air Transport Command, a new experimental project hauling freight in ex-airline DC-3s. Training Command alone ranked lower in popular esteem. We were "Allergic to Combat," the "Army of Terrified Copilots."

But you could buy the farm in ATC, no matter how secure it seemed. One of our trio did in Arabia. Another crashed with a load of aviation gas. The sole survivor, he was terribly burned. My own flying was scarcely more perilous than stateside duty and became the foundation of a postwar career. They paid, I profited; the fortunes of war were not fairly divided, but are they ever?

Has it been 45 years? A hotel I was in recently hosted a bomber group's reunion. I tried to identify the boys who once crewed B-17s and only found aging men. The grandmothers they squired were, of course, their war brides. (I know few veterans of that war who are not still with their first wives.) What do they think now, looking back? I asked friends who were deeply involved.

"Those were unforgettable days. They brought out the best in men, and the worst," said Bill, a B-17 waist gunner shot down on his 16th mission. "What Churchill said of England was true of us—it was our 'finest hour'. Our country will never again reach those heights."

Bob flew B-24s in Italy. "It was incredible, the biggest game of Russian roulette in history. Some guys changed position in formation because they felt they were going to get it, and got it anyway.

It was the flak. They didn't shoot at us; they just threw up a big rectangle of steel and we had to fly through it, going in and coming out. The good and the bad got it. There were no odds you could figure on. I remember that time with a sort of resignation. I survived because of luck and prayer. Determination had nothing to do with it. I went over, flew 32 missions, came home and still couldn't vote. I never again hit such highs and lows. In a way, it's good to have your extreme emotions behind you."

Don flew 65 P-51 missions with the RAF and USAAF before being shot down. "What do I think, looking back? Well, I was damned lucky. It was the most exciting time of my life. It was valuable—where would you get that kind of experience today?" Like the others, he minimizes his contribution. "Some did a good job of it; I was just there." He does not feel the war had any profound effect on his life.

Hugh flew B-24s and B-17s, 8th Air Force. "I flew 18 missions, then the war ended. We said they saw us coming and gave up. I wouldn't take a million for the experience or give a nickel to do it again —though I would if I had to. It gave me confidence I might never have had otherwise. I had the usual experiences but most of all I remember the people, the friendships."

Dick, a B-26 lead bombardier, was shot down on his 31st mission. "I enjoyed it. The values and qualities learned during the Depression and in school, then putting your life on the line day after day —those two things were stabilizing—they prepared you for the rest of your life. You became sort of fatalistic, not in a wild sense, but death didn't hold the terror that it seemed to for people who didn't go through it. It gave me new values. I don't think the world owes me a living because I fought in World War II, but I'd like to think somebody remembers now and then. But they don't."

He's right; people soon forgot. The whole enormous, incredible catastrophe that altered the course of history as had no other war itself became history and lost its interest—except for those who were involved. I recall my daughter's response when I asked what she was studying in 7th grade history: "Oh, some jerk named Hitler," she said. Recently a television reporter questioned high schoolers in a small city about the 21 names on a local monument. None knew who the men were or where and when they died and they didn't seem to care. Those 21 died, incidentally, in Vietnam. World War II is ancient history.

I asked others, "When you think back 45 years, what comes to mind?" and got much the same answers. They remember the people, the fear and elation, the appalling cost in lives and national treasure. Each had unique adventures and all remember what Hugh dismissed as, "the usual experiences." The usual experiences included being among the 14 to return out of 18 that left, of "flak you could walk on," of counting chutes from a smoking cripple, of watching a direct hit convert an F4U into a shower of scrap metal, of collisions in the pattern, of watching one friend survive a tour with relative ease while another vanished on his first mission, of staring at the empty cot of the fellow you sat next to at breakfast.

The details emerge slowly; the more that was endured, the more reluctance to recall them, even at this distance. The most terrible memories are the most personal, so the talk is mostly of training days, of the misery of life on a Pacific atoll, of dysentery in Nigeria, of the girls in Sydney and the dearth of them in Okinawa. The rest is locked away. In any event, it would be incomprehensible to anyone who wasn't there. Most were able to put it behind them and rejoin peacetime life; most have done well. I know of one who couldn't forget. His Convair nearing Kansas City became his B-17 nearing Cologne and he alerted his gunners to diving 190s. He's been sweating it out over Germany for 30 years now.

Second question: "How do you feel about today, about what has happened since the war?" "I'm grossly disappointed," said Bill. "The country did not keep faith with its fighting men." He values being a child of the Depression and blames postwar affluence for much he dislikes now. "We live in an escapist society; kids wrap themselves in fantasy and science fiction."

Bob agrees. "We were a tremendous people in World War II. We reached our zenith then. The feeling of national unity and purpose—we've never known it since. I once thought our generation was put upon by the Depression and the war—those were awful times, I still can't throw away food—but I've come to believe we were the blessed generation. We stood at the top and could have called the shots and dictated world peace. But we blew it." Yet he hopes for a reversal of the trend. "The pendulum may have reached the end of its swing. I hope so."

"We lost our nationalism," says Don. "You're almost ashamed to salute the flag today. Kids today are older and more mature in many ways than we were, but not smarter. This drug business is bad; I don't understand it. I don't understand the courts; today's criminal is in great shape. Vietnam was bad; the American people let their troops down over there. Disappointed? Not totally. This is still a great country."

Hugh: "Our generation was fortunate. We pulled together—women working in factories, that sort of thing. Esprit de corps. Basically we are a trusting people, too trusting. We want to believe the other guy has good intentions; it's a national weakness and look where it's led us. But I still feel I've lived the best 63 years of the century."

"Affluence has done a lot of harm," says Dick. "I'm glad I grew up in the Depression. I learned values early. Kids today have different values and standards, but neither did I share my father's viewpoint for that matter. He walked seven miles to school; I had a hell of a job talking him out of 50 dollars to buy my first car. My daughter didn't understand my standards. I wished she had, but times change. I couldn't expect her to see everything my way."

The others responded similarly: prosperity has been more curse than blessing—two no-win wars since 1945 hurt us badly—the average under-40 American has little understanding of the international picture—Cuba and Vietnam were colosal mistakes which we sometimes seem bent on repeating—our children are not taught history and therefore cannot appreciate the price paid for what they enjoy—there is too much emphasis on rights, too little on responsibilities—the get-mine-while-I-can attitude is deplorable, but understandable—the drug scene is frightening—and so on. "We have people who, if they thought it wouldn't affect their 'life styles,' would turn it all over to someone else," said one. "They couldn't care less whose flag is flying." "There wouldn't be the same response today," said another. "Some would cave in rather than fight—the 'better red than dead' element."

My questions were to American combat airmen, and I believe their views are shared by most other World War II vets, whatever their involvement. Their blunt comments, as put down here, could be shrugged off as the grumbling of disillusioned old men who live in the past, who couldn't accept inevitable change, but that would be to misunderstand them. These men have enjoyed good lives since the war. Time and again I had to steer them away from careers, families and retirement life back to what happened four decades ago and since. They are without exception cheerful; their traumatic experiences considered, they have adjusted amazingly well to changing times. They would not have prospered otherwise.

They are not convinced the world is going to the dogs, no matter how they come across. The apprehensions none can shake stem from firsthand knowledge of the cost and senselessness of war and how close their war came to being lost. They recognize the fragility of peace. It worries them to see our good life taken for granted; it appalls them to hear it debased. "We used to call it the 'American way,' remember?" said one. "They've made that sound silly. I'm almost ashamed to say it."

One reward of my airline years was the continuing association with airmen who began as I did in World War II and learned to fly because of it. We shared the same boyhood background and, to varying degrees, the same wartime experiences. We saw eye to eye. Years later came the influx of Korean War vets into airline ranks. There was little difference between us except that they were more knowledgeable about flying than we were at that stage. Still later, Vietnam returnees came into the picture and, with their time in KC-135s and Mach 2 fighters, were the best qualified pilots yet hired for airline flying. And they were great troops as well.

Whereas my flight engineer class in 1949 rented beds in a fraternity house and went to ground school by city bus, the Nam boy hit town in a Corvette towing a ski boat and bought a three-bedroom house, an indication of the dramatically changed economic climate. But those were surface differences. Our views on most things were remarkably similar. That we believed in the same basics should not have surprised us as it did. After all, we ancients of the grand old World War II collection are their fathers.

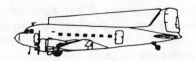

# A Ride to Remember

"Clear right?" The long blades turned slowly, inches from the side window then, belching gray smoke, the big radial came to life and settled into rough idling, shaking itself awake within its bulbous cowling. The needles rose on the ancient gauges—manifold pressure, rpm, oil pressure, cylinder head temperature—and pointed to the right numbers. It all came back. Starting large recips was a tricky business, it being all too easy to warp a cylinder due to hydraulic lock, burn up a starter or produce an embarrassingly loud backfire. The penalty for over-priming was an engine wreathed in flame, the memorized procedure for which read: mixture to shut-off, throttle wide open, keep it turning, pray.

But J.K. West put both to work with no fuss or fire and taxied out, keeping straight with throttles and gentle nudges of brake. Many the time I sat in a B-26, itching to fly; now, four decades later, I would ride in one, the next best thing. This is the only still flying anywhere. I mean the original B-26, the Martin Marauder, not the Douglas A-26 which became the B-26 when the Martins were retired. Yes, the "Widow Maker," the "Coffin Without Handles" and all the rest said of it.

J.K. worked the throttles forward, we slowly accelerated then hammered along the concrete and rose into the summer evening sky. Gear up, flaps up, climb power; the 18-cylinder Pratts' horrendous roar precluded all but hand signals between us. While I had gone to south Texas to see the priceless restoration perform, my experience was a joy ride. I wondered about the young men—boys really—who long ago set out like this, but with bombs in the racks and a flak encircled Luftwaffe field at the other end of the line of their navigator's chart. Only they can talk of that.

The *Marauder* is proof that a deadly weapon can also be a thing of rare beauty. Its lines are exquisite. It's one of those airplanes that make a pilot long to grasp the wheel and ease forward on the power. Its background is fascinating, its record remarkable.

In early 1939 the Army solicited bids for a high speed medium bomber. Martin designer Peyton Magruder conceived a 56-foot cylindrical fuselage with 65 feet of tapered wing mounted on a (then) novel tricycle gear. A pair of Pratt & Whitney R-2800s with four-bladed Curtiss Electric props supplied thrust. The Army was impressed, ordered 201 off the drawing board (a first in Air Corps procurement) and increased the order to 1,131 before the prototype flew. Actually, there was no prototype as such. After flight testing was completed, the first off the line was delivered for duty. It featured a power-operated turret, another Army first.

The wing loading worked out at nearly 50 lbs/sq. ft. which raised eyebrows among the knowledgeable. Considering typical wing loadings of that day: DC-3—25.5; B-17-34.5; P-39-37.8; P-47-41.6, Magruder's brainchild would be one hot airplane requiring a long takeoff run and a sizzling ride down final. And its flying, not to mention its combat role, had to be taught to youngsters fresh out of cadets.

Despite training accidents and mechanical problems with nose gear and props, the first B-26s saw action in the Southwest Pacific less than four months after Pearl Harbor. While results were mixed, the Marauder proved able to absorb incredible punishment.

But the training picture was alarming. It was "one-a-day-in-Tampa-Bay" and sometimes more down at MacDill Field where crews were taught. Its small wing (little visible means of support) inspired the nickname, "Baltimore Whore." Worse, it became the "Martin Murderer." Lose an engine on takeoff and you crashed, they said. The word spread: the B-26 was a killer.

No less than four times the uproar over training accidents led to investigations, one chaired by Senator Harry Truman, another by Major General Spaatz. Suggestions that the entire B-26 program be terminated were offset by continued glowing reports from overseas. When expertly flown, the Marauder clearly was the match of any other bomber in dishing it out and taking it. Its crews swore by it; there was no interruption of Martin's assembly lines.

Magruder added six feet to the wing which reduced top speed but improved handling. (To no one's surprise, the Army capitalized on the extra lift by increasing gross weight until wing loading was 56 lbs./sq. ft.) The pre-operational training syllabus was drastically revised. In the initial rush to qualify crews, many AT-6 graduates were assigned to MacDill, an unrealistic upgrading. Later students were given intensive twin-engine indoctrination in such types as the Curtiss AT-9, a tricky little affair with miserable engine-out performance.

Major Vincent Burnett, a highly experienced Army pilot, made the rounds of B-26 bases to prove that the dreaded killer, when expertly handled, was in fact a splendid flying machine. His demonstration, conducted for the most part with one prop feathered, is vividly recalled by those who watched it. Enthusiastic reports continued to arrive from Army B-26 units in the Southwest Pacific and the Middle East, where the RAF put its Marauders to the test in the Battle of El Alamein.

The introduction of USAAF B-26s in Europe did not come off as well. On May 14, 1943, the first mission was flown by the 322nd Bomb Group. Twelve crews left Bury St. Edmonds to bomb a power station at Ijmuiden, Holland. Crossing the target at 150 feet they encountered withering ground fire; one ship was lost and another sustained 300 hits. Three days later 10 returned, flying on the deck, and again met a murderous flak and small arms reception. The group commander fell first, then another B-26 was hit and collided with a third. A fourth crashed and two more went down on the way out. Messerschmitts jumped the remainder; not one made it back to England.

The disastrous low level plan was abandoned. Thereafter the B-26 normally flew at the medium altitudes which proved to be its natural element. Its maneuverability, along with its speed and rugged constitution, made it a difficult target for ground gunners. Many limped home on one engine. One unit history shows one with its right engine gone, its flat firewall exposed; it made it back to friendly territory and a belly landing. When it was over and the figures were tallied, the combat loss rate of B-26s was lower than that of any other American bomber in Europe. It was the safest of all bombers to fly in combat.

The remarkable B-26 story is not unique in aviation annuals. One is reminded of the Sopwith *Camel* of World War I. Its rotary engine (stationary crankshaft, cylinders spinning with the prop) produced vicious torque which snapped many a hamfisted student into the ground. Experienced pilots employed the characteristic to deadly purpose with the result that Camels claimed more victories than any other fighter of that war. Camel pilots were regarded with a certain awe, as would be their sons who mastered the Marauder 25 years later. The B-29, P-47 and C-46 are among other World War II types that overcame serious initial problems.

The last of 4,115 B-26s built in Martin's plants at Baltimore and Omaha was rolled out with *Tail End Charlie "30"* painted on its nose. At the war's end, the Army quickly phased it out. Economy was given as a reason, the Martin costing about $193,000 per copy as compared with $142,000 for the B-25, which was continued in production. It appears more likely that this great airplane never outlived its early reputation and was grounded because of it, "probably by some fathead general who was afraid of it," a Marauder veteran surmised.

It was not considered worthwhile to fly the European-based Marauders back home. Most wound up in rows at Landsberg, Germany, awaiting the breakers. A few Stateside examples found their way into private hands and were converted to executive aircraft, one being B-26C-20-MO, USAAF #41-35071. Built in Omaha, it was accepted by the Army in April, 1943, and based in Florida, North Dakota and Texas. It was declared surplus in June, 1945. Lee Cameron, a United Air Lines pilot, flew it in the 1949 Bendix Race, but failed to finish due to a mechanical problem.

Its whereabouts for the next 27 years are somewhat a mystery. It underwent considerable modification, including installation of a drop-down passenger door, was owned by two companies, later registered in Mexico for whatever purpose and somewhere or other landed gear up. But for a happy event it would have become beer cans long ago—the Confederate Air Force heard of it. During runup soon after reaching CAF headquarters in Harlingen, Texas, a main wheel retracted, causing extensive damage. And that would have been that, except for the devotees who make up that remarkable group.

"Colonel" Jerry Harville (every CAF member is a colonel) was determined that it would fly again. It entered the shop in October, 1975, and emerged recently, nine years later. "If we'd had the money, we could have finished in two," says Jerry, who remained with the project throughout. To watch him fussing about the glistening Marauder, you'd think it was his alone which, in a way, it is.

A book could be done about that restoration. Martin, when asked for blueprints, replied that all its records were lost in a fire. Every foot of wiring was replaced, and much of the plumbing. The plexiglass nose posed a problem, eventually solved by making detailed photographs of the B-26 in the USAF Museum. The replica is correct down to the size and number of screws. There was one happy surprise: the powered turret in CAF's museum was the exact model used on the B-26C. Jerry figures overall investment at $350,000, "and that doesn't include donated labor," he says.

And where does that sort of money come from? A CAF squadron membership is $350, a sponsorship ten times that; larger sums are welcomed. Corporations help with money and equipment; additional income is earned from air shows staged all over the country, the annual autumn bash at headquarters being the largest. I counted more than 50 WW II types in flight at the same time then. "Yet, said Jerry, "there's so much more we want to do . . ."

That morning he and J. K. led an inspection tour. The ship now bears registration N5546N, Serial 2253. The overhauled R-2800s swing three-bladed Hamilton Standards which, says J. K., don't give nearly the performance of the original Curtiss Electrics (which are on the CAF wants list.) The name on the nose is that of the wife of a member who donated funds for the project. The cockpit is strictly World War II except for modern nav and radio equipment, a new setup of push-pull mag switches—and the control wheels which are from a Lockheed *Electra*. Aileron and rudder trim controls are located overhead. The bomb bay doors are sealed, the interior is stripped and replica .50 guns are stowed at all emplacements. From most outward appearance, the CAF Marauder might just have flown in from a base in East Anglia.

J. K. first flew a B-26 as a ferrying pilot 42 years ago. He's an FAA-designated check airman on multi-engine types. I size him up as one whose name you wouldn't easily get on your ticket. The CAF is fussy about who flies its rare birds, particularly this one-of-a-kind.

My ride was more than fun; it afforded dramatic evidence of aviation progress since World War II. By today's measures, the B-26 is not a hot airplane, though it obviously requires careful handling, even when flown minus payload. Its wing loadings have since been increased three times on airliners, more for some military types; approaches at 130 mph are ho-hum.

But in its day, a "long" runway meant 4,000 feet, often bordered with trees. The B-26 had no sophisticated flap system to convert its wing shape from high speed to high lift, no reverse thrust, no autofeathering, no dual mains with anti-skid brakes, no drag chute. It featured a novel electric propeller, the proper maintenance of which was not at first understood. As a result, it was prone to "run away" during takeoff, its blades twisting into flat (high drag) pitch; in the worst instance it refused to feather, leaving a pilot with an unflyable airplane bent on rolling itself inverted. His sole option: chop the power and put it down straight ahead. In its day it was one ball of fire, a handful for the experienced, a nightmare for the student.

Martin's spectacular bomber was a hint of the future. The day of "eyeballing the situation" was ending. It would eventually be realized that pilot judgement was often faulty, that high performance aircraft must be flown by the numbers. The techniques drilled into today's multi-engine pilot are based on lessons learned the hard way at MacDill Field—and overseas. I watched a Marauder race across Aden airdome on a windless 115-degree day. Only the nosewheel left the sand.

So far as the CAF can learn, there are but three Marauders surviving. One is in the USAF Museum near Dayton. The most famous of them all is in the National Air & Space Museum in Washington. That B-26B flew 202 missions, more than any other American bomber in Europe, dropped 190 tons of bombs during 725 combat flying hours and collected more than 1,000 hits, thus more than earning its name, "Flak Bait." The third is in the Confederate Air Force collection, displayed at Harlingen when not on tour. (I learned later that one or two more B-26s are slowly being restored on the West Coast.)

I came away with tremendous admiration for the Marauder, the gutsy young men who made an honest woman of her and the enthusiasts who preserve this remarkable piece of flying history.

# Time Warp

As we approached the deserted airplane, sparrows darted from the wheel wells and perched atop the rudder, hurling curses at the intruders. There was no other sign of life. But for the squatters' protests, the silence was absolute.

The big machine itself would never make another sound. From a distance it appeared intact, but when we saw the empty engine pods; their contents were nearby, not on proper engine stands, but lying unprotected on the concrete. You don't do that to magnificent JT3D turbines, but the voice of this giant was forever stilled. Wheels were missing; the exposed axles rested on greasy wood blocks. The big airliner was a shell, gutted, dead where it sat.

Terry, from his Piedmont 737 copilot seat, had spotted nine large jets on an abandoned World War II field. Like his dad, he regards such a discovery in much the way an archaeologist regards a chip of mastodonic ivory. On a crisp wintry afternoon we rolled out the Cessna and flew down for a close look.

The ragtag fleet was parked helter-skelter—720s, DC-8s, one 727 in faded Eastern colors, one 707, all being "parted out," their vitals transplanted to keep distant sisters going. Some of their excised flap sections, gear struts and cockpit gauges are back in service, perhaps on the far side of the world.

The 707, one of the long-range jobs, drew us like a magnet. We remembered that one in particular, each from personal acquaintance. The airline name was painted over but the thin dark stripe along the windows, the trademark and small flag were unmistakable. Air France. *Chateau* someplace-or-other had once bestowed individuality, but no longer; the name of the honored castle or estate was obliterated. Near the tail was *707,* followed by, *Intercontinental,* in red script.

"Just think of the hours it spent over the Atlantic. Think where it's been," said Terry, "Paris, Moscow, Hong Kong, Rio, London,

Tokyo, Calcutta, all those places."

"You're reading my mind," I said, seeing it glistening under the O'Hare floods, ready for its overnight dash to Orly.

"Think of when we flew these. It's a time warp."

He is suddenly aware of what I realized at his age about the transitory nature of our industry. You enter the game and there are the airplanes. You come to know them in that certain sense known only to pilots. The airman-aircraft relationship cannot be explained by words and pictures. It must be experienced. The years roll by for man and machine until a day comes when you realize they're all gone and have been replaced by entirely different types. In retrospect, the scene altered subtly, but rapidly. Snapshots taken at an airline terminal are in five years dated, in ten, curiosities.

The career airman witnesses the birth, life and decline of many airplanes, and is reminded of his own mortality. As a high schooler bitten by the flying bug I watched the first DC-3 schedule touch the grass at Bowman Field in Louisville; that made the front page. Then one of the original B-17s landed; that went unheralded and we boys were kept away. The war produced so many famous machines—the P-51, P-38, B-26, Wildcat, B-24, Spitfire, Lancaster—the list is long. They flew by the thousands, became legends, then all but vanished. A few still fly, a few are in museums, some are extinct. In the Egyptian desert I saw long rows of Beaufighters, Marylands and Baltimores; I believe one Beaufighter survives in a museum.

I remember walking through our first Convair 340. Brown paper was taped over the carpet and plastic covered the seats. Its cabin exuded the nice smell of a show room car. The first DC-7C enthralled us. Our boss said it was a hint of things to come, and indeed it was. The Electra was our introduction to turbines. We studied the lean cowlings and enormous props, listened to its ominous deep hum and wondered. We came to know them and other types very well. In turn, each was the pride of the fleet, then junior equipment working milk runs and finally it disappeared and was scarcely missed. Out of sight, out of mind.

An ex-KLM DC-7C, after a brief time with a travel club, wound up at Greater Southwest Airport which itself was abandoned when enormous DFW was built. Shorn of engines and, like the Air France jet, taken over by birds, it slept in the weeds until its owners were told to clear it away. Terry and I asked for its control wheels. The owners said, "How about the airplane? Move it within 60 days and it's yours, all of it." At least the skipper's wheel from *Red Sea* did not go for scrap; it's mounted in my den.

Our first 707 was delivered with much fanfare. It was not simply another step forward. The National Society of Professional Engineers named it one of the 10 engineering achievements of the past half century. The loose designation "707" covered a range of engine/airframe combinations, all seemingly identical to the untrained eye. The 720 was to all purposes a medium-range 707; its different number, so the story goes, was demanded by a major carrier late in ordering jets. It wanted to introduce a "new" Boeing and intimate it was an advancement, which it wasn't.

We flew six versions of the basic 707 design. Despite significant handling differences, one rating was good for all. Compared with its sisters, the 720-027 we bought was grossly underpowered. A huge blast of thrust was needed to move away from the gate. "It won't taxi over a wet cigarette butt," grumbled one old-timer. "It won't get out of its own way," said another. Departures at Mexico City were downright frightening. When the official responsible for its purchase retired, one 720 driver suggested giving him a Mark V with a Falcon engine. But, once under way, the 720 with "little" engines would climb to 41,000, given time, and was easy to land. Our ex-Qantas 707-138Bs had short fuselages, big engines and tanks. On domestic runs they'd inch up to Mach .86 unless you pulled thrust way back, which we never did in those cheap fuel days. The competition ate our smoke.

The 707-327C, the "Intercontinental" with big cowl doors and all the latest gadgets, was in all ways magnificent; no other word will do. That marvel was assigned to the Texas—Hawaii scheduled owned by the graybreads. Then we were contracted by the military to fly the Pacific. Surprisingly, I got that, and why so many of my seniors passed it up mystified me. So, 27 years after soloing, I was flying left chair in the biggest and best on international routes, no small thrill for an old Georgia boy.

Those hours are remembered in terms of hairy maximum gross load takeoffs, unbelievable expanses of blue sea, fuel gauges that monopolized attention, confusing navigation, coral islands, tiresome deadheading in coach seats, plush hotels, fleabags, poor radio communications, sunrises right off calendars and grinding fatigue. It was a gypsy life. You were never completely sure where you were or what time it was and you always craved another night's sleep. I wouldn't have missed a minute of it.

I still have a cassette tape of a midnight departure from Honolulu in a 707-320C at max gross takeoff weight—336,000 pounds—made with a little Sony recorder I picked up in Japan. I just played it back. I'd almost forgotten how those big P&W JT3s sang at full thrust. I could sense again the heavy feel of the Boeing lifting into its slow sweeping turn away from the city and out into the total darkness off shore, its initial shuddering ceasing as gear doors closed and flaps retracted. Four minutes after brake release I hear myself call for climb power. Next stop—Clark Air Base in the Philippines where it would still be night when we found it 10 hours later.

The moldering Air France hulk brought it all back, and I was no better or worse off for it. Airplanes you once knew well are reminders of whatever they did for you. Or to you. Each leaves its mark. In 1944 a friend landed in England after 30 missions. When we met years later, he said he had not been in an airplane since. The mere thought of flying still made him sweat. "If I had to sit in that cockpit again, I think I would be physically ill," he said. Had he seen the remains of a B-17 rusting in the weeds, he would have gone the other way.

It all depends.

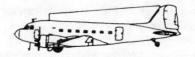

# The Grand Old Lady

My first DC-3 hours were disappointing. I had long admired Mr. Douglas' huge (it was then) pride and joy from behind the fence and decided that piloting it was the world's finest job. But staid transport flying would come later; first, there were wild oats to sow. The Hurricane and P-40 enthralled me. I spent hours in their cockpits awaiting my chance. Instead, our group was sent to the steaming west African coast to copilot C-47s (militarized DC-3s), the last thing we wanted.

In 1942, Pan Am was laying out trans-African routes for the Army. Airline captains were recruited to get things going and to train young Army pilots. They wore military issue suntans with distinctive insignia, an ensemble we dubbed the "lion tamer's suit"—beyond their hearing.

A balding TWA veteran with bifocals took me in hand; he was old enough to be my dad. I took the green leather right seat and looked back at the prop, big R-1830 radial engine and long tapering wing. We sat ridiculously high. More disturbing was the confusion of gauges and controls inside, the keeping track of which was certainly beyond the ability of ordinary humans.

The old man lit a cigar. "You got any heavy time?"

"No, sir. Single engine. AT-6s."

"All right. Keep your eyes open, ask questions—and call me Fred."

He came alive, flipped switches, moved levers, adjusted this and that in a preflight drill lasting half a minute. Then he said, "Clear on your side?" I nodded. The big Pratt shuddered, belched smoke and fired. I looked back at the steel blades slicing past my seat. He brought his side to life, kicked off the brakes and away we waddled to a chorus of internal creaks and groans, the instrument panel dancing on its rubber mounts, all of which he accepted as normal, except for one piercing screech which he silenced by yanking a long handle beside my seat. There was a sloppy, loose-jointed feel to everything, as if the airplane was falling apart.

He ran them up together, exercised the props, checked carb heat and mags then took position, reaching under the pedestal for something. "Tail wheel lock," he said. "If your captain forgets, remind him." He worked manifold pressures up to 46 inches and off we lumbered, slowly gaining speed. The tail rose, affording a splendid view of tall trees growing taller. I glanced at him. He was puffing away and glancing out the side window like a bored Sunday driver, but we tracked down the runway as if on rails.

He reached down for something on the floor, then lifted a long lever. We were in fact airborne with the gear coming up and skimming across the jungle in a shallow climb. The altimeters crept through 200 feet. Above the din he yelled, "It won't climb like this with a load." Food for thought.

We struggled up to 5,000 feet where he demonstrated turns, power management during climb and descent and stalls clean and dirty. Control response obviously was sluggish but there was nothing half-hearted about the way it dropped a wing in certain stalls. The maintain-flying-speed point was well made.

"You've got it," he said. I took the wheel and tried a turn. Lean into it and wait. We slowly banked and the nose sagged. The elevators were responsive but required effort to move. The ailerons were rubbery, as if the linkage included springs. After an hour of watching me slop around in the hot choppy air, Fred took us home. Landing was a complex procedure involving continuous fiddling with power, trim and flaps. We arrived over the fence at 85 and touched down ever so lightly with a distant squeal of tires. He could fly the monster. Sweat-soaked (you always were over there, day or night), we climbed out.

"Well, what do you think?" he asked.

I was extremely disappointed, a natural reaction considering my meager experience and naive notions, but I pretended eagerness. Training was completed the next day, that is to say I learned to trail the cowl flaps, extend gear and flaps and hold it straight and level. And recite what no DC-3 pilot will ever forget, "Gear down, locked, green lights, pressure, I got a wheel," to which the pilot flying would respond, "I got a wheel." By the definition of the airline types who ran that show, I was a qualified copilot. That was the day of, "Gear up, you've got it, gear down, I've got it." We neophytes were "commissioned ballast."

And away we went across the sand and rock and dense forests that make central Africa both miserable and magnificent, struggling off rough gravel strips with too many tons in back to plodding through sandstorms that reduced engine life to 200 hours and incredible torrents that drowned them both. A good day was 10 hours of wrestling through stifling chop. Yet, compared with what the C-47 crews were doing on the treacherous Hump, our life was easy.

I quickly came to admire this amazing "airliner" which lifted almost any burden strapped to its back and hauled it through appalling weather to wherever it was needed. It groaned and creaked, it ran rough, it ran hot, it leaked, it staggered into flight, it wallowed along flexing its wings in a horrifying manner, it settled back to earth with an almost audible sigh of relief, yet it failed few of the thousands of pilots who staked everything on it. Its success at tasks for which it was never intended surpassed the record of some World War II aircraft doing what they were designed to do.

It was damned good training. Our civilian skippers found African flying a far cry from domestic schedules and kept us busy; we learned fast. Once you got its feel—which came quickly—the C-47 was fun to fly. It was a most forgiving airplane if you gave it your best effort. Carelessness or inattention drew sharp reminders that she was, as two admiring biographers called her, a Grand Old Lady who brooked few liberties. Clumsy handling at the flare could produce a bone-jarring arrival followed by a determined attempt to veer. The old girl could be ground looped, or stood on her nose if over-braked. Touch downs in gusty crosswinds required the complete attention of an experienced driver. On occasion it was a handful of flying machine.

Postwar DC-3 flying was white collar work. Fill out the flight plan and climb aboard a nice clean airplane filled with nice clean people. Refrigerated air was pumped in until time to go. No more did we sip warm grapefruit juice filched from the cargo but cokes on ice delivered by a sweet young thing. Maximum takeoff weight was a mere 25,000 lbs. as compared to the Army's 27,500 (which was routinely exceeded. On long ferry hops, 30,000 was not uncommon.)

Premium schedules had been taken over by DC-4s and -6s. We new hires worked the short hauls, flying from one smooth runway to another, almost always VFR so as to turn off the radios which radiated heat like ovens. Airways clearances were obtained through company stations on high frequencies; fields with towers were worked on 278 and 396 kilocycles when close in, fine tuning with the "coffee grinder" just below the mag switches. Beneath them, suspended on bungee cords, was the compass which was unreadable in rough air. We rarely cruised above 8,000 feet.

The low freq range remained the primary airway and approach aid out in the boondocks. Expertly executing a range approach to 400 feet was an art. A large ADF was mounted behind the throttles, face up. Like the range, it worked best when needed least. And there was the light line, a help on clear nights when you didn't need help. These vestiges of prewar flying were soon gone, however. Every field got a VOR, the larger ones an ILS and we began calling towers by thumbing in 118.7. Range stations and airway beacons were dismantled. With new radios installed, the DC-3 trudged on, in most respects unchanged.

Our fleet was a hodge podge of prewar models, half of which had seen military duty, surplus C-47s and others picked up here and there. There was little attempt at cockpit standardization. If one came with two ADFs or an autopilot, they were left in place. All had Pratt & Whitney R-1830 14-cylinder radials with Hamilton Standard props. There was little difference between them. One had experimental coupled autopilot/throttle gear installed. It would fly the ILS and control airspeed almost as smoothly as the sophisticated equipment now in vogue. Tom Braniff, our boss, turned it into an executive ship and thereafter it was "Uncle Tom's Cabin."

The Three was billed as a three-mile-a-minute airplane and if mileage was divided by three, you'd usually have the destination in sight when the time ran out. Realistic schedules were figured at 165 to 170 plus :05 on the ground—three from gate to takeoff, two from landing to shut down, and you could make that in those light traffic days. In freakish winds, groundspeed could reach 250—or sag to 80. Rule of thumb fuel consumption—90 gallons an hour. The tanks held 820 gallons.

Taxying required special skill. The true artist navigated with throttles and rudder; braking, except on tight turns, drew scowls from the left seat. "Free, rich, trim, trail and locked," the pre-takeoff litany for checking controls-mixtures-tabs-cowl flaps-tail wheel, was occasionally chanted without verification. An unlocked tail wheel produced violent shuddering during roll out, after which we'd remain in the cockpit until passengers had deplaned.

You didn't watch the DC-3 fly itself, jet age fashion. It had to be flown every mile of the way. You were a pilot, not a "flight manager." Don't misunderstand. No one who flew the DC-3 in thunderstorm weather or in freezing rain or fought to keep it on an icy runway longs to repeat any of it. Nostalgia is for layover talk. But, most of the time, it was good work; at times it was downright soul satisfying. I remember padding along at 5,000 feet on a smooth evening, the trials of a long day forgotten, watching familiar landmarks appear and slowly slip beneath the nose, those superb 1830s thundering, fresh coffee in hand, all needles in the green, the lights of home a dim glow on the horizon. There were worse ways to earn $250 a month.

Perhaps it was that I flew the Three at an impressionable age, or because it was a most impressive airplane, that I recall more about it than about types flown for longer periods much later. Twenty-five years after my last trip I sat in a feeder DC-3, automatically taking the right seat. Without conscious thought, I released the seat latch and rolled forward, then swung the arm rest around, again without reminding myself. On the right were the can-like cowl flap controls, on the left the flap position indicator, down there the knob regulating air flow, on the floor the gear latch and little compartment with fire bottle handles. I knew exactly where to look. It was as if I'd flown it yesterday—and I wondered if I still could. From the right seat, that is, where I logged most of those memorable hours.

You know, I think I could even now, all these years later, but I'd want a good man in the left seat to keep an eye on things until we learned if the old girl remembered me.

# Mean Storms Ahead

During my last year on the line, I talked with friends already retired. How were they faring? What was life like on the outside of the fence where we all started?

Almost all deplored the way the job had gone downhill since they quit. They were quite sure the challenge and enthusiasm they remembered had been erased by technology and regimentation. "Today you sit there with the manual in one hand and the autopilot switch in the other and a radar man telling you what heading to hold and how fast to fly—I'm glad I'm out of it," said one about what had happened "since they took my wings away."

"It's just another job," said another, "nothing like when you and I flew DC-3s to Chicago. Remember? Nine stops. Thunderstorm Alley. That was something." You'd think he wanted to do it all over again. Were he able to arrange it, he'd need another copilot.

Curiously, many career pilots who readily accepted change as necessary while on the line conclude that all change has been for the worse since they dropped out of the picture. I didn't see it that way then and I don't now. I vowed to "stay current," to keep up with the changing skill and, should I be taken with downbeat notions, to keep them to myself. Retired pilots should keep quiet if they can't say good things.

I envy today's skipper in his "glass cockpit." He can program his aircraft to fly itself from lift off to roll out—climb, enroute navigation, holding, approaches, go-arounds, landings, braking—and the black boxes do a smoother and more precise job in most respects than he can. Our 747-200s and -SPs provided a hint of things to come with their Inertial Navigation System, auto-throttles, coupled autopilots and automatic brakes. The uncanny precision with which that monster slid down the ILS and flared was something else, but it never made me feel less essential to the process.

I would have welcomed today's aids while wrestling a sluggish old Boeing 720 around a race track pattern in winter chop, at the same time figuring how long we could hold. The new aids free a pilot to do what he's there for—to think, manage, plan ahead. Call him more manager than pilot, he must still learn to do it without the computers, and reprove himself every six months thereafter.

From what I read, heads-up-display is next—flight data projected onto glass dead ahead through which the runway appears at break out—or at touch down, for an unfavorable surface wind is about the only factor ruling out a shot at arrival. The suggestion that technology is reducing crews to mindless button-pushers is self delusion on the part of those who wish it were so.

While I envy today's pilot his new technology, I feel for him otherwise. To the considerable mental stress inherent in his work have been added horrifying personal dreads.

A number of global economic and political factors have produced the merger/takeover mania that is turning American business inside out. One economist dubs the process, "creative destruction." Capitalism is razing old structures to build new ones, he says. By whatever name, its effect are mind-boggling. Just prior to my retirement the real meaning of "creative destruction" was revealed to the good people of our company. Under the "open skies" rules of deregulation, we watched our line expand at a rate never before seen in the industry. Sixty days after I was retired, the card castle collapsed. Few of us dreamed it would come to that.

It was a shock to us, a surprise to everyone else; the general feeling was that we had asked for it. Outsiders had all the reasons for our failure—and all the reasons it couldn't happen to them. In retrospect, none of us comprehended "creative destruction," of which airline deregulation is but an element. We were so sure it couldn't happen to us we didn't worry; today's pilot is sure it can happen to him. He's worried.

He now knows his line could go under. Turn out the lights, lock the door and that's that. Try not thinking about that. Being a "grandfather line" is no protection, nor are four decades of success. Look at what happened to Frontier. A merger is no assurance of improvement as witness the Pan Am—National union. The sale of Pan Am's lucrative Pacific division to United is an incredible development to anyone familiar with airline history. Consider huge TWA's almost comic dilemma, and the Eastern mess. Size is no protection. Mighty United's claim that its shuffling of investments in hotels and pension funds has made it immune from takeover reads more like an effort to convince itself than to discourage raiders.

Had anyone 20 years ago predicted that one shrewd investor

could gain control of one of the "Big Four" by 1985, he would have embarrassed his listeners. Once in charge, a raider can do as he pleases with an operation built during a half century of hard work—and to the people who run it. On the one hand, he may prove a better manager than the old team which warned he was not "fit," (which would hardly be an astounding achievement in some cases).

On the other hand, he may regard his acquisition as a money machine to be drained of the last dollar by trimming routes, selling aircraft and borrowing against the resulting "streamlined" operation. If it fails (indeed, bankruptcy may be induced), he can tear up employee agreements, ignore debts and start up a completely new airline on whatever terms he chooses.

Whether the corporate raider wears a white hat or black, he's certainly from a different mold than a Jack Frye, Tom Braniff, Pat Patterson or Eddie Rickenbacker. One wonders if the wizard clever enough to seize control of an enterprise built over 50 years has what it took its founders to create it in the first place. Only history can judge the "creative destruction" that made him possible. Perhaps, as some economists maintain, the new breed of leaders are what were needed to modernize an industry that became stagnant. We shall see. Meanwhile, the convulsions continue and no one can say what shape the industry will have assumed when the dust clears.

Meanwhile, many a pilot is worried. He wonders what cockpit seat he will warm a year from now—that is, if he still has a job at all. Can his line survive another fuel crunch or another recession, much less the increasing competition of new discount carriers? What positions, flying or otherwise, is a 45-year-old professional airman qualified to fill? What's happening to his pension fund? Had we on my airline the complete picture we would have been as concerned. But we were naive. We thought it would all work out.

As a sidelight, those of us already retired when our line failed were not home free. No indeed. There were serious—and federally approved, please note—shortages to all pension funds, the pilots' included. We were assured that enough assets were available to bring all funds up to date in the unlikely event of bankruptcy. We were misled to put it politely, in fact, many retirees will draw less that half the promised amounts for the rest of their lives. All of which became common knowledge after we went down the tubes, giving today's 55-year-old another bleak prospect to consider.

Worst of all, there are certain dismal situations today requiring a pilot to share his cockpit with another crewman who, because of inter-labor disputes involving strikes and pay scales, thoroughly despises him. At least, we didn't have any of that. A pilot strapping in with 275 souls in back is entitled to the cordial and respectful cockpit atmosphere I remember. And it is grossly unfair to load him with worries that have nothing whatsoever to do with the difficult work at hand. Isn't it interesting that, in all the reporting of the present turmoil in the professional airman's world, there is rarely ever any mention of pilot attitude as it affects safety?

I feel for today's airline pilot and I wish him well.

# The Big One

"Come see for yourself," said Tom Cole, leading the way down the tunnel and through the oversized doorway. Even having seen the pictures, I was not prepared for a cabin 185 feet long and 20 feet wide. Four-bedroom homes are built on less square feet. You had walked onto other large airplanes but you went *into* this one, as when boarding a ship. As we strolled the aisles Cole recited dizzying numbers—374 fares, three galleys, 13 blue rooms, 15 flight attendants, 47,210 gallons of fuel, 174,000 lbs. of thrust, 710,000 lbs. max gross for takeoff. "Fill the seats, top the tanks and load as much freight as the payload of the largest 707," he said.

That cabin never flew, being a mock-up in Seattle. "May we see the real thing?" I asked. Tom, typical of Boeing's enthusiastic PR team, sent us to Everett. There, inside the world's largest building, was the world's largest airliner—the 747. The first one. It would not emerge until seven months later or fly until four months after that. But it was complete, standing on 18 wheels with the immense turbines in place—and what an awesome sight to one introduced to flying by a 14-passenger DC-2. That many would sit in the "upper deck lounge" of this monster, reached by a spiral staircase, no less. I stared unbelieving, like a hayseed gawking at the Empire State Building. The whole proposal was unbelievable—but there it was, glistening under a thousand lights, incredibly real.

Of course, there was no chance I'd occupy that lofty cockpit. I envied those who would. Then, miraculously, our airline ordered one and posted an invitation to bid: "Wanted: seven crews; equipment—B747." The left seat was seized by the top seven graybeards (who were under 59; older skippers remained on 707s at 747 pay, this costing less than jumbo training). The copilot slots went to 707 captains while 727 captains took the flight engineer's panel, all taking pay cuts in the move. That captains willingly downgraded to the right seat, much less the engineer's, says it all about the 747's appeal. There was my name in the awards—sixth among the copilots.

We went to United's school in Denver for lectures and simulator, then to Los Angeles for flight training in UAL ships. Our single 747, N601BN, was the 100th off the line. It was painted bright orange and arrived amid much fanfare, and dubbed "The Great Pumpkin" by one reporter. That stuck, but to us it was "Fat Al."

We scheduled a round trip between Dallas and Honolulu every day, seven days a week. That's 15 hours aloft covering 7,746 statute miles. You'll never do it, said industry experts; eight to 10 hours was considered maximum for a long distance airliner. With Fat Al we rewrote the book, shuttling out and back with streetcar regularity, surprising ourselves as much as anyone else.

At four-and-a-half years of age, 601 had spent 57% of its life in flight while its sisters averaged 35%. Although the 100th 747 built, it led its nearest competitor by 90 days in the air. Never before had an aircraft racked up time so rapidly, nor has that record been matched since. It was good being part of that. Incidentally—and crucially—our Hawaii run earned profits from the first.

All of which said good things about Boeing and Pratt & Whitney. The airframe represented a stupendous engineering achievement. It was all new, not an enlarged 707. Its monstrous JT9D turbofans were new technology engines with no military background as had been the case with most powerplants previously hung on airliners. Reliable and trouble-free, it took a bit of getting used to. (Care was required during start up and taxying; it was prone to over-temp, particularly with a wind on the tail. The copilot kept a close eye on EGT gauges and a hand on the start levers until takeoff. And, if thrust levers were retarded to idle at high altitude, as when starting descent, one or more of the fires might go out).

Rumors about problems were rampant. "The 747 is in deep trouble," said one aviation writer who should have known better. Such comment amused us. In fact, the big Boeing with its novel engines was phased into service with less fuss than perhaps any previous airliner. Ours served us well and inspired crew confidence. Passengers loved it. A Honolulu tower man, knowing we flew a multi-colored fleet elsewhere, asked, "Braniff, are all your 747s orange?" to which we replied, "Affirmative."

Any pilot with 707 or similar experience easily learned it. Sitting way, way up there was startling at first but posed no lasting problem. In a few hours the view became completely "right" (and being able to look down on those DC-10 and L-1011 mini-jumbos stroked the ego).

The economics of jumbo operation were thought-provoking to say the least. A full house 747 could make you rich; empty, it would quickly drown you in red ink. Sagging load factors shortly after their introduction led to a number being stored in the western desert where, at least, they weren't burning 27,000 pounds of fuel an hour.

Initially, there were ground handling problems. Our HNL people were hard pressed to clean, restock, fuel and load the big airplane in two hours, but they pulled it off on time almost every day. More than once inbound Flight 501 arrived 30 minutes late, yet returning Flight 502 blocked out on the dot. That reflected maximum effort.

After six months I went back to the left seat of the 707, never dreaming I'd fly Fat Al again. I'd had a taste of the big time I would never forget. But eight years altered the picture to the extent that I flew good old 601 to Hawaii again, this time from the left seat. Not surprisingly, it performed as well as when spanking new, though the well worn cockpit was evidence of its hard life. By then we had several more, including a magnificent 747-200 with all sorts of new gadgets, plus some "little" SPs, real hot rods by comparison. The shortened SP got up and went. We flew them to Europe, South America and the Far East. London, Frankfurt, Brussels, Paris, Santiago, Hong Kong, Seoul, Guam, Anchorage—those were memorable trips in a wonderful airplane. I remember them often.

Look what's happened since: 620 747s have been built and Boeing has orders in hand for 50 more; so far, 70 airlines now have them (1986). As many as 69 passengers (a typical Electra load) can now be seated on the extended upper deck of the latest 747-300. With all-economy seating, a total of 550 fares can be accommodated. The 747-400 with 12 feet more wing plus six-foot winglets will fly in 1988. That should be a jewel.

Prices have soared in the meantime. Whereas the first -100s brought about $24 million, today's -200 goes for $98 million, the -300 for $115 million. The -400 is available (if you sign up now) at roughly $125 million. A lot of money. A lot of airplane.

Thinking back on this big airplane's remarkable story, three things come to mind. Of all the big numbers, its weights impress me most. I learned to fly in an RCAF Fleet biplane; the Canadians had 600 of them in World War II. The 747-100 I flew as copilot weighed, when at max gross, as much as all of them—plus nine AT-6 Harvards. The new −400's ramp weight will be 850,000 pounds. That's more than the weight of the Union Pacific's 4-8-8-4 "Big Boy," the largest steam locomotive ever built—39 *tons* more, that is. Impressive.

Secondly, children born when I was shown that cabin mock-up are now 18. They cannot remember a time without 350-ton passenger airliners, Mach 2 warplanes and space travel. Can they possibly witness the same astounding progress? I think I was born at exactly the right time.

Finally, the 747 is stamped, ''Made in U.S.A.'' I'm proud of that.

# Weeding Out

$M$oving. No one dreads it more than a collector. If you saw these quarters you might conclude I'm a pack rat, defined as, "a person who collects, saves or hoards useless small items." I deny that. My items are useful—to me, at least—and, unfortunately, they are not small. They took years to accumulate and they occupy much space. Now the whole collection must be dismantled and packed again, not to mention unpacked and set up. Collecting can be a pain in the neck.

There's one thing about moving: it's a good time to weed out, get rid of things that don't matter. I did some of that prior to moving here yet the van grossed out a ton heavier than estimated. This time I've got to be unemotional, even ruthless.

Where to start? I'll try upstairs where my books covering aviation history through the end of World War I fill old Globe-Wernicke book cases with glass doors. About 500 titles, painstakingly acquired over 40 years. You wouldn't believe how long I waited for some of these. Most of the standard works are here, *Winged Warfare; Fighting the Flying Circus; Outwitting the Hun; Recollections of An Airman; Up and At 'Em,* plus some rarities—*Down the Flare Path; Flying Minnows, The Clouds Remember*—and several privately printed memoirs, sad letters from France usually ending with condolences from the commanding officer.

Oh yes, here's a mint copy of *King of Air Fighters,* Ira Jones' much sought after biography of Mickey Mannock, the legendary RAF ace. Jones, with 40 victories confirmed, should have written his own story. This copy is "signed by the author," a catalogue phrase to make a collector's mouth water. At least 80 of these books are autographed, in fact. I paid too much for most at the time, but the lot would fetch at auction (as Christie's says) four times or more my investment, not that profits cloud the judgment of a dedicated bibliophile.

Weeding out this batch would be like culling coins from a pile of Krugerrands. There's no question about the Globe-Wernickes; my grandfather bought them in 1920. And they wouldn't look right half empty, would they? What about all these pictures? Here's a photo of Armstrong, Aldrin and Collins, framed with their signatures. Can't let that go. And an original painting of a Fairchild 24 we once owned, done by Bob Carlin, the gifted artist and a friend of long standing. The 24 was a lovely old bird. Keep that.

This numbered print of Doolittle's B-25 is signed by the general himself. More prints—Hartmann's 109, Coppens' Hanriot, Scott's P-40, Sakai's Zero, two of Boyington's Corsairs—each signed by the artist and the celebrity depicted. All keepers. Here's one I'd forgotten: a 727 I used to fly, signed by Jack Steiner, the Boeing engineer who masterminded its creation. This blown-up snapshot of an orange 747 tucking up its 18 wheels could go except that I was in the left seat at that instant. It's valueless to anyone else.

The den—that's where the bulk of it is. Get the wall stuff first. "Join the Air Service and Serve in France—DO IT NOW." World War I recruiting poster. That should go in the same room with the WW I books in the new place. This original of an RCAF Harvard rolling above a Fleet Finch is special. Both aircraft bear the numbers of Canadian trainers I flew. Tells a story, doesn't it? And this DC-7C in our line's colors. N5906. I logged a few hours in that one. Get back to the art work later.

As for these mounted sticks and wheels—oh my, but were they hard to find. That skinny one is from a DC-3. This with the pistol grips is from an Electra. That's from a B-17. And this is a P-51 stick. There's a good place in the new house for all 12 of these. Is it silly to cherish such relics?

Look at these cluttered shelves. What's this? An ash tray made from a Spitfire piston with the RAF crest engraved. Could you throw that out? These stone bookends were cut from rubble left when the House of Commons was bombed. The Lindbergh bookends and Wiley Post-Will Rogers lamp go way back. Sure, the lamp works. This plate came from Wake Island, this one from Panama, the wood figure from Bangkok. A hundred souvenirs of places visited, all meaningless to anyone else. A little red London bus, brass Brandenburg Gate, serpentine lighthouse from Land's End, scrap of coral from the Guam invasion beach, figurine from Seoul—they remind me, and only me. Someday all will be tossed out, but someone else will do it.

This wood propeller is unique. Beautifully crafted, isn't it? It was carved from wood from the wreckage of a Zeppelin brought down in England in 1916 and given to my father; he knew I'd value it.

What's in this box? My helmet from training days. Queer looking thing. Still fits. RAF "hooks" (sergeant stripes), uniform buttons (shine them until they blinded like diamonds, or forget the weekend pass), Army patches, wings, airline service pins for five years, 10, 25, 30. Why hoard these trinkets? Papers—orders, log sheets, reports, letters—big stack, too much to go through now.

See this old pocket watch? It's a Waltham. Still keeps as good time as when Paul Braniff carried it in the lumbering Stinson with which he started an airline. He pledged it against a load of gas at Tulsa and never redeemed it. Now I ask you! Look at this scroll attesting to loyal service, signed by General H. H. Arnold. Actually, he didn't sign any of the many thousands mailed to vets. That sheet and two bits would buy a cup of coffee in 1946 but I value it as though old Hap had brought it to the door. Ought to get it framed. Wonder if my RAF discharge is somewhere in this pile?

These file cases are a real mess. Eight deep drawers crammed with what? Photos, brochures, newspaper clippings, letters—look, a 1950 Colonial Air Lines timetable, probably from that trip to Bermuda. Should be worth something now. Letters from old friends, some of whom I've known for 40 years yet never met. Book collecting puts you in touch with fine people—authors, artists, editors, publishers, readers. It is a world unto itself, a good place to spend time, an easy way to spend money.

This bundle came from readers of my magazine articles and what thoughtful individuals they were to take time to say what they thought of what I wrote. Some were less than flattering, to put it mildly, but their comment was valuable all the same as I told each and every one. Writing is lonely work, as frustrating and fatiguing as a long flight through bad weather. The flight at least includes the reward of arrival, the satisfaction of knowing you did most of it right. No way I'll part with that reader mail.

Now the long shelves of since-World War I books. *Atlantic Highway,* transocean travel from windjammers to jets in 239 pages. Real potboiler. Not bad illustrations, though. Worth having just for those. *Under My Wings,* autobiography of a Pan Am pilot. Two copies; get rid of one. And two copies of *Flight Deck* and *Vision.* Keep one each. Wonder why these old magazines were saved? Yes, I remember; here's that feature on GB racers; the rest must also have worthwhile reference materials. Go through them later.

Lot of good stuff here, too. Full run of Jane's. Everything you want to know about 75 years of aircraft. A letter hand written by Fred Jane is pasted inside the first (1909) edition. John Taylor, the present editor, tells me there may be no more than 25 full sets anywhere in private hands. Many top writers have favored me with autographed editions.

Time for a break. Fix coffee, read the mail. Here's *The Log,* the well-done journal of the British Airline Pilots Association. Always has good book reviews. Look at this—*Brief Glory, The Life of Arthur Rhys-Davids.* Well! That name fairly leaps from print at anyone who has read about the first air war. What a scrapper that fellow was, what a tragedy his fall at age 20. He is mentioned in numerous accounts, but only in passing. Now, at last, his full story. The reviewer is enthralled. Order it today—and might as well get those other titles on the list I was saving for Christmas. I'll have another list by then.

Come to think on it, what's the mad rush to do any of this? Might discard something really valuable. Keep it all. Get back to it at the new house when the dust settles.

# A Flight Into History

A professional pilot is by nature forward-looking. A critical departure from a marginal runway at maximum gross weight is intensely interesting at the moment but is no sooner completed than forgotten. The probabilities—and possibilities—involved in climb, cruise, descent and landing now demand his attention.

This ingrained thought pattern is reflected in the average airman's view of aviation. He cares about the future and, aside from personal experience, has scant interest in the past. Few aviation histories have been penned by pilots, or read by them. The publisher of air books who counts on pilots to buy them is in for a surprise.

I am in the minority with an interest in history and wish I had concentrated on it instead of math and science, for which I had no flair. But writers of the 1930s said piloting was a technical pursuit; bone up on trig, physics and chemistry, they warned, or you'd never make it. Unwittingly they wrote pure bunk; they weren't pilots. An individual who can't balance his check book or wire a doorbell can learn to fly an F-16 or command a jumbo as quickly as a science major. In fact, he often makes the better pilot, being less prone to preoccupation with technical specifics.

Recently we went exploring historic sites in our adopted state—by air. The coast of North Carolina is a series of narrow sand reefs called the Outer Banks. It protrudes into the Atlantic at points well known to seamen—Cape Fear, Cape Lookout and Cape Hatteras. By car it's a dull drive with few glimpses of the sea beyond the dunes. By air it's a wonderful excursion into history—providing you know its history to begin with.

That coast is bordered by restricted and warning areas. It is wise to study the Sectionals and seek local advice before going. (A private twin wandered into the area unannounced and collided with an intercepting fighter. It fell into the sea with seven aboard.) We landed at Kinston and talked with an instructor who made useful suggestions.

The Cherry Point Marine base controller heard our tour proposal then vectored us through her area, clearing a departing "Fox Four" to maintain 7,000 until past us (we never saw him), and turned us loose at the shore with a new transponder squawk and advisory frequency to monitor. We descended to 1,000 feet and headed northeast, just off the beach and beyond the restricted area.

Some 600 vessels are known to have foundered off the Banks, earning it the reputation, "graveyard of the Atlantic." Historians say the total exceeds 1,000. The 300-mile stretch from Currituck Beach to Cape Fear drew sailors like a magnet. Why? The answer is in your library. Charts pinpointing wreckages are locally available.

Ocracoke is a neat little fishing village with a 3,000-foot runway, well maintained as are all North Carolina fields I've seen. Its nondirectional radio beacon (Pamlico, 404 kc.) is strong (being most often used by ships?) A Piper Warrior II parked beside us. A young man got out, unfolded a bicycle and pedalled off to town, explaining it as his weekend relaxation. And where was his girlfriend? He said he couldn't afford one and aircraft rental charges. At his age I would have gone for flying, too.

Cape Hatteras is 25 miles further up the coast. We circled the famous lighthouse and landed at nearby Billy Mitchell field, the site from which the outspoken general demonstrated that "dreadnaught" was no longer apt for battleship. Some brushing up on that incredible event brings the place into focus. On the ramp were several aircraft, their owners having flown in for a day on the beach.

We gazed at the sparkling sea, its docile surf lightly caressing the sand, and tried to imagine its savage fury in a winter storm. I'd like to go back then, but not in the 172. We continued northeast toward the main points of interest, Kitty Hawk and Roanoke Island.

By the early 1500s, Spaniards had established settlements in the south. British officials urged Queen Elizabeth to challenge the threat of total Spanish domination of the New World by seizing part of it in her name. Seven vessels with 600 men aboard sailed from Plymouth in April, 1955, under royal charter. Sir Richard Grenville commanded the fleet from his flagship, the 160-ton *Tiger*.

On June 26, the colonists made landfall and laid out the first English-speaking settlement on these shores. As North Carolinians are quick to point out, this was 22 years before John Smith's pioneers made camp in Jamestown, Virginia, and 35 years before the *Mayflower* landed in Massachusetts. And now it lay just over the nose, narrow forested Roanoke Island where they built their fort. The fleet left 108 plucky souls to fend for themselves. Here was born Virginia Dare, the first child of English parents born in America. England was soon at war with Spain and the pioneers were all but forgotten. Five years passed before a sizeable relief force arrived. The fort was deserted and overgrown with weeds. On a tree was carved a single word, CROATOAN. No other clue as to the fate of the "Lost Colony" was ever found.

All of which comes to mind when you look down at the little island, wondering where the crude fort had been. Though the little colony vanished, it put Spain on notice that Britain would challenge any northward expansion. Smarting from the disastrous defeat of their armada in 1588, the Spaniards gave later British colonists little trouble.

From overhead Dare County Regional, an extremely nice three-runway facility on Roanoke Island, can be seen the Wright Brothers National Memorial, seven miles to the north. By coincidence the Dayton brothers' momentous success was achieved within sight of the first English settlement on our shores.

It was inevitable that a European power would dominate the New World and establish its system and tongue as the standard. That fell to the British. Powered flight was also inevitable; many keen minds were at work on the riddle by 1900, but it fell to the Ohio brothers to pull it off. How strange that our great nation and perhaps its most famous invention had their beginnings within sight of each other on this remote North Carolina coast.

We put down on the 3,000-foot strip at Kill Devil Hills. Two gaudy 172s were hopping passengers at $12.50 a head. The billboard promised a view of the coast as it was first seen by Wilbur and Orville plus a look at ship wreckages. It is a short walk to the stretch of sand where the Wrights succeeded; by all means go there, step off the short distances of those first faltering hops, think on what we do in flight today and try to tell me history is a dull subject. The invention proved on those bleak dunes would revolutionize warfare and transportation and lead to space exploration.

The momentous events at Kitty Hawk and Roanoke Island complement each other. It was not simply the miracle of flight but the privilege of exploiting it that began there. What the ill-fated Lost Colonists founded 400 years ago evolved into a society whose members enjoy unprecedented freedoms, among them this: I can fly my own airplane anytime I like to any place in this broad land. If I maintain personal qualifications and follow common sense safety rules, I need no passport or official permit to fly for business or pleasure, anytime, anywhere. Wealth is not a condition; the privilege of flight is available to anyone of average means. How many other societies offer so much?

Our trip to that fascinating region was thought-provoking. Among other things I wondered why, at the several fields we used, I saw only one airplane bearing an American flag—our Cessna. And it just occurred that but for what happened at Roanoke Island you might be reading this in Spanish.

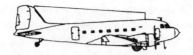

# Challenger Aftermath

Instead of the noon news there was a view of the ocean and the announcer was saying, "Coast Guard and Navy vessels are proceeding to the area." Then he mentioned "Challenger" and it dawned—the space shuttle was down, somewhere out there beneath the blue sea.

There followed a graphic replay of the launch—the slow, twisting climb, the monstrous explosion and the twin boosters insanely vaulting skyward while NASA's man droned on about speed and climb as though all was well (what was the fellow watching, anyway?) Then the awful dribble of smoking pieces falling like a Roman candle's shower of sparks. And the unbelieving expressions of relatives trying to make sense of the madness. Think no less of newsmen for that; you watched, I watched, and in a small way we shared their horror.

There is no settling the account once and for all, nor will there ever be. So long as we travel about our planet or within its thin skin of atmosphere or venture into the limitless void beyond, we must pay as we go in heartbreaking installments. There is no record of the first man or woman who died in surface travel or perished at sea; we know more about the conquest of the air and space, though that is the wrong term for we have conquered neither, nor will we ever. In space, as in all other travel, we can only try to minimize the risk.

The first human to leave earth in a man-made contrivance was Pilatre de Rozier who rose in the Montgolfier balloon from Versailles Palace in 1783. Two years later, as his fiancee sobbed in disbelief, he became flying's first fatality when his combination hot air-hydrogen "aerostat" erupted in a ball of fire. More than 50 brave pioneers were lost in balloon and glider mishaps before the Kitty Hawk success.

Lt. Thomas Selfridge was Orville Wright's third passenger. Structural failure caused loss of control, the frail craft fell and the young officer became the first airplane fatality. Yuri Gagarin was the first to orbit the earth, 51 years later. He survived only to die when his jet crashed. Russian press accounts were typically cryptic, but somewhere someone wept for the first astronaut.

Along the way uncounted thousands of airmen and their passengers died in the extravagantly expensive advance to modern aviation. After every accident it was asked, why do we go on? Is anything worth this price? The same questions are heard in the Challenger aftermath.

Much has been learned from flying accidents. Certain safety devices and procedures in use by all airlines today resulted from accidents that claimed friends of mine. Have the improvements been worth their lives? There is at least some consolation in knowing that, for every life lost in their accidents, many thousands since have travelled safely because of hard lessons learned. We may someday come to regard Challenger in that light.

Every airline's policy manual includes a detailed procedure to be implemented after an incident, major or minor. Among other things, full cooperation with the press is stressed: provide complete information about what happened, avoid speculation as to why.

NASA's top people bungled, as though the possibility of disaster had never entered their thinking. Was there any layman with the least conception of the dreadful risks involved who hadn't wondered . . . what if the skyrocket explodes, or they can't slow the shuttle for reentry . . . how will they tell us? If NASA had a contingency plan, no one could find the book. Five hours passed before a news conference was held at which hedging officials revealed nothing that had not been gathered from TV replays. We expected better.

While NASA's record of getting appropriations is the envy of other agencies, it has done a poor job of explaining itself to us laymen who send Congress the money. We want to believe that manned space exploration is worth the risk and cost, and that it is important, perhaps imperative, that we match the Russians and go them one better when we can. National defense is at stake, they tell us. We have watched scientists conducting mysterious experiments in weightlessness and been told their findings will produce wonderful things for life on earth.

Personally, I'd like some details. Tell me how our defense has been affected by the first 24 shuttle missions; surely that can be explained in general terms without compromising security. Just tell me what the other side already knows. And tell me about the experiments—what has been learned so far? And, since every precious hour in orbit is crammed with scientific studies, how is there time to carry out experiments sent in by school children?

NASA's efforts to make us feel involved in its program are somewhat patronizing. What is supposed to be a crucial scientific investigation occasionally appears as a magnificent stunt. If so much hinges on what is to be learned out there, why are doctors, congressmen and teachers given seats instead of technicians?

There are parallels between these pioneering manned space voyages and the first flights in aircraft. The early balloonists were as much heroes as today's astronauts, having little inkling of what they would find aloft. Then as now, there was no lack of bystanders eager to go along. The greatest balloon ever constructed lifted 50 passengers at an exposition in France; in four months 35,000 people rode up to 1,500 feet. Orville Wright was seven at the time. Although the hydrogen-filled ''aerostat'' was a slave of the fickle wind, ascents to 20,000 feet and higher and nonstop rides covering 1,000 miles were completed. Much was learned in the 120 years preceding Kitty Hawk.

The first airplanes were frail curiosities. Hops lasting minutes required weeks of preparation. The new science quickly revealed its unforgiving nature. Men and women were injured or killed when their slow, crude, unstable craft came apart in flight or dove into the ground for reasons not then understood. Yet there were always new romantics willing to take up the challenge at the risk of their lives and fortunes, none of whom dreamed where their efforts would lead. World War I quickly converted the wealthy sportsman's toy into a weapon to be reckoned with; the postwar commercial development of flying resulted.

Now, with manned space travel, we are back at square one. The great adventure that began in a courtyard outside Paris and became practical in North Carolina is being tried in a new way on the Florida coast. All went well at first as it did for de Rozier and the Wrights, in fact, success seemed almost easy. Twenty-four thundering climbs into orbit and as many grease job touch downs—and then the catastrophe.

In the aftermath, history has repeated itself yet again. Self-appointed experts came up with the exact cause right away (in surprising displays of ignorance in some cases), but such post-mortem guesses amazed no one. Clearly, communications were not what they should have been between technicians who understood the machinery and NASA officials pressed to meet launch schedules.

The tendency to stick with a plan for its own sake or to preserve an image is insidious for it leads to the complacent assumption that because the plan worked before it will work again. It becomes easy to shrug off serious questions as unimportant. It has happened many times in aviation with tragic consequences.

There is one interesting difference between the loss of the space shuttle and the loss of an aircraft. Challenger's builders and operators cannot sidestep responsibility by pointing at the crew. And, this time the answer to—why did it happen?—will be as sought after as the answer to—what happened? That has seldom been the case in aviation probes.

# For Jill

It was a beautiful spring morning, a fitting time for it. Margaret and I climbed into our 172, rose in the crisp air, headed southeast and leveled at 7,500 feet. Watching the greening landscape slowly drifting past, I thought about our purpose. It was solemn but not depressing, this flight that neither of us would forget.

And I thought about her, born in England during Queen Victoria's reign and as proud of her British heritage as of her adopted homeland. Juliet—she despised the name but accepted "Jill"—was vivacious, fun loving, keenly interested in people and events. Her enthusiasm for life was infectious.

Watching Claude Grahame-White beat eight rivals out to Boston Light and back was a clear recollection. "Oh, the excitement of that tremendous crowd when his flimsy little aeroplane came back! I'll never forget it. That was in 1910, and when you think of what pilots do now, going to the moon and back!" She also remembered the drone of Zeppelins during the first London blitz and seeing one caught in the searchlights.

We altered course to avoid a military training area.

An exceptional student, she passed the Cambridge entrance exams, no mean feat. Then her family moved to the United States. She met Jack, a young English minister, and they were married. Jack and Jill went up the hill and a tortuous climb it proved throughout their lives together. She immersed herself in church work as organist, choir director, teacher and organizer. Her energy was astounding. She kept three headstrong sons in tow with soft-spoken words about loyalty, heritage, manners, going by the rules. She got their best by the example she set. To have disappointed her was unthinkable.

Far ahead and high above us were the thin white tracks of New York—Florida jet traffic, but the coast was not yet in view.

She loved flying. When the boys were grown, Jack and Jill

managed a trip to the old country, their first flights ever. He was nervous but she thought air travel delightful, having implicit faith in crew, machine and airline. "At Gander they had to fix one of the engines," she said. "Then—and how I wished you had been there—the pilots took it up for a test and came back and flew right past us, down low, going like blue blazes and we all cheered. What a sight that was!" and it must have been, that old Pan Am Connie buzzing the field. She loved things like that and never forgot them.

She would have reveled in our smooth progress across the morning countryside and the splendid view of farms and towns and roads. Once, after a similar ride, she told me, "I'm so envious! Do you know how fortunate you are to do this as your life's work? And to get paid for it—really now!" And another time, "Flying brings things into proper perspective. It puts you in your place, if you know what I mean." I did. She always went right to the heart of things.

She wanted to understand things. "I can look at the blades and understand how a propeller works but the jet engine, tell me about that." Or, "Show me those slides again; I've got some questions." She never became blase about progress. "When I think back on those awful voyages lasting eight days, and now this Concorde does it in less than four hours! That must be a marvelous trip." She appreciated aviation progress and the price it involved.

I remembered her expression the time I said, "Here, you fly it." She took the stick without hesitation and did better than I had on the first try. "If I were younger I could learn to do it right," she confidently announced when we landed, and indeed she could. The interest and enthusiasm that mark a good pilot were there. She immediately understood the joy of flying for its own sake.

I should have done things like that more often. Now I realize how much they meant to her and how she would remember the details for as long as she lived. I should have done many things differently where she was concerned. Once in a rare moment of remorse, she said, "Looking back over my life, it's not what I've done that bothers me half as much as what I've left undone." That said it for me.

She authored two books, conceived and sold crossword puzzles, wrote poetry, painted, sketched and invented atrocious puns, circulating them without mercy, going into gales of laughter at the moans they drew. She maintained continuous correspondence with overseas relatives and friends, her own children and theirs, never forgetting a recital, Boy Scout camp, birthday or anniversary ("You soloed 40 years ago today. I still have your telegram"), praising or chiding when she thought either was due.

She tackled the most intricate needlepoint and embroidery projects, often from her own designs. A voracious reader with a penchant for mysteries, she adored Agatha Christie. Her priorities were God, family, friends; she lived by an inflexible code with optimism, good humor and grace.

Ahead lay the shoreline, a strip of white sand separating brown land and blue sea. It drew closer and we looked down at the surf. She loved the sea.

Jack died in their sixty-third year of marriage. His ashes were scattered over the Atlantic by a flying grandson from his airplane. "It's a sort of link between here and the old country," she said. It was his wish and hers.

As fiercely independent as ever, she continued alone in their small retirement home amid the happy clutter of snapshots, postcards and souvenirs sent from all over the world by sons and grandchildren, insisting, "I don't want to be a bother to anyone." She was always busy. When an uncontrollable tremor of her right hand prevented writing, she typed and changed to the left for sewing. The steady flow of letters continued as did her exquisite handiwork. She proudly plodded on, ever cheerful, always thinking up nice things to do for the rest of us.

Jill and those like her, native and immigrant, are our beautiful people, not the shallow crowd with that label. Strong, loving, hardworking, optimistic and utterly selfless, they accept life's lot without question or complaint, giving all they have, asking nothing in return. We are blessed with many like Jill. They have class. The real source of our strength and the reason for our greatness, they are a national treasure beyond price.

The end came quickly. First, an emergency operation lasting far too long, though she emerged alert. "She's one tough lady," the surgeon said. We knew that. Characteristically, her immediate concern was for the rest of us. "I'm being an awful bother and I don't like it at all. I'll be fine. Go back home, all of you." Then, when partial recovery seemed assured, a sudden relapse. More surgery, more this time than the weary old lioness heart could withstand. Within hours she was gone.

It was the way she wanted it, quickly and without it causing problems for anyone. "I am ready to go now," she said the day before. She would have been miserable as a semi-invalid with dignity and independence compromised. She had a horror of heroic measures, of "being a bother." We kept reminding ourselves of all that, and yet. . .

The memorial service was brief and dignified. Her 12 descendants—"my greatest riches," as she always called them— were all present in the small chapel listening to the words, each lost in his own thoughts. It was much too short a tribute for her magnificent 89 years, and yet it was in all ways perfect.

We reached the coast and crossed it, still flying eastward toward the morning sun. In a few minutes we throttled back and fulfilled her final request by consigning her ashes to the deep. We looked toward the eastern horizon, far beyond which these same blue waters washing the sands of her adopted homeland also lapped the shores of her beloved England. Then we reversed course and started homeward.

Rest in Peace, Mother.

# Counting My Blessings

You don't have to wear a tie. The phone doesn't ring at two in the morning. You don't live out of a suitcase anymore. There's no more recurrent training, no more sweating physicals and check rides, no more cramming for silly exams, no more watching the clock, no more feds, no more trying to sleep in the daytime. Not when you're retired.

There were things about the job I detested. Airline flying was not always as nice an employment as outsiders imagined. The hassle involved, most of it foisted on us by desk-bound industry and federal nitwits fearful of involvement if we bent something, became horrendous during the last years, and I'm sure it's worse today. Once you were fired up and under way, the job was as much fun as ever; then you did things your way. I don't dwell on that best part, but on the frustrations. That helps keep the slowly fading picture in proper perspective. It wasn't all good, I remind myself; remember those midnight calls. "We need you for a ferry hop, Take it to Seattle, deadhead home." I don't miss that. Count your blessings, boy.

Being away from it isn't all that good, either. I've had four years of it now. How has it been? The first month was wonderful, just like an annual vacation. After 60 days I was restless. It was time to bring the manuals up to date and get back to work. I had loafed long enough. I felt guilty.

Airline flying was a way of life, not a job. You were a slave to the calendar and clock. All family activity revolved around the answer to, "When do you go out again?" It takes months to change, to ignore circled days on the kitchen calendar and realize there won't be any more trips next week, next month, ever.

Years ago I lay for a week in a hospital bed. My window overlooked a street filled with healthy people leading normal lives. The world went on without me. I was resentful. I felt bypassed. It made me appreciate what good work does for self-respect. Retirement was something like that at first. I was on the outside, not because of a mistake or because I had failed a physical or proficiency check, but because I was no longer wanted. At age 60 an airline pilot is discarded; that's the long and short of it.

These personal reflections are, I suspect, typical. Some friends welcomed retirement to the point of quitting a year or two early to get away from flying and into something else. Others dreaded the end, fought it and sank into bitterness and self-pity. Those pathetic few rapidly deteriorated physically and mentally, having retired from life. The majority accepted the inevitable and went on to other things.

But it was not easy in my case. It was tempting to ponder the "age 60 rule." One line from Federal Aviation Regulations, Part 121 (airline operations), said it all: "No person may serve as a pilot on an airplane engaged in operations under this part if that person has reached his 60th birthday." The underhanded way that was conceived rankled if you let it. There was no real basis for that, no evidence to support the notion that another day makes a pilot less able.

It was also tempting to recall pilot response. There was little said when the rule was adopted other than by the good men grounded overnight by the stroke of a vindicative pen. A movement begun later to have the rule rescinded drew surprisingly little support. Clearly, most pilots approved of their age limit. I cannot explain their short-sightedness, much less their sense of what's right and wrong. Were the retirement age dropped to 55 tomorrow, you'd hear them yell. But rehashing all that is pointless and corrosive.

In my late 50s I began reading articles about retirement—"Preparing for the Autumn Years"—that sort of thing. (The Autumn Years, for pete's sake! Me? I was always the kid in the outfit.) I felt silly reading such things but the clock was ticking so maybe I should pay attention. After admonitions to get finances in order, every adviser stressed the importance of having something to do after retirement. This is excellent advice.

A consuming hobby or sport can fill the bill, and I don't mean checkers on a park bench. Several friends have built and flown airplanes which are works of art. Others travel. One couple took off in an RV to really see the sights here and in Canada. They were gone six months and had a great time. Others have expanded sideline businesses, farms or ranches. More than one fellow pilot's income now exceeds what he made while line flying. Proving the ability to continue earning is exactly the right therapy in their cases. All the truly contented retirees I know are busy people.

The relationship between a professional airman and his work produces a thought pattern not easily abandoned. Piloting requires study, imagination, thought and frequent periods of intense concentration. A pilot's relationship with his management and his associates is much closer than that known in most other fields. The seniority system enforces a lifetime marriage between pilot and company. You put down roots. There's no jumping from line to line seeking a better deal. Walking away from that close atmosphere and its personal contacts is traumatic. The necessary adjustments demand the same self-discipline as flying.

Most retirees are ready for grounding; I wasn't. Build an airplane? I haven't the patience; we bought a 172. When I'm fed up with some manufactured project (like writing this), I call the field. The red and white Cessna is rolled out when I park. Last week I climbed northbound toward Virginia. There's no better way to clear away the cobwebs. Maybe I'd land someplace, maybe not. Greensboro slowly fell behind and the foothills came into view on that crisp fall afternoon. The sky was crystal clear and the ride rock solid. I only fly these days in ideal conditions.

My Cessna 172 is a great little airplane with avionics rarely used. I tried an ILS one day, VFR, down to 100 feet, just for fun. Piece of cake. But it provoked no yearning to do it again with 400 passengers—though I could. They take away your job, not your skills.

Danville's three-runway municipal caught my eye. I could put a light 707 in there with no sweat. I debated landing, then elected to head west toward the mountains. Our local TV weatherman calls them "those gorgeous mountains" and indeed they are when ablaze with autumn colors. It is a spectacular sight. All gauges were in the green, the tanks were nearly full and I was right on schedule, meaning the time over Danville was of no significance whatsoever. The digital readout showed groundspeed at 90 knots, not that it mattered in the least. Outside temperature—45; I eased on a modicum more of cabin heat.

A drive, popular with locals, is to the mountains to admire the autumn foliage. From aloft I could take in more at a glance than a motorist sees all day. The view from a Chevy on the Blue Ridge Parkway can't compare with that from a Cessna at 2,500 feet. Looking down on the bumper-to-bumper cars, I was glad we bought the plane. I turned south, well clear of the TRSA, and slowly overtook a 100-car Norfolk Southern freight moving along at a fair clip behind six diesels. I'm almost used to the 172's leisurely pace, in fact, I now enjoy it. Those guys way up there at flight level four-one-oh don't know what they're missing. Mach .85? Big deal.

It was a day for contrails. High above were the thin white tracks of long distance traffic. One trail, splaying into a broad cloud of vapor, caught my eye. A 747. I swapped cockpits for a moment to live again in his world of sights and sounds and concerns and it all came back as if I'd sat in his seat yesterday. He was playing the game by strict rules with the cards they dealt him while I wrote my own rules and stacked the deck.

I strapped back into my little airplane, turned east, eased back the throttle and started a DC-3's 300-feet-a-minute rate of descent toward home. My unknown compatriot in his wondrous jumbo continued on his scheduled way over the horizon and I envied him but one thing—the fresh coffee he could promote with a call to the forward galley. And I reminded myself that, among many other annoyances, he has to wear a tie.

# Other Bestsellers From TAB

# Other Bestsellers From TAB